REMEMBRANCES OF RIVERS PAST

BY THE SAME AUTHOR: Matching the Hatch
Salmon of the World

Ernest Schwiebert

Remembrances

of Rivers Past

The Macmillan Company NEW YORK, NEW YORK
Collier-Macmillan Limited LONDON

These collected memorabilia are some of the milestones in more than thirty years spent seeking rivers of greatness. These pages are dedicated to the people who shared these times and places, and to the rivers we may yet share, since daydreams of those unfished rivers in the future are as rich as our remembrances of rivers past.

The Macmillan Company
866 Third Avenue, New York, N.Y. 10022
Collier-Macmillan Canada Ltd., Toronto, Ontario

Designed by Joan Stoliar

Library of Congress Catalog Card Number: 71-167929

First Printing

Printed in the United States of America

ACKNOWLEDGMENTS

Special acknowledgment must be made to several airlines for their assistance in travel arrangements for promotional considerations. These carriers include Pan American World Airways for its role in the expedition to Nepal, Scandinavian Airline System for its generous cooperation in several trips to the salmon rivers of Norway, Loftleidir for its many courtesies in my several summers in Iceland, Braniff International for its assistance in trips into the Argentine, and the little Austral for its assistance with internal transportation to Patagonia and Tierra del Fuego.

Permission to reprint material written by the author and published elsewhere has been most generous, and the following publishers and periodicals are also due special acknowledgments: *Remembrances of Rivers Past* contains material that first appeared in the annual catalogue of William Mills & Sons, 21 Park Place, New York, 1963, and later in the quarterly *Rod & Gun* under the title "Schwiebert Takes You Down Memory River," Hearst Publications, Summer 1970. "Memories of Michigan" was first published, by special arrangement, in *Fisherman's Bounty*, Crown, New York, 1970, and later under the title "Magic Days When Boy Meets Trout" in *Sports Afield*, Hearst Publications, December 1970. "First Blood," *Flyfisherman* magazine, Saint Louis, March 1971. "Ounce of Prevention," *Flyfisherman* magazine, Saint Louis, March 1972. "Song of the Catskills," in a somewhat different form, *Sports Afield*, Hearst Publications, May 1971. "The Strangest Trout Stream on Earth," in an abridged version, in *Field & Stream*, Holt, Rinehart & Winston, July 1965. "Legend and the Letort," *Esquire*, New York, May 1961. "Charity on the Little South," *Sports Afield*, Hearst Publications, September 1971. "Grasshopper Wind" is an altered version of an article in *Fishing Yearbook*, Fawcett Publications, Spring 1961. "Raspberries in the Rain," *Flyfisherman* magazine, Saint Louis, April 1970. "The Time of the Hendricksons" was first published in a different version in the 1968 annual catalogue of William Mills & Sons, 21 Park Place, New York, and later, in an expanded version, in *Sports Afield*, Hearst Publications, April 1972. "River of Regeneration" includes material that was published in a different version under the title "We Found A Salmon Shangri-la" in *True* magazine, Fawcett Publications, May 1963. Subsequent trips resulted in the present expanded form of the article, which was abridged under the title "Sweet Prize of a Bitter Land" in *Sports Afield*, Hearst Publications, August 1971. "The Rainbows of Pichi Traful," under the title "Dry

5

Flies in a Dinosaur Landscape," in *Flyfisherman* magazine, Saint Louis, November 1971. "The Fickle River of Giant Salmon" contains material first published under the title "The River That Makes Fishing Widows" in *True* magazine, Fawcett Publications, August 1967, and later, under its own title, in *Sports Afield*, Hearst Publications, February 1972. "La Fiebre de las Bocas," under the title "In the Land of Giant Rainbows," *Sports Afield*, Hearst Publications, February 1971. "Homage to Henryville" appeared, originally, in a limited edition titled *The Gordon Garland*, published by the Theodore Gordon Flyfishers, New York 1965. That same version was published in a later trade edition entitled *American Trout Fishing*, Alfred Knopf, New York 1966. The new version included in this book has been rewritten to reflect changes in both the Brodheads and its cast of characters. The present version is published with special permission from the publishers of its earlier forms. "Fishing in the Land of Fire" appeared, much-abridged, in *Field & Stream*, Holt, Rinehart & Winston, November 1967. The present version includes material gathered in subsequent trips and was published in *Sports Afield*, Hearst Publications, March 1972. "Laerdal Memories" first appeared in a shorter version in the annual catalogue of William Mills & Sons, 21 Park Place, New York, Spring 1964. There were several trips to Laerdal, and their anecdotal material and experiences were included in the enlarged version titled "Where Fishing is a Blood Sport" in *Esquire*, New York, October 1967.

Contents

Remembrances of Rivers Past   9

Memories of Michigan   19

First Blood   28

Ounce of Prevention   33

Song of the Catskills   37

The Strangest Trout Stream on Earth   59

Legend and the Letort   72

Act of Mercy   89

The Rainbow of Rosh-Ha-Shanah   92

Charity on the Little South   98

Grasshopper Wind   101

A Duck Is Better Than Nothing   115

Raspberries in the Rain   124

The River of the Spirits   129

The Time of the Hendricksons   144

River of Regeneration   152

The Rainbows of Pichi Traful   167

Night Comes to the Namekagon   172

The Fickle River of Giant Salmon   179

The Canary in the Mine   194

Tigerfish of the Himalayas   197

La Fiebre de las Bocas   215

Homage to Henryville   229

Fishing in the Land of Fire   259

Laerdal Memories   275

Remembrances
of Rivers Past

SNOW is falling softly outside, and we are months away from fishing except in our thoughts. The rivers are black and almost silent among the rocks. Winter cold stirs in the rattling branches, but the secrets of spring are working deep in the earth, and our rivers already hold the fly-hatches of the coming year.

Memories are a major part of fishing. Their pleasures reach back through the years to favorite rivers and familiar pools. The mind is a rich assemblage of recollections, planning tactics for the future and remembering the companions of other seasons. Some of those companions will no longer join us for the fly-hatches of the coming spring, and the continuing life of the river is a yearly reminder of our own mortality.

There are memories of both fish and fishing. Sometimes fish are taken and sometimes they are lost. Anglers often remember lost fish more clearly than those that surrendered, and fishless days remain as stubbornly in the mind as the happier memories of success.

Fishing memories are never limited to fish, since there are other lessons along rivers. The experience of many is mirrored in the life of each man, and a fly-fishing life is no exception. Like the familiar cycle of fly-hatches, our rivers repeat their lessons until both seasons and secrets are layered in the mind, like mossy ledges above a favorite riffle. Each fisherman can find echoes of his sport in the experience of others, and there are always echoes of your fishing in my remembrances of rivers past. Memories of fly-fishing are as bright as a riffle over sunwashed gravel, and boyhood memories of Michigan are as fresh as recent days on the Laxámyri and Miramichi.

There are similar milestones in all lives spent along trout waters. The small fish that started my lifelong pilgrimage was caught with grasshoppers in a meadow creek. Its riffle-bright lessons were faithfully studied for two summers and prepared a solid groundwork for the future. My first fly-caught trout took a wet Cahill on the Pere Marquette. The technique was perilously close to worming, since the line was simply trailing in the current. The fish barely measured ten inches, but it seemed like a sailfish. It was lying in a sweeping bend hung with willows, followed the swing of my flies into the sunlight, and hooked itself solidly. The episode is familiar, but it ended countless hours of bait-fishing, and the praise of my father and his friends was a heady reward.

We celebrated on the stream, and with that ten-inch brown in my wicker creel, it seemed that I had finally joined their world. The memorabilia of that world are familiar still, and the mind savors them again: fishing coats stained with parafin and citronella, the rhythm of summer rain on canvas and the melancholy of whippoorwills at nightfall, silkworm gut tippets coiled and soaking, creels lined with mint and freshly-picked ferns, pockets bulging with English pipes and fly-boxes and countless gadgets and tobacco, fly-rods bright with varnish and elegant silk wrappings, coffee boiled on a gravel-bar fire, and sour-mash whisky from a stream-washed cup.

Their world of fly-hatches and fishing talk became mine that pale August morning, and we celebrated the occasion with my first cup of coffee while my father and his friends toasted the triumph with a stronger catalyst.

The following summer my first dry-fly trout succumbed on a warm evening along the Little Manistee. Its current was dark with cedars and hemlocks, sweeping down a gravelly reach of water into a quiet pool. Rises bulged and died tight against a deadfall. Caddisflies were coming off and the trout were taking them freely. The small spentwing Adams settled above a fish and rode the current and disappeared in a quiet rise. The slender rod throbbed as the trout worked deep along the bottom, and I was captured too.

Trout became the consuming passion of my boyhood, and each summer was spent on trout water. Winters were occupied tinkering with tackle and learning to dress flies. Like most beginners, I typically measured success in terms of weight in my creel. The first limit catches seemed like victories, although one summer an old Michigan fisherman chided me about my frequent baskets filled with trout.

He's only jealous, I thought angrily.

The old man seldom came in with fish, and I was sure he was a poor fisherman, but I watched him secretly from the willows a few weeks later. It was a still reach of the Little South, full of tangled deadfalls and overhanging trees. Fishing it was difficult, and I usually lost several flies in the branches or lost fish among the logs.

His casting was flawless, working low under the branches and placing dragless floats tight against the holding places. The old man fished a half mile of water without losing a fly or making a poor cast. There were fourteen rises, and he hooked and landed thirteen trout, releasing each of them gently. It was obvious that he could creel a limit of fish any time he wished, and that his basket was empty because he chose to release his catch.

The memory of his pale fly-line working rhythmically in the sunlight, and settling on the current shadows deep under the trees, has lasted through the years. His lesson was digested slowly over many summers. It was difficult to understand a fisherman who was not interested in keeping the fish he caught, and I continued to kill every legal trout foolish enough to take my flies. My skill improved steadily and there were many limits of trout before I realized that I had emptied many favorite holding-lies myself, and the secret places of those rivers were less special without trout.

Boyhood rivers are home rivers. Their images and lessons last all our lives, and mine were summer rivers flowing over pale bottoms of sandy gravel. Pines and swamp cedars and hardwoods sheltered their pools and runs. There is still the bittersweet sound of their names in my mind: the gentle Manistee and the strong Pere Marquette and the tea-colored Two Hearted in the Hemingway country of upper Michigan, and I struggled against their currents in huge man-sized waders that accordioned comically down my legs.

Their memories still crowd the mind. Twilight has a well-remembered softness on the Little Manistee, and its trout still dimple softly in the hemlock shadows. Mating spinners swarm on the Pere Marquette, filling the late afternoon sunlight with the butter-colored sparks of their egg-sacs, and the dark swamp-colored currents of the Black conceal many secrets. There is a tumbling kind of lyricism in rivers, and their moods are as varied as April weather on the storied Au Sable.

Sometimes boyhood rivers ultimately prove too small a challenge, and a restless angler wanders farther afield. There are countless rivers to explore across the world, and their memories are as rich as those of boyhood in Michigan.

There are other memories mixed with fishing. We travelled north in those boyhood summers through a landscape of orchards and small towns and cornfields, until the pastoral countryside dropped behind and the world of lakes and forests began. Thoughts of the north country in those years were enough to fill me with delicious shivers of anticipation. The rolling farm country ended and the paved highways finally changed to gravel, reaching farther north into the jackpines. Mist sometimes shrouded the northern lakes and tamarack bogs at daybreak, and the tumbling trout streams were totally unlike the sluggish silt-filled rivers farther south.

The mind drifts lazily in eddies of recollection, like a canoe at midday in midsummer. It remembers things like otters rough-housing on the swift-flowing Pine, ruffed grouse and woodcock in thickets along the Boardman, and hours spent watching old Len Halliday dressing Adams spentwings at his feather-littered workbench in Mayfield where the pattern was born. There are flowers in the weedy shallows of the Namekagon in northern Wisconsin, raccoons that forage for crayfish in the shallow riffles of the Brule, giant herons that fished with me at daylight on the Ontanagon, and I remember the heavy mating flight of big *Hexagenia* drakes the night I took my first brown over twenty inches on the Big Pere.

Several teen-age summers were spent in Colorado and Wyoming, moving nomadically from river to river. There are many memories of Colorado. They began on the tumbling Fraser and the Colorado itself near Hot Sulphur Springs. There were many hours fishing the late morning hatches on the headwaters of the Arkansas. Both watersheds have since been decimated by impoundments and mine tailings, but some of those boyhood rivers survive. There are still good fish in the wild Roaring Fork below Aspen. Its bottom is a checkerboard of dark basalt and pale pieces of marble, and its fat rainbows are completely invisible in its camouflage. There have been many frustrating hours with smutting trout on the weedy Platte and equally fruitful hours on the weedy stillwaters of the Frying Pan, where the fish dimpled softly to hatches of tiny *Paraleptophlebia* flies in September. Colorado rivers have a special place in my memories.

Wyoming is another special place. Its rivers are born in the high meadows and snowfields of mountains like the Big Horns and Medicine Bows and the Tetons, and its memories are varied. Flying ants once triggered an incredible rise of fish on the Encampment, and there were days of excellent sport on the North Platte when the trout were taking tiny bark beetles. Wyoming had heavy cutthroats in those boyhood years, and I took several over four pounds on the jade-green pools of the Gros Ventre, the meadow flats of Slough Creek, and the huge many-channeled Snake. Herds of elk cropped and grazed in the rich meadows of the upper Madison, buffalo wandered myopic and absent-minded in the Ojo Caliente meadows on the Firehole, and a cantankerous moose once routed me from a marshy reach of the Yellowstone.

Those western rivers were completely unlike the boyhood rivers in Michigan and Wisconsin. There is a wild sweep and distance in their landscapes that dwarfed the quiet tree-sheltered currents where I learned to fish. There are such landscapes in the sprawling South Park basin of Colorado, the grayling headwaters of the Big Hole in Montana, and the labyrinth of cottonwood channels that mark the course of the storied Gunnison. Western memories are like September twilight in the Rio Grande country, where flight ducks ride the warm winds from the pueblo valleys farther south and blood-colored sunsets linger on the Sangre de Cristos.

Rivers tumble ceaselessly in the mind. Their currents are bright in sunlight and leaden in rain, and there were always new rivers in the weather of early manhood. Those years were spent in Europe, and experiences on its rivers awakened both a sense of tradition and a storehouse of memories.

Bavarian rivers were my baptism there, and the first European trout fell to my April flies on the Pegnitz above Nürnberg. It was working steadily in the mossy current and came softly to a small nymph just after daylight. The fish measured a fat eighteen inches and the riverkeeper laid it in his basket lined with lichens and wild flowers. It was a good morning, and we celebrated at lunch with fresh sausages and rich potato soup and dark beer in a half-timbered inn. Many hours were passed on the tranquil weed-channels of the Wiesandt, with ruined castles and watermills and villages reflected in its gentle currents. Memory fishes the *Sprungzeit* hatches again on the Lauterach, where we hunted boar and roe deer in the dark afternoons of winter, and returned for trout fishing when the river orchards were perfumed with springtime.

There were other Bavarian rivers in the summers that followed, and the mind returns to them with pleasure. It savors an evening in Oberammergau when the famous *Passionsspiel* performance had ended, and I returned to the inn to change for fishing. Families stopped their evening walks to watch from the footbridges and applauded each trout. There was fresh snow on the mountains one April morning on the Leizach, and we finally stripped off our parkas and sweaters as the sun warmed its valley. We stopped for lunch at the steep-roofed farmhouse where the women boiled our fish, and served them with small potatoes and melted butter. There are many such memories, and my mind happily returns to the millrace at Fischen-im-Allgäu, when I gave the woodcutter a two-pound grayling and he took me home to celebrate with *Kirschwasser* at his cottage on the mountain.

Europe is the place of many memories now. Its people and its landscapes are well-remembered friends, and fishing there has become like going home. The mind returns to water meadows on the Risle and the Test, and the Traun with its petulant regatta of swans, where we fished from the timber walkways and stayed in the little fishing hotel at Marien-brucke. Those were fine years on storied beats, and on the bitter evenings of midwinter I remember the five-pound rainbow at Oberstdorf, caught the morning before we took a magnificent stag after a long twilight stalk on the Nebelhorn.

Since those years my fishing has been focused on the rivers of the Appalachians and Adirondacks. Pilgrimages were made each season to the shrines of American fishing—rivers like the Beaverkill and Neversink in the Catskills, the swift Battenkill and the tumbling Ausable, the Brodheads in Pennsylvania and the pastoral Musconetcong in New Jersey—and fishing memories still accumulate like tree-rings in the buttonwoods above a favorite pool.

Trout were the catalyst of my fishing, but the contemplative pursuit of trout inevitably leads a venturesome flyfisher to salmon. The fish of smaller rivers are introspective souls, perfectly attuned to the Waltonian moods of angling, but there is something primordial about salmon.

Salmon addicts are men whose moods are as varied as those of the salmon themselves. There is a manic celebration of their victories and brooding over their failures. Sometimes the fish disdainfully refuse hundreds of flies, only to engulf those same patterns recklessly in some imperceptible change of mood. Fishless days are common with salmon, and the species is legendary for its fickle moods. Such moodiness is even found once a salmon is hooked—sometimes they bulldog or sulk stubbornly on the bottom, and sometimes they cartwheel in a fight that lies somewhere between the explosive performance of a tumbler and the poetry of a ballerina.

Memories of salmon fishing are rich with the music of salmon rivers. The pilgrimages of a salmon fisherman first lead north to home rivers like the Machias and Narraguagus in Maine. Canadian rivers like the Miramichi and Grand Cascapedia and Restigouche soon follow, and a typical salmon-fishing odyssey will ultimately explore the wilderness rivers of the Labrador, like the sprawling George and the River of Whales and the Adlatok. Their names alone evoke a mixture of poetry and magic for fishermen around the world.

The pilgrimages of a salmon fisherman inevitably lead to Europe and its Atlantic islands. There are rivers of greatness in both Norway and Iceland. The pastoral memories of haymeadow pools on the Flåm, the incredibly clear currents of the small mountain-walled Naerøy, and the charming farmstead beats of the Laerdal are treasures. Sometimes my mind returns to the glacier-fed Driva and a valley filled with the lacework patterns of countless waterfalls. There are timber casting platforms on the swift little Stryn, and the Gaula is a wild cataract where it spills into its brackish sea-pool, with a fishing house that has the giant outlines of past trophies carved into its sitting-porch floor.

There are exciting memories of the tumbling Årøy steeplechase and the currents hissing through its Platforms of Despair. The storied Alta a hundred miles below Hammarfest marks the northern limit of my fishing odyssey. Arctic rivers like the Målangsfossen and the Alta are familiar friends, and I remember their sounds and smells and supper fires on their rocky beaches long after midnight. There are pools on the Laxámyri and Langá in Iceland where the salmon lie in weedy channels like the chalkstream trout of England, and there is the fickle Vossa—where I killed a fifty-one pound cockfish on a bright Dusty Miller.

Patagonia is another lode of memories. Fat rainbows rise steadily at twilight in the tree-fern pools on the Pichi Traful. Heavy hatches of caddisflies trigger evening rises of big browns on the Quilquihue, and we fished its foothill country in the purple twilight of the Andes. Trophy fish are common on sprawling rivers like the Limay and Collón Cura and Caleufu. Knowledgeable anglers make annual pilgrimages to the Boca Huechulafquen on the Chimehuin, and the smaller outlets of the swift Correntoso, hoping to equal or surpass the fly-record browns already taken in those waters.

There are other trophies too. Big rainbows are found in the mouths of the Paimun and the River of Swans and the Limay. Sometimes they can be taken under the plunging waterfalls of the Lagoon of Tears or among the tangled deadfalls of the swift Calcurrupe in Chile. Giant brookies are found in the mouths of several bone-chilling rivers that drain the Andean threshold of Chile, and it seems likely that a new world record will ultimately be caught in the *boca*-shallows of some Patagonian river like the Auquinco or Corcovado or Pireco in March. Big landlocks are common in the remote headwaters of the Situación country and in the weedy currents of the Traful, where hundreds gather in pewter-colored schools over the pale gravel of the Campamento Pool.

Tierra del Fuego is the southern limit of my fly-fishing odyssey. It has rivers with sea-run browns from the remote fjords of Chile to the Straits of Magellan and Cape Horn. Its weather is foul and its fishing is incredible. The fish are sea-bright as freshly minted coins. Sheep grazed in the sheltered places. Small herds of antelope-like *guanacos* moved restlessly on the high grass benches. Thousands of waterfowl nested in the bottoms, and the pale saltpetre lakes were filled with flamingoes. Tierra del Fuego has an awesome emptiness that dwarfs both the rivers of Michigan and the western landscapes of my teenage summers. Its treeless barrens reach west toward the fog-shrouded forests of the Darwin Range, and its winds sigh over rocky beaches to the sea.

These are the milestones of a fly-fishing life. Its pilgrimages have filled the years of youth and manhood, and its memories tumble down the years like a favorite reach of water. Many stories form my remembrances of rivers past, and like fishing on such home rivers as the Beaverkill or the Brodheads, stories of fishing are best when shared.

Memories of Michigan

AUGUST mornings were bright on the wind-riffled surface of the bay, and beyond the shallow inlet, there were whitecaps on the darker water of the lake. Its surf rolled and broke on the beaches. Ore boats moved slowly south along the horizon. They steamed toward the mills at Chicago or travelled lazily back, empty and riding high in the water, bound for the ironfields of Lake Superior.

The town was almost forgotten. There were only five or six houses to remind its oldtimers of the lumber port that had once boasted five hundred buildings. The logging drives had stopped. Brook trout were coming back in the little river, although the delicate grayling were gone, and its gentle currents had slowly filled the harbor with sand and silt.

The piers and jetties were gone, and only the ebony skeletons of their pilings remained where the summer people fished for perch. Outside the inlet channel to the harbor, the rolling waves pounded and flowed through the pilings that remained to mark the breakwater. The pale beach reached for miles, marred only by the weathered bones of a schooner lost in a winter squall a century before, its broken timbers like the ribcage of some ancient whale imprisoned in the sand.

The post office and general store had a high falsefront, and a single gasoline pump stood in the dusty street. There was a tiny clapboard church and its weed-filled cemetery. The broken windows of the Grange Hall had stared at the jackpine landscape since farms were abandoned in the thirties, and the school was the only building that had been painted in years. The saloons and rooming houses and sawmills were gone. There were few echoes of a thriving past except in the skeletal pilings of the harbor and cellars long forgotten in the weeds.

There were several cottages on the lake in those boyhood years. It was often too cold for swimming, but its unspoiled beaches were empty. Sand dunes rose hundreds of feet above the lake, pale with beach grass and dark with trees. Those Michigan summers were peaceful times when my father fished and worked at his research, or prepared his lectures for the coming term.

My fishing began with catfish and perch and pumpkinseeds. Many summers have passed since that long-ago summer when I was first introduced to trout. After the foolish perch and pumpkinseed shallows below the cottage, trout were a revelation, and since that first morning they have obsessed me with a single-minded passion that has paled other fish to unimportance. Only salmon have ever distracted me from that single-minded odyssey in the years that followed.

Those first hours are still fresh in my mind. Long before daylight I was awake. The week of hot weather ended in a squall off the lake, and I listened to the lashing wind and rain on the roof. It was still dark when we finished breakfast, but the sudden storm front had passed.

Getting the grasshoppers for bait was sport in itself, and we gathered them in the wet grass. They were sluggish in the cold just after daylight, and we searched the meadows with our fruit jars, picking grasshoppers like berries. My classroom was on the headwaters of the river. Its meadows were willow-bordered, its origins deep in the springs of a cedar swamp.

It was dark with willows and conifers above the meadows. Some places it flowed through quivering bogs of sand and marl, and it reached the sunlight in a logging pond. The shallows were filled with stumps and deadfalls. There was a beaver house below the inlet. Its occupants once frightened me into jettisoning a rod just before midnight. They discovered me during a night fishing session and their warning tail-slaps were a series of explosions in the darkness.

Courage failed and I ran. Fifty yards down the logging road I stopped. My mouth was dry and there was an ache in my side. Several minutes passed until my breathing returned to normal, and I went back sheepishly for the rod with my heart still beating wildly.

The pond was less formidable in the morning. Brook trout were deep over the emerald moss of its channel, cruising in nervous schools. They were bright with color in these swampy waters, and they cruised beyond the range of boyhood casting. Below the pond was almost a mile of dark swamp-colored water we never fished. It was densely grown with hemlocks and cedars. The mileage below was a pleasant reach of meadow water, marked with a serpentine row of willows. Halfway through the meadow, the stream was bridged with a simple tractor span of planking and logs. There was a hill above the bottom of the meadow, with an old cemetery in the jackpines.

My parents restricted me to the meadows, but the temptation of the pond was strong. It caused a number of furtive expeditions. These attempts were fishless, but nagging memories of fish prowling the mossy channel always brought me back.

The meadow was easier. The first hole was below a sluice culvert, where the current poured under the road. The deepest place was tight against the roots of a giant elm. My equipment was a stiff bait-rod and a precious Meek casting reel. The agate guides and cane were intricately wrapped with silk. The rod was perfect for worms and minnows and grasshoppers.

It was cool the morning I caught my first trout. The wind was almost cold off the lake, but it was warmer on the river. Our approach to the sluice-culvert hole went infantry style, crawling flat in the roots of the elm. The grasshopper chosen for sacrifice was worked past the lid of my pickle jar, squirming and protesting with brown juices that stained my fingers.

It was lowered into the current tight against the roots. The action was instantaneous. There was a wild splash and the rod dipped, and I derricked the trout into the branches. My father laughed and extricated it from the tree, and we sat in the grassy shade admiring its colors. Foot-long brook trout are still treasured in the adult world, and in boyhood it seemed like a salmon.

Later I became skilled at snaking fish high on the banks, but twice I hooked trout that broke off. The best of the summer was a plump fifteen-inch brown, and in trying to quiet its wild flopping, I fell into some bankside nettles. There were never any fishless days after that first session under the elms, and I often took fish to twelve inches.

My consistent luck was a source of amusement in the general store. Its freezer was always filled with ice cream and trout. The locals kept their fish there and its contents were a kind of angling scoreboard. Daily catches were common knowledge.

That summer I fished every possible minute, while my father was usually busy with his writing. My packages of trout soon surpassed his and the general store regulars laughed.

You be right nice to your boy, they winked at him each time we deposited our fish. *You buy him enough ice cream,*

they laughed, *and he might tell you how he caught them trout.*
You're right, my father smiled.

There was a swift run below the sluice culvert where cattle forded the stream. The current eddied and deepened above some tangled deadfalls. Bog willows sheltered the run. There were usually good fish in the deepest place, but the boggy ground trembled when we approached and they were skittish. They always bolted and disappeared under the deadfalls. It was a good lesson.

Willows covered the water downstream, except for a single swirling hole. It always held good fish. We crawled close through the grass and peeked at the water to fish. Crayfish burrows were clustered like swallow-nests in the banks. The fish held deep where the sun-filled current slipped back into its leafy tunnel, and sometimes we lost them in the willows.

There were several open runs between the willows in the half mile that followed. The hay meadow bridge was below. The current was dark under its planks and timber cribbing. It boiled out from the willows where the debris of past freshets were tangled in the fence.

Big trout lived under the tractor bridge. We sometimes watched between the planking, where the narrow patterns of sunlight reached the bottom. It was almost impossible to fish there because of the fences close above and below the bridge. Its big browns were a challenge we continually failed to solve that summer.

The downstream meadows were filled with cattle and plowhorses. The fish hid under the banks. The livestock seldom frightened them, but it was difficult for us to approach. We crawled the banks, staying well back from the current, and fished our grasshoppers against the grass. These meadow trout ran smaller, and took our bait with eager splashes. There were bigger fish in one place where the foam eddied up into a soapsuds crescent against a fence.

It was still and deep, and once I hooked a fish there that

easily snapped my leader when I tried to horse it on the bank. It looked immense, and I repaired my leader with trembling fingers.

The fishable water ended at the cemetery, and fishing there was a little frightening. The grass was thickly tangled in its cast-iron fences, and its headstones leaned at strange angles or lay flat in the weeds. Wind stirred through the jackpines on most days, but when it was still, there was a faint odor of fading wreaths and flowers.

It was a logging-camp cemetery from the lumbering years in Michigan. There was no trace of the camp or its canvas-tent church. Those lumbering years have a colorful history, with more than their share of Bacchanalia. There were killings and gambling tents and tenderloins and hanging trees. Cemetery hill had once been covered with tent camps when the valley was lumbered and the logging pond was built, and my boyhood imagination often explored those lumbering years. There was no doubt in my mind that the cemetery was filled with sinful men and camp followers, or that its graves were an unhappy residue of a jackpine Sodom and Gomorrah.

Night fishing in those lower meadows below the cemetery was filled with delicious shivers of fear. There was swamp fire sometimes in the marl bogs downstream, and moonlight danced and gleamed on the polished headstones.

Later that summer, one of the local fishermen caught a six-pound brown in the marl bogs. It was taken with a night crawler. It seemed to prove what a man could accomplish if he would only brave the demons of Hell (boyhood imagination could conceive no other destination for the loggers and their girlfriends) in the dark of the moon. The temptation of such fish was considerable, but my fear of the cemetery and the swamp prevailed. It was the mysterious swamp fire and the dead that tipped the scale toward caution.

The man who caught the big brown looked old enough to have been a logger. It was possible to imagine him topping timber and felling trees during the day, and wasting his wages in sinful revels (once I had seen him drunk on the courthouse lawn in Manistee) in the tenderloins all night. When I finally decided the old man was a lumberjack, his brave expeditions into the swamp seemed less impressive. No lumberjack would be afraid of a cemetery filled with friends.

The cemetery was too formidable for me. Except for my traumatic encounters with the beavers in the logging pond, my nights were properly passed in bed. Those hours were spent listening to the sullen rhythm of the lake, and the wind in the pines above our cottage. Thoughts of fishing filled my head until sleep finally came, as they sometimes do years later, and I fished back through success and failure.

Sometimes I tried to solve fishing problems in those moments of half sleep, and I often returned to the little river and its frustrations in my mind. Such nocturnal problem solving always seemed to return to the tractor.

It had been a raw windy morning the first time I discovered the big fish under the bridge. Gusts of wind tossed the willows and the sun glittered on the riffles. The slender leaves writhed in the wind, turning green and silver as they moved.

When I reached the bridge, several trout were working in its shadows. The wind rose and gusted across the meadows, and the trout began rising again. There were five of them.

The wind was blowing terrestrial insects into the stream. There was an obvious relationship between its rising gusts and a subsequent increase in activity among the fish. Four of them were deep in the shadows of the planking. The fifth was working tight against the cribbing. They were all browns. Excitement rose inside me when I looked down through the bridge floor. They ranged from above fifteen inches to a dark spotted fish of two pounds.

They looked huge. My fish had averaged about nine inches that summer. The tractor bridge became my secret enigma, and I often dreamed of arriving in triumph at the store with such trophies.

Because of the fences at the bridge, there was no way to

fish them. It was like a wire cage with a planking roof. The problem caused some restless nights. Its solution was devised in some moments just before sleep, and it seemed foolproof enough that I slept soundly.

The bridge planking would be shifted aside carefully, until I could lower a grasshopper directly to the fish. *The leader should be heavy,* I thought, *and I can weight it with sinkers to hold it steady.*

There were no other fishermen the morning I tried it. The trout eagerly accepted several grasshoppers I threw into the current above the bridge. Everything seemed perfect, and I coaxed my biggest grasshopper from his pickle-jar prison. The leader was tested and ready. The fish were right under me. It was now or never. The planking was heavy, but I moved it soundlessly until a bright streak of sunlight exploded across the bottom and the fish bolted wildly upstream.

Several years later I returned. It was a sentimental pilgrimage back into my boyhood, but that past was gone. The town had all the symptoms of mindless progress. There were ice-cream stands and a shiny diner. The drive-in movie stood in the meadow where we had watched the deer on August evenings. There was a supermarket, and the automobile graveyard sprawled down from the white service station into the shallows where I had fished for perch.

The fishing was changed too.

Memories of those first grasshopper summers crowded my mind. The men who had helped me learn about trout were all gone, part of the timeless cycle of the seasons now, and without them something was missing on the Au Sable and the swift-flowing Pine and the dark swamp-colored currents of the Rifle and the Black.

The wind off the lake still smelled cool and clean. Clouds moved swiftly inland. The logging camp cemetery was still there, headstones askew and sprawled flat in the tangled weeds and grass. Two men were fishing the culvert under the road, and I stopped to talk.

What are you using? I called.

Cheese, they answered.

The little river still wound lazily through its meadows and the wind moved in the willows. There were three new houses in the pasture upstream. The logging pond and its beaver house were gone, and there were no fish where the tractor bridge had been.

First Blood

IT has been more than twenty years since that first Leadville summer. The haying was almost finished, but several days of rainy weather had made the bottoms too wet for mowing. The irrigation ditches were dry except for the rain. Their flow had been returned to the little stream that rose high on the northeast shoulder of Mount Massive. The turbid water had settled and cleared again. The current was still high, but the pools were fishable.

Clouds obscured the mountains across the river bottoms, and the morning train climbed achingly along the grade past Malta crossing. It whistled and strained slowly toward Tennessee Pass and the Pacific watershed. The rain had stopped on the bunkhouse roof just before daylight, and the radio promised clearing weather.

Hatches should be good, I thought.

There was no haying scheduled that morning, but I had chores in the horse barns. There was manure to clear and shovel, and I worked slowly until the water ran swiftly in the stone gutters behind the stalls.

It's finished, I announced at the house.

You're off fishing? asked my aunt. *Will you be back in time for lunch?* She was baking fresh bread.

I'll take a sandwich with me, I said.

My tackle was in the main bunkhouse. I took my rod down from the finish nails on the wainscoating wall and pulled on my waders and jacket. It was a two-mile walk through the hayfields to the serpentine line of willows that marked the creek.

It begins in the snowfields below the summit of Massive, and flows through high meadows filled with tiny flowers. There are quaking bogs above eleven thousand feet, several hundred yards above the timberline. It flows through the chain of tiny lakes and beaver ponds, filled with small cutthroats and brook trout. There is a large beaver pond a half mile above the ranch, and I sometimes took a horse to fish it in the evenings. The pools below the pond held brook trout and some rainbows, but the slower pockets sheltered browns. The creek tumbled wildly down its final boulder-filled ravine to the valley floor, less than a hundred yards south of the ranch. It wound through willow channels, looping toward the river in the distance, and its lower mileage was entirely brown-trout water.

Its deep pools and cut-bank runs often seemed empty, but the fish were there. It was possible to fish for hours without catching a brown. There were always a few small rainbows near the ranch, but when a fine drizzle misted across the hayfields and triggered a hatch of flies, the seemingly barren currents were alive with browns.

The creek enters the river in a long, sweeping bend with deeply undercut banks. The currents are smooth-flowing over pale gravel and sand. Grass trails in the waist deep eddies against the banks, and although it always seemed like a perfect reach of water for trout, I had never seen one rising there. It was strange and I thought about it sometimes in those last moments before sleeping, half-hearing the coals shifting in the pot-bellied stove and the mice scuttling in the bunkhouse walls.

The solution occurred to me that morning, while I was walking down through the meadows. My approach to those last fifty yards of the creek had always been from upstream, walking on the open paths along the water. From the paths it was possible to see every pebble on the bottom, but it was also possible for every trout to see approaching fishermen.

Idiot! I thought angrily. *Cross the stream in the riffles above and wade up from the bottom!*

The opposite bank was thick with willows and the drift-wood tangles of the spring snow-melt. It was slow going and I fought through, carrying my rod high or butt-first through the brush. Half-wild cattle bellowed and crashed off like buffaloes into the willows, and I was sweating when I finally escaped into the open river bottoms. The creek joined the river fifty feet upstream, and I waded up slowly to the gravel bar and sat down to rest. There were a few mayflies hatching. They were fairly large flies. Their pale wings had a slight olive cast and they looked like big Cahills rising off the current into the willows.

Since that summer I have learned they were *Ephemerella inermis*, but then they only set me searching my fly-boxes for pale dry flies. There was a fresh Light Cahill in one compartment, its rolled woodduck wings and pale ginger hackles stiffly cocked and unsoiled. It was knotted to my tippet carefully, and I studied the deep run along the grass. The mayflies were still emerging sporadically, but no rises showed in the quiet currents.

Weather is capricious at nine thousand feet. Clouds drifted off the high slopes of Mount Massive, where they had been gathering since midday, and a gentle squall misted across the valley. The fine drizzle scarcely disturbed the stream, and seemed to trigger a full-blown hatch of the pale mayflies. It happened almost imperceptibly. The flies emerged from the smooth current, fluttered awkwardly in the rain while their wings dried, and flew off uncertainly into the brush. Their hatching went unnoticed until a sudden rise engulfed one tight against the grass, and its disturbance spread downstream on the current.

Big fish! I thought excitedly.

There was a second rise, porpoising and showing a thick well-spotted bulk. *No wonder I've never seen a fish here*, I thought. *He's got the whole place staked out!*

Working carefully into position, I checked the leader for knots and frayed places while the big trout rose again. The cast dropped softly and cocked the fly above the fish, reached its feeding station and disappeared in a showy rise, but there was nothing when I tightened.

Damn! I sighed. *Might put him down!*

The rises stopped and for some reason I stood motionless in the current and waited. Just when I had decided that it was hopeless, there was another impressive rise fifteen feet above the place where I had missed the first fish. It seemed unlikely that two fish that size were in a single run, and I waited nervously while the big trout settled into its methodical feeding-pattern. It took a dozen fluttering duns before I tried a cast that fell perfectly, and the trout rolled lazily and took the fly.

The reel protested and the rod bucked with its writhing and head-shaking fight. The twelve-inch browns I had taken that summer were forgotten, along with the sixteen-inch rainbow taken in the ranch-house pond. The runs stripped line off the reel, reaching high into the riffles above, and threatened to escape into the heavy river currents downstream. Several runs bored under the cut banks and trailing grasses, ticking the leader across the willow roots, but the tippet held safely. The trout fought desperately when it saw the waiting net, working its tail just out of reach. Just when it was close, it bolted off again until I worked it back.

Finally it came to the net and its bulk threshed in the meshes. *It's better than twenty inches!* Excitement surged through me, and I waded ashore with the trout twisting powerfully. *Four pounds at least!*

It was the biggest trout I had ever seen and I killed it quickly, but in the weeks that followed I always passed that pool with a touch of sadness. There is nothing so empty as a pool without trout, particularly when the guilt is yours.

Ounce of Prevention

THERE was frost on the hay-meadows beyond the river. Two pintails flew downstream, wingbeats whistling above the swift current. Whiteface cattle were grazing in the cottonwoods. The mowing crews had finished cutting the hay-crop, and their huge stacks of bales looked like Indian pueblo ruins in the river bottoms.

Gunnison mornings are like that late in August. The river is low and its side channels trace riffling patterns of lacework across the valley floor. The river cottonwoods move restlessly in the wind. The cold nights would change their color soon.

Breakfast sizzled in the tiny cabin below the Cooper ranch house. Our tackle hung on the porch nails, and we suited-up and wriggled into our waders. It was getting hot when we crossed the bottoms above the ranch. The baling crew was already working in the fields.

Good luck! yelled Frank Klune.

We waved and he disappeared into the brush along the main river. The first pools are tangled with brush and deadfalls from the snow-melt of early summer. The trout hold deep under the logs. It was a long walk from the ranch and its outbuildings, and the sun was high above the Tomichi bottoms. The wind stirred in the high country, following the river and scattering leaves into the current.

It felt good and I stopped to wipe my sweating face. There were no fish working. Regular hatches of small *Paraleptophlebia* flies had been coming off each morning at ten-thirty, and I sprawled in the warm grass to watch the water.

The flies began hatching on schedule, emerging on the surface and fluttering along the current. The trout began taking the nymphs, and occasionally the flash of a nymphing fish showed deep along the logs. Soon they moved to the emerging mayflies, and their quiet rise-forms dimpled and swirled. The hatching flies increased steadily, until the trout were working along the full length of the run.

The hatch had lasted a week on the Cooper Ranch mileage of the Gunnison. We had collected many samples of the tiny duns, and I carefully tied several imitations each evening, using the light of a gas-fired lamp. The naturals had dark slate-colored wings, pale gray legs and tails, and a darkly ringed body with a faint olive cast. Our imitations were dressed with dark blue dun wings and hackles, and bodies of bleached peacock quill wrapped over a base of yellow silk. The bodies were coated with clear lacquer, turning the silk underbody a delicate pale olive.

The pattern worked perfectly that morning in the meadows above the ranch. There were fish rising everywhere in the pools and pocket water and along the high undercut banks. It was easy fishing. The trout came frequently and the current was covered with the tiny mayflies. It was simply a matter of marking a fish's position from its rises, and dropping a cast to get a dragless float down its feeding current.

There were dozens of small stocked rainbows and occasional wild brown trout. The rainbows were in the open riffles and runs in the tail shallows of the pools. The browns were more furtive. They chose currents tight against the logjams and the trailing grass of the banks. Some were holding in the deep, heavy runs and chutes at the heads of the pools. The browns were bigger, dark with their secret hiding places, and there were several of twelve to sixteen inches that morning.

It was almost noon and I was hungry. There was a deep pocket filled with brush-piles that looked good, with a shallow run upstream.

I'll fish that, I thought, *and then I'll walk back.*

Nothing was rising along the brush, although it seemed perfect for a good fish. I watched for signs of a feeding trout, but there was nothing. Finally I fished the brush-pile currents anyway, working slowly upstream and dropping the fly along the jackstraw tangle of driftwood. My imitation was matted and frayed, and was floating badly.

The water upstream looked less promising, and I was about to stop fishing when a soft rise caught my eye. It was working unobtrusively in the shallow run that fed the deep pocket along the brush. The fish porpoised and I watched it roll full length as it took a tiny dun. It was a heavy trout and my pulse was suddenly racing.

There was a fresh dry-fly in my box and I knotted it nervously to the leader. The nylon settled into place and I oiled its hackles. The big trout rolled again, and I watched its spotted length settle back in the smooth current.

Five pounds! I thought wildly.

The run was scarcely deep enough to cover such a fish, except that it was sheltered by overhanging willows. It porpoised again, its dorsal showed after the rise, and its tail wriggled with satisfaction as it disappeared again. There was no question about its diet. The tiny *Paraleptophlebia* duns fluttered along the current and were sipped almost casually, like a gourmet savoring a fine vintage of Chablis.

The leader slipped through my fingers as I prepared to cast, and I felt a wind-knot in the tippet. The knot was close to the fly, I cut it off and snipped the wind-knot and knotted the tiny dry fly back on the leader. The fish swirled heavily as the nylon threaded into its final loop, and I watched its rise-form drift downstream with the current.

Hastily I seated the knot against the hook and studied the trout's position. There was a slight downstream wind, which made the right hook-cast easy. The current tongues were more complicated than they seemed at first glance, but I crawled through the shallows on my knees to reach a better angle. The fish was still working. My position made a cross-stream cast possible, with a slight upstream loop of slack leader.

The line worked back and forth in the sun, drying the fly carefully, and I dropped the cast above the fish. The leader straightened and settled. It caught the wind and fell in a perfect downstream hook.

Beautiful! I thought.

The fly cocked itself on the current and reached the feeding station and disappeared in a soft head-and-tail rise. The line tightened and I gently raised the rod. The fish threshed in surprise and anger, and spray showered high in the wind. Then it panicked and bolted up the run, and shook its head sullenly and was off.

Damn! I said angrily.

The hastily tied knot had slipped.

Song of
the Catskills

IT was a filling station on a high ridge above
the Hudson. There were jawbreakers in a glass apothecary jar
and a rack of green Lucky Strike packages, and hundreds of
colored gum-balls filled the penny machine on the counter.
The pump circulated gasoline through its tall glass cylinders,
bubbles tumbling and churning as it filled the Oldsmobile. We
stood in the shade of the station portico, watching a helper
check a patchwork inner tube for leaks.

We searched through floating pieces of ice in the cooler
and opened two root beers. It was hot and we drank thirstily.
The river wound across its pastoral valley floor. There were
locusts in the trees, and the hot wind stirred the acrid smell of
gasoline. Beyond the river and its villages and farms there
were mountains.

It's like a picture, I thought.

My father finished his root beer and racked our bottles in their wood crate. *What are those mountains?*
Catskills, said the helper.

The gasoline spilled over and streaked down the dusty fender. That afternoon was more than thirty years ago, and it was still a time for childhood summers beside lakes of reeds and lilypads, fishing for pumpkinseeds and bluegills and perch. It would be many years before I fished the rivers in those mountains, rivers that have become the classic Catskill shrines of American trout fishing.

Their source lies in a surprisingly small group of ridges west of Catskill and Kingston on the Hudson. It is still a wild and beautiful region behind its facade of roadside diners and elaborate summer colonies and *borscht*-circuit resorts. The high Catskills rise west of the Hudson, rolling ridges covered with forests and smoke-colored in the distance.

The summits are a series of somber outcroppings, wounded with the grinding scars of ancient glaciers. Hawks and eagles soar on the winds that sigh through these hemlock ridges, and bears and wildcats are killed each season. Sometimes there is even the report of a cougar.

There are still thousands of deer in the dense forests of hardwoods, hemlocks, and pines, deer that wax fat on the apples of colonial orchards long abandoned and overgrown with trees. Wild turkeys are coming back on the Schoharie ridges. Grouse and woodcock are plentiful enough for men who know the covers. Sometimes there is a horned owl flushed from a hemlock thicket, or a pileated woodpecker threading through the trees.

Catskill rivers are still beautiful, although some of their solitude has been surrendered to diners and automobile graveyards and drive-in movies. The wilderness that existed when the Dutch settlers named the river and the village of Catskill has retreated into the highest ridges. These settlers lost livestock to the cougars that lived in the foothill valleys that drained toward the Hudson. *Kaaterskill*, the Dutch called the little river that came down from the ridges of Blackhead Mountain. *The river where there are panthers.*

The region is a mother of rivers. Catskill Creek is no longer a major trout stream, but its sister river across the Blackhead ridges is the famous Schoharie, winding out toward its junction with the Mohawk. The East Branch of the Delaware has its source on Bearpen Mountain, which turns the tumbling Schoharie north. There are two minor Catskill rivers, the Callicoon and the Mongaup, which rise in the timbered hills of Sullivan County and join the Delaware between Port Jervis and Long Eddy.

But two mountains are the genesis of the most famous Catskill trout streams. Doubletop rises 3,868 feet in the western Catskills, and its maternal springheads are the source of three watersheds—tumbling little Dry Brook, the gentle Willowemoc, and the legendary Beaverkill, the most famous trout stream in America.

Slide Mountain reaches 4,207 feet west of the Hudson at Kingston. Its forested shoulders are the beginnings of the Rondout, the swift-flowing Esopus, and both branches of another legendary river—the classic Neversink.

This round handful of Catskill rivers is the wellspring of American trout-fishing literature and tactics. Their pools and riffles have been fished by every major American fishing writer since George Washington Bethune, and the Neversink and the Beaverkill have been the home rivers of great anglers like Theodore Gordon, Reuben Cross, George LaBranche, and Edward Ringwood Hewitt.

Fishing pressure and reservoirs and pollution have decimated the Catskill rivers until the Rondout, the once-famous rainbow water on the Callicoon, and the Mongaup are seldom rated major trout fisheries. Reservoirs on the Schoharie, Esopus, Delaware, Rondout, and Neversink have eradicated some first-rate mileage of river, but in some cases they have created good trout fishing in their impoundments and impressive runs of big spawners in the spring and fall. The cold tailings of some reservoirs have improved and extended the trout habitat downstream, while others have released insufficient flow to purge their rivers of silt and sustain both spawning and the principal fly-hatches.

Some fishing mileage in the Catskills is controlled by private clubs and estates, like the Tuscarora Club and the other huge retreat on the Dry Brook assembled by tycoon Jay Gould, who was born in the Catskills and forged an empire that included both Western Union and the Erie Railroad. There is extensive private water on the headwaters of the Esopus, Willowemoc, Neversink, and Beaverkill, but there is still excellent public fishing on the principal Catskill rivers.

The beautiful Schoharie is a native brook-trout river in its headwaters on Indianhead Mountain. Its tumbling runs and riffles above Hunter are the classic image of mountain trout water, and in the open valley at Lexington it has changed into a series of sweeping riffles and smooth flats. Its principal tributaries are well-known streams in their own right, particularly the Bataviakill and East Kill that join the river from the north, and the West Kill that begins high in the grouse covers on Hunter Mountain.

The watershed has a rich history of famous anglers down the years, and its most famous regular is Art Flick, who once operated the charming West Kill Tavern near the river. His classic little *Streamside Guide to Naturals and Their Imitations* is based on the fly-hatches of the Schoharie, with color photographs of its principal mayflies and the exquisite dry flies Flick ties to imitate them.

Other famous anglers gathered at his inn. Preston Jennings did much of his field work for *A Book of Trout Flies* on the Schoharie and its sister rivers. His pioneer work was the first American attempt to classify and imitate stream insects with the discipline of British fly-fishing writers a century before. Dana Lamb often fished there too, and his feeling for the region is found in little books like *Not Far from the River* and

Preston Jennings

Woodsmoke and Watercress. Lamb often came with his sons to the West Kill Tavern, when the April mayflies were hatching or flights of woodcock had settled into the alder thickets above Lexington. Leslie Thompson was another regular on the river in those days, along with Raymond Camp, whose outdoor columns for *The New York Times* were known to a generation of sportsmen. Thompson and Camp badgered Art Flick into writing his book, helped with the streamside work on the Schoharie, and Thompson painted exquisite watercolors of the mayflies they collected.

Their river and its hatches also played a role in my book *Matching the Hatch,* and it included an episode the first morning I ever saw the river. The night before we camped in sleeping bags beside the Esopus, and we crossed the mountain from Bushnellsville just after daylight.

Mist hung over the river at Lexington, and we crossed the bridge and turned into the meadows below the town. The flat flowed smooth and dark in the mist, and the sun filtered through weakly as we walked through the wet grass.

The surface of the pool was covered with tiny mayflies and fish were working everywhere. *Look at them!* I gasped.

What are they taking? my father asked.

We collected several specimens and studied their bluish wings and bright olive bodies.

Bluewinged Olives, I said.

The trout were rising steadily now. Several were making impressive swirls and porpoise-sized rolls, and we rigged our gear hastily, clumsily stringing our rods.

Nervous? laughed my father.

We shouldered into our wading jackets and edged stealthily into the current. Two heavy fish boiled above me and I knotted a sixteen Bluewinged Olive to my tippet. The line worked out into the rising mist and settled the fly softly above the fish. The tiny dry-fly floated over its feeding position. It rose softly to a mayfly just before my imitation reached its riseform, and it swirled again to a natural just after the fly drifted past. The whole sequence was repeated several times.

They're choosy! I yelled.

My father was working on another fish two hundred feet upstream. *This one won't take either,* he said.

The hatch lasted thirty minutes. We cast over fish after fish until our arms ached. Finally my dry-fly was floating badly and a two-pound brown inhaled it softly. The reel protested and the hatch was over when it finally stopped splashing and surrendered.

Let's check his stomach, I said.

The autopsy was revealing. The fish had been concentrating on the nymphs before they hatched and fluttered down the current. Its stomach was sausage-tight with dozens of dark olive-bellied nymphs. The half-drowned imitation must have looked like a hatching nymph, struggling to escape the surface film of the river.

They were nymphing, we shook our heads.

Such choosiness is common on Catskill rivers, and successful fishermen must understand both their annual cycle of fly-hatches and the artificial flies that imitate them. The skilled angler must also observe what stage of the hatch the fish are taking. We had seen rises to emerging nymphs, and had assumed they were rises to the adult mayflies we could see riding the current.

There are many memories of the Schoharie, from the tumbling runs of the Jeanette water several miles above Hunter to the heavy water at the covered bridge below Blenheim and the Gilboa Reservoir. It has been ten years since I last fished the Blue Bell stretch at the schoolhouse above Lexington, where a huge blue-painted bell hangs in the playground, and its April hatches were mixed with snow squalls. There was another blizzard morning when we walked down through snow-capped tombstones to the Cemetery water and found a heavy hatch of Hendricksons.

There was also the summer when the river was a lukewarm trickle, seeping through the sun-bleached skeleton of its bottom. The stream thermometer found temperatures better suited to smallmouths, and Art Flick suggested the springhole where the Bataviakill entered the river.

Flick shook his head unhappily. *She's so low and warm,* he said, *that I can't bear to look at her!*

We took several bass in the Schoharie flat below the Bataviakill, working upstream into the heavier run of water where the tributary currents mingled with the river against a series of boulders.

My line worked out and dropped the big stonefly nymph against the boulders. There was a heavy swirl in the darkness and I was into a strong fish.

Bass? yelled my father.

It was difficult to tell and I countered a half-dozen stubborn, bulldogging runs before the fish surrendered, fat and threshing in the meshes.

It's a good fish! I carried it ashore.

Didn't act like a bass, my father joined me.

The fish was slender and heavily spotted. *It's a brown!* I laughed. *It's a good three pounds!*

We worked the nymph free and nursed the fish gently in the cold currents of the Bataviakill. *Shame to kill him,* said my father. *The river needs him to spawn.*

We released him in the darkness.

Schoharie fishing has come back since that summer, and in his farmhouse at West Kill, Art Flick still dresses his exquisite dry-flies, faithful to the sparse hackles and wood-duck wings and slender bodies of the Catskill school. Flick still works his magic on the river each season, but his charming West Kill Tavern is gone. It was lost in a tragic fire that engulfed its rambling clapboard frame, licking at the tiger-maple chairs and antimacassar-covered couches, smouldering in the worn Oriental runners, and melting the glass nineteenth-century cases of woodcock and grouse.

Esopus Creek rises on the north shoulder of Slide Mountain

and flows west before winding back in a long question mark course toward the Hudson. It is still a wild little river at Oliverea, tinkling down ledges and gravelly riffles until it reaches Big Indian. Its main channel begins at Shandaken with a series of strong runs, boulder-strewn rapids, waist-deep flats and sprawling pools in the shadow of Panther Mountain.

Its flow is quickened with water carried through Bearpen Mountain from the Schoharie, destined for the faucets and fireplugs of Manhattan. This flow is chilled in its subterranean tunnel, maintaining unusually low midsummer temperatures and a fine head of water in the Esopus below its Allaben outlet portal, but it can also mix torrents of pewter-colored siltiness into the river from its encounter with deposits of marl inside the mountain.

There are sparkling little tributaries like the streams at Stony Clove and Woodland Valley, which are charming and well-known trout fisheries themselves. These little rivers are a refuge from the artificial spates of the portal, and often hold big spawners in season.

The New York Board of Water Supply completed its Ashokan Reservoir on the lower Esopus in 1912, forming a sprawling lake that covered a dozen miles of trout water. It also became a tiny freshwater ocean that has fine rainbows and browns in spring and fall spawning-runs.

The river has its share of tradition too. Henrik Hudson anchored off its mouth in 1609, and the Dutch settlers who named the Catskills had already settled the region only five years later, in spite of bloody raids by marauding bands of Esopus Indians. Like its sister rivers, the Esopus has held a circle of famous disciples in its spell. Their headquarters is probably the Folkert store in Phoenicia, the combination gun-shop, tackle store, newspaper stand, ice-cream parlor and bus stop whose real purpose is a message center for news of wood-cock covers and the fishing.

Paul O'Neill once wrote wry, penetrating articles for *Life* in the halcyon days when its editors would explore any project once it caught their fancy, no matter how outrageous its subject or cost. O'Neill has since retired from its masthead, but his classic article *In Praise of Trout—and Also Me* appeared in the magazine before his departure. Its passages treated the wonder of the sport, focusing on his own experiences with the Esopus, and it firmly established O'Neill as its writer-in-residence.

Other regulars have included fishing experts like Jim Deren, Ray Ovington, Ed Sens, and Al McClane. Deren has run the Angler's Roost in Manhattan for many years. Ovington collated his experience and the original Sens nymph patterns in the book *How to Take Trout on Wet Flies and Nymphs*, the bible of standard wet fly practice for the Catskill rivers. McClane was frequently seen on the river in his early years as fishing editor of *Field & Stream*, and his work was often punctuated with references to the Esopus, particularly rainbow water like Seven Arches and the Greeny Deep when the spawners were running in the spring.

The river is a mixture of enigmatic moods. Failure is common on the Esopus, with its uncertainties of temperature and clarity, but its generous days are superb. There was an evening at Phoenicia many years ago, with a heavy hatch of big *Isonychia* drakes that triggered a massive rise of trout. We took fish after fish, working up into the heavier currents at the head of the Bridge Pool, until it was getting dark and only the biggest fish were still rising.

One heavy trout was slashing at the fluttering mayflies in a strong rip between the rocks. The line worked out and dropped my big slate-colored variant over his position.

There was an explosive rise. The reel screamed as the fish bored straight into the rapids upstream, jumped wildly in the darkness, and powered back past me. *Look out!* I yelled. *It's a big rainbow and we're coming through!*

My father reeled in. *Good luck!* he said.

The fish was still running, cartwheeled end-over-end and

stripped backing from the reel. *He's still going!* I groaned. *He's got most of my line already!*

The fish turned toward my father and pole-vaulted high in the darkness. *Four or five pounds!* he yelled.

There were three more jumps and the fish reached the rocky rapids downstream. There was too much line and backing in the current to control. The fish was running again in the rapids, gathering speed until the line raked and caught on the rocks. The fragile nylon parted.

What happened? yelled my father.

It was a big rainbow! I groaned unhappily.

He laughed and waded toward the shallows. *I know it was a big rainbow,* he said, *but what happened?*

That's what happened! I said. *Rainbow!*

Neversink fishing has been decimated since completion of its reservoir, but its tradition remains as rich as any river in the Catskills. Its fame is secure as the home river of Theodore Gordon, the bachelor fly-fishing genius who evolved the Catskill style of fly-dressing and adapted British dry-fly theory to American waters. Gordon is considered the father of American trout fishing, and his writing was collected by John McDonald in *The Notes and Letters of Theodore Gordon*. The book verifies his major role in the evolution of American trout-fishing practice. It gives us important insights into the frail, tubercular little man who invented the Gordon Quill and other classic flies. Gordon fished the Neversink faithfully the last years of his life, suffering the harsh winters beside his pot-bellied stove to dress exquisite flies for wealthy clients, and died in the old Anson Knight farmhouse near the Neversink in 1915.

The river has also been home water to great anglers of other generations. Edward Ringwood Hewitt had his famous mileage above Bradley before the reservoir was built. Most of his pools are under water now, except for the few cribbing dams that remain above the impoundment on the mileage of the Big Bend Club. Hewitt wrote ten books and pamphlets on fishing, capping his career with *A Trout and Salmon Fisherman for Seventy-Five Years* in 1950. The old master was a tireless innovator in fisheries management and fly-fishing, and carried on a cantankerous, lifelong partnership astream with the equally famous George LaBranche, whose *Dry Fly and Fast Water* is another Catskill classic.

The fly-dressing tradition known as the Catskill school began with Gordon on the Neversink. It continued in the delicate flies dressed by tiers like Herman Christian, William Chandler, and Roy Steenrod. Although it was Gordon who developed the Light Cahill from the older Catskill patterns, Chandler is responsible for the pale modern dressing, and Steenrod was author of the famous Hendrickson.

Two other great anglers were regulars on the Neversink in the last years of their lives. John Atherton often fished with Hewitt, and his experiences on the river are recorded in the pencil drawings and passages of *The Fly and the Fish*. The late Larry Koller lived at Monroe near the river, and fished it regularly from a hunting camp at Long Eddy. His books like the *Treasury of Angling* are filled with fishing pictures and experiences gathered on the Neversink.

The river is born in two branches high on opposite shoulders of Slide Mountain. Its clear little West Branch drops down a lovely valley through the Forstmann estate and the beautiful Connell mileage. These upper reaches are all private water, tumbling musically down pale-gravel riffles and sliding through ledgerock pools. There are wild brook trout with darkly-mottled backs and bright-spotted flanks and orange fins. The main river also supports them as far downstream as the reservoir, perhaps the largest river south of Maine that still holds wild brookies. These headwaters are all private except for a brief mileage available on the tumbling East Branch above Claryville, where the country church has a wooden trout for its weathervane.

There is a lot of public water left between the dam at

Edward Ringwood Hewitt

Neversink and the big private estates below Bridgeville, where the late Ray Bergman described a great afternoon of Green Drake hatches in his classic *Trout*. However, the flow released from the reservoir is erratic, often insufficient to purge its boulder-strewn bottom of silt and sustain its once-great hatches. Fishermen can still find first-rate sport around Bridgeville and Fallsburgh when conditions are right, particularly in April and May, during the heavy hatches of Gordon Quills and Hendricksons.

There are many memories from the Neversink. Len Wright shared his mileage with me on the upper river one cold April weekend, catching wild trout on small wet flies in its sweeping riffles and flats. There was a brace of heavy two-pound browns from a deep flat on the Connell water above, while phoebes caught tiny *Trichoptera* flies above the riffles and deer browsed in abandoned orchards.

Still the most persistent memories of the Neversink are those hours spent with Larry Koller on his hunting-camp water below Bridgeville. There were afternoons with sunlight slanting through the pines, following hen grouse and their broods along paths deep in fiddleback ferns. The last evening I took a big brown fishing the ledges above Long Eddy, with cooking smells of a woodcock cassoulet drifting down to the river. Koller is dead now, and no longer fishes the river or stalks whitetails or walks up grouse on the ridges. His friends ended his funeral in that simple hunting camp above Long Eddy, and scattered his ashes into the river.

The winding East Branch of the Delaware is almost too much river to cover with trout tackle, and most of its best-known trout mileage was inundated with the filling of Peapacton Reservoir. That mileage is permanently lost, although the huge pools that have always wintered Beaverkill fish have been improved and extended downstream, and some really big trout are regularly caught in the reservoir.

Cold tailings released from the dam have transformed the

East Branch and the main Delaware into trout water as much as a hundred miles downstream. Fishermen can find small-mouths and walleyes sharing their river with big browns and rainbows since the dam was completed. The mileage between Shinhopple and Hancock on the East Branch itself is probably the most productive water for trout-minded fishermen, and like the Esopus with its cold tunnel water from the Gilboa reservoir, the East Branch stays cold all summer.

Most fishermen find its chest-deep pools and half-mile flats forbidding, but men who know the river catch some huge trout. *It's tough fishing,* argues Harry Darbee, the professional fly-tier who lives in the Willowemoc nearby, *but when the hatches are coming it can be great!*

The rise and fall of the river and its temperatures below the Downsville dam make it difficult to predict and locate hatching activity. *It scrambles the hatches,* continues Darbee. *We see all the hatches on the East Branch, but we see the tiny Bluewinged Olives and Orange Cahills all summer.*

Big water like the East Branch requires methods familiar to trout fishermen on western rivers, but unknown to eastern anglers who fish only the relatively small Catskill streams. Most big trout on the East Branch are taken Montana-style on big nymphs and bucktails.

Chuck-and-chance-it, explains Darbee.

Such tactics are a game of percentages, working nymphs and bucktails on a deep bellying swing of a sinking line. Each cast is dropped across the current, fished out with a slow pumping rhythm of the rod, and another cast is made with a half-step downstream. The fish are covered thoroughly with a series of concentric teasing-circles over the entire pool. It is a deadly method on big trout.

There is a long flat not far below Shinhopple. It has a strong riffle tumbling into its head, and turns and deepens into a hundred yards of waist-deep water before it slides into a half-mile pool under high slate ledges.

Jeff Norton and I fished it carefully one evening with little luck. *They're here!* he insisted.

I laughed and made another cast.

You wouldn't believe some of the brutes I've seen working here! he shook his head ruefully.

You're right, I grinned.

The cast looped out and dropped the big Muddler against the ledge where the current gathered deep and smooth. There was a fierce strike and an awesome splash. The fish broached like a marlin and fell heavily and the nylon failed.

Wind knot! I examined it unhappily.

That trout looked mammoth! Norton said weakly. *Looked like a ten-pound brown!*

Alligator gar! I laughed.

Roscoe is the village where two of the most famous trout rivers in America meet in the Junction Pool. Both are born high on the hemlock ridges of Doubletop Mountain, tumbling down through abandoned farms and dense stands of hardwoods and conifers. Their headwaters are a thousand riffles whispering into deep pools under ledges dark with lichens and bright with flowers. These are the beginnings of the Willowemoc and the storied Beaverkill.

Their tradition is mixed with a long history of famous anglers. Theodore Gordon often left his farmhouse near the Neversink to fish them, and there he influenced his most famous fly-tying disciple in the late Reuben Cross, who lived many years at Lew Beach on the Beaverkill. Gordon was a secretive man who seldom shared his skills with other fishermen, but he gave Cross several flies during their days along the rivers. Cross worked until he could copy their style faithfully and he codified the techniques of the Catskill school in books like *Tying American Trout Lures* and the classic *Fur, Feathers and Steel.* Cross tied some of the most elegant dry-flies ever dressed, and his customers still marvel at their deli-

Theodore Gordon

cacy and proportions, wondering how such a powerfully-built man could perform such miracles with his huge hands.

Other famous fly-tiers were also regulars on these two Catskill rivers. Louis Rhead wrote *American Trout Stream Insects* in farms and boarding houses along the Beaverkill in the years before 1916. Skilled fishermen like Ray Bergman, Lou Petrie, John Alden Knight, Herb Howard, Preston Jennings, and Roy Steenrod were all regulars forty years ago. Bergman and Knight wrote a cornucopia of first-rate books on fishing, and Steenrod was another Gordon disciple who divided his streamside hours between the Neversink and the Beaverkill watershed. Gordon willed the famous collection of flies sent to him from Hampshire by Frederick Halford in 1890 to Steenrod. Following in the footsteps of Gordon, Steenrod invented an American classic—the Hendrickson pattern.

Willowemoc history begins with Thaddeus Norris, who wrote about its fishing in his *American Angler's Book* in 1860. Other writers who followed included Ladd Plumley, long-time editor of *Field & Stream* in its early years, and expert fishermen like William Schaldach, Samuel Camp, George La-Branche, Edward Ringwood Hewitt, John Taintor Foote, Ray Holland, Emlyn Gill, and John Alden Knight were frequent contributors often found on the Willowemoc and Beaverkill.

Other regulars like John Woodruff, William Bradley, Scott Conover, Charles Campbell, L. Q. Quackenbush, and A. E. Hendrickson all had famous Catskill flies named after them. The tradition of Catskill fly-tying still lives in those patterns and the skilled hands of men like Art Flick on the Schoharie, Walter Dette on the Beaverkill, and Harry Darbee on the Willowemoc. Sparse Grey Hackle and Guy Jenkins are living *dramatis personae* telling stories of those years before the fireplace at the Angler's Club of New York. The fly-boxes of Theodore Gordon have a place of honor on its mantelpiece, while Sparse and Jenkins spin their tales of past days on Catskill rivers, smoking and sipping pungent pot-still whisky.

Willowemoc fishing is filled with *pianissimo* moods, particularly when the rhododendron and dogwood are blooming along the river. Its headwaters are small in the private mileage above Livingston Manor, where the holdings of historic little hotels like the Hearthstone and Ward's DeBruce Club are closed to public fishing. Most of the water downstream past Livingston Manor to its junction with the Beaverkill is still open to anglers who ask permission.

Those hotels were our Mecca then, sighs Sparse Grey Hackle owlishly behind his steel-rimmed spectacles, *and from Gordon Quill time to the Potomanthus hatches in July, they were always full of serious fishermen.*

Harry Darbee is the present Dean of the Willowemoc. Darbee lives in a farmhouse perched above the river, not far from the Covered Bridge Pool that artist John Atherton used in his exquisite pencil drawings of the river. His rooms are filled with fly-boxes and feathers and gamecock necks, mixed with stacks of mail from bankers and corporation presidents and stockbrokers ordering flies. There are gamecocks in the backyard, and sometimes Darbee will show his rare Andalusian blue duns.

Beaverkill fishing above its junction with the Willowemoc is mostly limited to private clubs, except for the famous Covered Bridge water painted years ago by Ogden Pleissner. Clubs like the Brooklyn Flyfishers and the venerable Beaverkill Trout Club have been historic shrines, with more than a half-century of tradition and mystique.

The cacophony of modern life is muted there. The stream is a charming mixture of riffles and smooth bedrock pools and fast runs along the country-road cribbing. There is a classic tree-sheltered glide at the bottom of the farmhouse meadows that are headquarters for the Beaverkill Trout Club, and its members often close their day on the Home Pool. Sometimes it seems almost open and inviting, but there are somber moods when the river goes sour and its fish are not coming. There was a generous evening years ago when it surrendered a three-pounder to my tiny nymph as the members gathered on the porch for dinner.

That's a good way to finish the day, Bob Abbett laughed as we released it, *but it's a tough act to follow!*

Beaverkill fishing below the Junction Pool is another matter altogether. Its fifteen miles are mostly public water and its fish see a parade of anglers. The fishing is less idyllic and its character is mixed, ranging from placid flats to churning rips like Hendricksons and Horse Brook Run.

There is a prelude of open riffles, played on strings and woodwinds in a lyric mood, but the dissonance of drums and trumpets lies just downstream, with the counterpoint of whippoorwills and wind-music in the trees. Fishing the Beaverkill is a complete symphony.

The first pools are famous water, including the chest-deep slick at Ferdons where the Hendrickson was born. Barnharts is a similar pool below, with a long shallow tail that is fine dry-fly water in the evenings. Hendricksons is a wild blaring of trumpets, tumbling over boulders and ledges, and Horse Brook Run is a churning rip downstream where the current-loving rainbows lie in the cold flow of the tributary.

Cairns is a great flat of productive water where the currents from Horse Brook Run reach down a length of underwater ledges. Its length is often blessed with free-rising trout and Cairns has always been popular.

Wagon Wheel is almost an extension of Cairns, and Schoolhouse lies on a bend away from the old highway. Lockwoods has always been famous for big trout on flies, particularly during hatches of big drakes. Mountain is a theatrical pool with its sheer granite face rising from the river, and Lower Mountain has a perfect dry-fly current down its sheltering ledge. Painter Bend has no connection with brushes and palettes. Like the Catskills themselves, it is named for the panthers that infested the region a century ago.

Hain't seen no painters meself, farmers said on the lower

river in past seasons, *but 'spect they still some painters back in them mountains someplace.*

Old legends die slowly among country people, but Painter Bend remains worth the hike from the road. The famous pool in the village of Cook's Falls is two hundred yards of strong boulder-broken water the length of town. Its bridge was the setting for an apocryphal story, involving a city fisherman taking fish on a famous British pattern.

What're they taking? yelled some boys overhead.

Cowdung! the fisherman answered.

There was a long silence from the bridge. *Hey Mister!* they yelled finally. *You ever try horse manure?*

Cemetery and Barrel Pools lie downstream from Cook's Falls, although I never fished them enough to know them well. Like the churchyard stretch on the Schoharie, their mood made it difficult to fish under the dressed ranks of headstones above the river. Chiloways is like Mountain Pool, with a wall of granite covered with rhododendron and wildflowers and lichens. Baxters is the last reach of water before the Beaverkill reaches the Delaware at Peaksville, with enough varied water to occupy an angler for hours.

This is the storied Beaverkill, still the most famous trout stream in America. Its fishing is almost entirely public from Roscoe downstream to Peaksville, and the new fly-fishing-only water offers the best public fishing in the east.

Familiar rivers have a strange charm unlike the challenge of wilderness water. It is a sense of tradition mixed with time, with footpaths worn under the boots of generations, and a patina like the fading barrels of a familiar doublegun. There is also the sense of heritage passed from a parade of famous anglers. Such tradition is typical on the Beaverkill and its sister rivers, and the Catskill fisherman who watched it all was Richard Robbins. His eyes failed him in his last years along the Beaverkill, and sometimes he hailed another fisherman to change his flies. Robbins lies buried in an unmarked grave in the Riverview Cemetery at Roscoe, above the stream he fished more than half his life, and his enthusiasm for the Beaverkill never waned.

Don't get discouraged! he exclaimed when the midsummer hatches were sparse and the river was low and warm. *It's still early and come a rain to cool her some—you'll see the fishing come back!*

There are still men who fish the river who remember Robbins on the Beaverkill, particularly along the easily waded flats of the lower river. The regulars share whisky and stories in the Home Pool along the cellar bar at the Antrim Lodge. Some nights when the mist is layered over the hills, it is not difficult for them to imagine Robbins fishing the river and having him hail to them for a change of fly in the failing light of age and evening.

The Strangest
Trout Stream on Earth

STEAM rises high on cold September mornings, drifting across the river. Skeletal trees lie in bleached jackstraw tangles beside the smoking wasteland of geysers and hot springs downstream. The steam lingers over the river like fog, smelling of sulphur deep in the seams of the earth. It lingers in the pale windless mornings like an encampment of cookfires. The river eddies over its ancient ledges, flowing cold and swimming-pool green into a reach of trailing weeds.

Chutes of boiling water spill into the river across a richly-colored outcropping of lava, hissing steam when they reach the river. Fish rise softly to the daily hatch of tiny *Paraleptophlebia* flies, rolling and porpoising only inches from the scalding currents.

The Firehole River in Yellowstone Park is unique among the famous trout streams of the world. Its smooth weed-trailing currents are like those of the famous Hampshire chalk-streams in England, where dry-fly fishing was born a century ago, slow and rich with insect life and fat surface-feeding brown trout. These fish rise freely on most days, dimpling for minute insects beside weed beds and undercut meadow banks, but unlike the cold British chalkstreams, the Firehole is warmed by thousands of boiling springs and geysers like Old Faithful.

Sulphurous fumes and steam blossom high above its buffalo-grass meadows in a weird smoking landscape. The trout sometimes rise inches away from steaming currents that could literally cook them alive. Geysers rumble ominously beside inviting trout-filled runs, causing the fisherman to watch their smoking vents with a worried frown while he tries his luck. Other bankside geysers sometimes erupt, showering the river banks with lethal torrents of boiling water. Black volcanic sand bottoms the difficult stillwater bends of Biscuit Basin, and the swifter reaches are broken with strange lava ledges. Such fast-water runs sometimes produce rainbows, but the Firehole is primarily a brown-trout river.

Its warm currents spawn almost continually year-round hatches of the many-brooded *Baetis* mayflies, and its meadows are alive with terrestrials like ants and leafhoppers. Firehole trout take such minuscule insects with soft little rises that often hide surprisingly large fish; unlike the chalkstream browns of England, these Firehole fish seldom see insects larger than size sixteen flies. Most Firehole hatches are smaller, and such minute insects emerging on mirror-smooth currents cause some of the most difficult trout fishing in the world. The cold mornings of September and October sometimes find trout rising to such minutae in clouds of geyser steam that obscure the river. The wind carries strange fumes long imprisoned in the molten viscera of the earth, and on such mornings the Firehole seems like a river of the netherworld, the strangest trout stream this side of the River Styx.

John Colter discovered the Yellowstone country in 1807,

after participating in the earlier Lewis and Clark expedition, but Jim Bridger first explored the Firehole Basin. His outlandish catalog of exaggerations about Colter's Hell gave the Yellowstone its own Bunyan-like mythology as much as fifty years before President Ulysses Grant signed the law making it into a National Park.

Bridger delighted in spinning his Yellowstone tales, and one yarn described a river that was glacier-cold at its source and flowed downhill so fast that friction heated the water and cooked its trout. The Firehole was that mythical river. Bridger exaggerated about its currents, but there are places where its bottom is actually hot. The lava crust which forms the river bottom is so thin in places that it is heated by the boiling springs and geysers underneath. Downstream from Ojo Caliente spring, which spews frightening torrents of scalding water into the Firehole, there are places where the rhyolite bedrock is so thin that the bottom feels hot through the soles of English wading brogues.

Although the Firehole is heavily populated with good trout that rise freely to almost daily hatches, fishing over them can be extremely frustrating. Minute insect-forms and quiet currents can pose problems for anglers unfamiliar with such fishing, and brown trout fished over by thousands of eager Yellowstone visitors are unbelievably sophisticated.

The average fisherman finds them almost impossible, and the experienced fly-fisherman who is unprepared to match fly-hatches smaller than size sixteen will end his Firehole sessions talking to himself. Selective feeding, which finds the trout refusing anything that does not resemble their natural foods, is the rule rather than the exception.

Through some fifteen years of experience with these Firehole browns, I have found them relatively easy only during the June mayfly hatches and the September grasshopper fishing, other times are frustrating.

My first session on the Firehole occurred in the Nez Percé meadows, which border the highway. These meadows have beautiful open water that quickens the pulse of the most knowledgeable angler, although its trout are perhaps too accessible to the tourist hordes. Hundreds of free-rising trout dimple there every day, readily visible from the highway, and this stretch of the river attracts a lot of pressure. Its brown trout are tourist-shy and difficult. The first morning I fished the Nez Percé water was cloudless and bright. Trout were rising everywhere to some minute Bluewinged Olive mayflies, but catching them was another matter. None of my flies was small enough, and the best fish seemed frightened witless by my 4x leaders. There were some sixteen Blue Quills in my flyboxes, but they looked like battleships beside the naturals, and the fish refused them.

The second morning was easier. The hatching mayflies were larger, and the current was riffled with wind and drizzling rain. The looping meadow bends of Biscuit Basin surrendered fifty-odd trout under these less difficult conditions, and I felt my Firehole problems had been solved.

The third morning I returned to the Nez Percé meadows, determined to vindicate my earlier failures there. Good trout were rising everywhere in the bright September sunlight. Minute mayflies rode and fluttered down the deep channels between the ledges and undulating weeds. For several hours my 4x leaders and sixteen flies proved worthless. Two days later I left the Firehole, frustrated and fishless and talking to myself, and resolved to return the following year with a lighter rod and smaller flies and finer leader tippetts.

That was fifteen years ago. Since then our tackle has witnessed a minor revolution: lighter fly-rods are commonplace and size twenty-two flies have become available in the best tackle shops and modern nylons have produced practical 8x leaders. The Firehole has since yielded many of its secrets during subsequent visits, and careful studies of its character and its fly-hatches have paid off over the years. Those studies revealed the unique qualities that make the Firehole one of the strangest and best brown-trout streams on earth.

The river rises in Madison Lake above Old Faithful and flows northward through a plateau of rhyolite lava, looping its placid currents through clustered pines and straw-colored meadows and steaming geyser basins. Since the Firehole drains the principal geyser region in the Yellowstone, considerable temperature and ecological changes occur where the river receives its hydrothermal discharges. Other changes occur below its small cold-water tributaries. These changes and their remarkable effect on both the fish and the fly-hatches have been ferreted out in some fifteen years of Firehole observations.

The river is closed to fishing above Old Faithful campground to protect both its qualities as drinking water and the best nursery-areas in its headwaters. Such natural spawning is important to the management of the entire watershed. These headwaters are cold from the springs and snow-melt on the Continental Divide, seldom rising above fifty-six degrees in midsummer. Their chemical properties are average for good western trout waters and both the hatches and the growth-rate of the trout are typical. Below the tourist area at Old Faithful, with the influx of its strange pools and geysers and boiling springs, the Firehole changes radically. Even more changes occur below Riverside Geyser, where the winter river-temperatures are typical, but the summer temperatures hover at sixty-odd degrees and alkalinity is almost doubled. Such increased alkalinity improves both the fly-hatches and the potential trout population. These changes are progressively increased until the Firehole reaches Biscuit Basin. The intense hydrothermal flowages there are partially balanced by the waters of the Little Firehole, which enters the main river not far above the Biscuit Basin footbridge. The Firehole is shallow here, flowing over broken strangely-patterned ledges, and the average size of its trout has increased. Fly-hatches are more numerous, and some big browns are found both in the lava pockets and under the undercut banks of the Little Firehole itself.

Below this Biscuit Basin water, the alkaline richness of

the river is greatly increased and its river temperatures seldom drop below fifty degrees, making for excellent fly-hatches and greater growth-rate of the trout and better wintering. This stretch is scenic water, with serpentine bends in meadows bordered with spruce and lodgepole pine. There are some swift-flowing side channels and black-lava bottoms, where wise old browns savor minute mayflies along their grassy banks. The river is friendly and shallow here, and its trout are easily frightened by bad casting and a careless approach and heavy leaders.

The experienced Firehole fisherman fishes only to specific rises and spends much time on hands-and-knees, creeping and crawling to get within casting range without spooking his quarry. The stretch from the mouth of the Little Firehole to the bottom of the Biscuit Basin meadows, where a short loop-road provides parking near the river, is a mile of first-rate water.

The next two miles, between the loop-road and the Iron Bridge just off the highway, is varied water that offers both good browns and an occasional fat rainbow in the faster places. Ledges and deadfalls shelter some selective lunkers. Park rangers warn that grizzlies frequently cross the river in this stretch, and the angler should be watchful there. There are several convenient places for parking. The water above the Iron Bridge is excellent, and was described by Ray Bergman in his familiar classic *Trout*, in the passages about the Firehole and its exceptional dry-fly fishing thirty years ago. Both cold and hot springs add their seepage in this mileage of river, raising its median temperatures while decreasing its alkalinity. The stretch is especially good for caddis hatches and the fishing is excellent.

Between the Iron Bridge and the Midway Geyser Basin, where the river again parallels the highway, is a mile of broken water with both browns and rainbows. Here the Firehole is a series of fast runs and shallow lava-pocket pools, with occasional hot springs and comical geysers, like the miniature volcano with a *putt-putt* rhythm like a tiny one-lung engine. Temperatures remain relatively warm, although several hot springs raise the alkalinity somewhat. Hatches are good, and there is an occasional lunker brown among the potholes that scar the bottom.

The water that lies between the highway and the steep geyser-covered shoreline is often obscured by clouds of sulphurous steam. The geyser waters stain these banks with varicolored deposits where they reach the river. There are several first-rate pools beside the highway, but their trout are hardfished and shy. Above the Midway footbridge, where torrents of steaming water tumble into the river, the Firehole trout rise steadily to the hatching flies, only inches away from temperatures that could cook them alive. The exaggerations of Jim Bridger about the river were partially true.

Below the Midway footbridge, there is an excellent fourmile stretch of river, accessible from two places off the Fountain Freight Road. About a mile below the Iron Bridge, there is a twin-run trail that forks down to the river. Temperatures on this water never sink below fifty-eight degrees in winter, providing hatches and optimum feeding conditions throughout the year. Its trout grow deep-bellied like Florida bass. The alkalinity is high, creating rich weedy water and heavy flyhatches.

Another half-mile on the Fountain Freight Road is the turn-off to the Feather Lake picnic-ground. Anglers leave their cars there and hike down to the river bottoms below the trees. There are side channels and undercut banks here, where some really large trout lie hidden, and several excellent pools. One side-channel pocket above the picnic area was the setting for an important Firehole lesson on a September evening long ago. The river looked shallow over an open gravel bottom, and a fish was rising tight against the grass. The rises seemed insignificant. Since the Firehole browns had treated me shabbily that afternoon, even a small fish was a prize, and I worked stealthily into casting position. Kneeling in the shallow current, I watched the rises and selected a tiny Adams to imitate the minute brownish caddisflies on the water. The cast settled right and the float looked good. The little dry-fly flirted with the bankside grasses and disappeared in a sipping dimple. Suddenly the hooked fish exploded from beneath the grass, porpoising and wallowing wildly in the gravel shallows. The leader sheared like a cobweb when the mammoth brown tunneled into the upstream weeds. The lesson was important, and I have never attempted to judge the size of a Firehole brown by his rises again.

Above the Fountain Freight Bridge, there are clearings and meadows where buffalo and elk are often found grazing. The water above the bridge is fast and broken, tumbling over terraced lava ledges and outcroppings. There are good trout in the pockets. Rainbows are often found in these swift well-aerated places.

Below the bridge, violent Ojo Caliente spring spills its steaming waters into the river, raising temperatures and alkalinity to the highest levels in its fifteen-odd miles. Downstream the currents are slow and choked with undulating beds of weeds, over a bottom that varies from rhyolite bedrock to insect-rich layers of marl. Fly-hatches here are excellent. Two cold-water tributaries, meandering Fairy and Sentinel Creeks, add their flowage to the Firehole below Ojo Caliente.

This reach of the river provides optimum wintering conditions for its trout. When the midsummer temperatures rise too high, which has happened sometimes since the earthquake of 1959 changed the underground hot springs, the fish congregate in the cooler current-tongues below the two feeder-creeks. Gene Anderegg and I spent a week on this water once, taking some heavy browns that were selectively feeding in the mouths of these tributaries and the cold runs below them.

The Firehole returns to the highway in the Nez Percé meadows another mile downstream. This is one of the best dry-fly stretches on the river. Large browns populate its deep pools and main weed-channels, but it is almost too popular and easily accessible from the highway. The deep stillwater pool just above the mouth of Nez Percé Creek produced an eleven-pound brown in grasshopper season a few years back. The trout free-rise in this mile of water on most days, and because they are so hard-fished through the tourist season, their tippet-shy selectivity is a challenge.

Nez Percé Creek adds its cooling currents and alkalinity to the Firehole near the highway, stabilizing the temperatures and alkaline riches of the six miles below. About a mile below the mouth of the Nez Percé is the famous Rainbow Riffle, which has given up some slab-sided trout with carmine flanks and gill-covers. There are also some heavy browns in this stretch, but with the highway beside the river, they are hard-fished and easily spooked. These educated Firehole lunkers usually lie in the weed channels and runs along the opposite bank, beyond the range of the average fisherman and the rock-throwing children of the tourists. There is some big water here and felt-soled chest waders are needed. Two miles farther downstream, there are some first-rate pools and pockets above the Cascades of the Firehole, but they are adjacent to scenic turnouts and parking areas, and are heavily fished. However, after September there are few visitors in the Yellowstone, and the skilled angler will find them productive.

Two miles below the Cascades, there is a reach of relatively unproductive water above the Firehole Falls. Downstream is some better fishing in the half-mile of side channels and pocket water that lies between the falls and the campground at Madison Junction. This stretch is seldom fished, because most anglers become preoccupied with the more accessible meadows of the Madison and Gibbon Rivers below the camping area, but in late autumn, when the spawning browns and rainbows from Hebgen Lake are stopped by the Firehole Falls, this bottom half-mile of river will regularly produce trophy-sized fish.

The river ends in its meadow confluence with the Gibbon, which drains the Norris Geyser Basin to the northeast, and the two rivers join to form the Upper Madison. Some thirteen miles downstream on the Madison is the town of West Yellowstone, and the western entrance to Yellowstone Park. Regular air service to West Yellowstone is welcome news for Firehole devotees from Los Angeles to Boston, since it is possible to leave either coast in the morning and cover the Biscuit Basin stretch before nightfall.

With few exceptions, the fly-patterns needed to fool these ultra-selective Firehole browns are small. There is some variation in the distribution of the natural hatches with the fluctuations of alkalinity and temperature. For example, the best hatches of the larger *Ephemerella* mayflies occur in the upper reaches of the river, between Lone Star Geyser and Biscuit Basin. The brief early-season hatches of big drakes are concentrated in the weedy silt-bottomed water that provides the proper environment for the burrowing *Ephemera* nymphs. Caddis hatches are heavily distributed on the entire river, especially below Biscuit Basin. The large *Acroneuria* and dark-colored *Pteronarcys* stonefly nymphs, known erroneously as helgrammites on western rivers, are numerous in the fast-water stretches, with particularly dense concentrations in Rainbow Riffle and above Riverside Geyser and the Iron Bridge. Minute mayflies like the *Paraleptophlebia* and *Baetis* groups are thick, especially in the quiet weedy stretches, and are numerous enough to form a staple diet for the Firehole surface-feeders.

Since most fly-hatches are small on the Firehole, the typical flies in the boxes of its regulars are on hooks between fourteen and twenty-four. Typical patterns are traditionals like the Dark Hendrickson, Light Hendrickson, Red Quill, Blue Quill, Bluewinged Olive, Iron Blue Dun, Pale Watery Dun, and the Adams. Terrestrial imitations like ants, jassids, beetles and grasshoppers are also effective, along with standby wets like the Partridge and Olive, Grouse and Green, Partridge and Brown, and the Gold-ribbed Hare's Ear. Regional patterns like the Muskrat Nymph, Montana Nymph, Whitcraft, and Muddler are also useful, and during the big *Ephemera* hatches, the Dark Donnelly Variant and Red Quill in sizes ten and twelve are needed.

Perhaps the most unusual quality of the Firehole lies in its management regulations. Millions of visitors pass through its valley every season, and the Firehole is probably the hardest fished trout stream anywhere. Public water everywhere else has degenerated to put-and-take stocking under fishing pressure, with the result that we have trout streams without trout, except on scheduled fish-truck days. Even big western rivers like the Snake and the Yellowstone and the Big Hole, while far from being fished-out, are declining noticeably each year because of excessive kill-limits and thoughtless irrigation methods and rapidly increasing numbers of fishermen. The Firehole lies within a few hours of all these bigger rivers, and although it is fished even harder than the remaining public mileage of eastern streams like the Beaverkill and the Brodheads in the shadow of New York, its fishing has remained pretty much the same in my fifteen years experience.

Local experts like Bud Lilly and Pat Barnes, who operate famous shops in West Yellowstone and fish the Firehole regularly, point out that the river has not been stocked in the past twenty-odd years.

How can the Firehole remain the same without stocking? asks a typical first-timer.

The answer is surprisingly simple: the river has been restricted to fly-fishing for almost thirty years, and its kill-limit is only five trout per day. The result is a watershed in perfect natural balance between its spawning potential and the wild trout harvested each season, even with the extremely heavy fishing pressure.

There has been a slight decline in the number of big trout and the average size in recent years, although a heavy population of fish to sixteen inches is still present. Perhaps the unique qualities of the Firehole should be recognized and its kill-limits even more restricted. Regulations making it a fish-for-fun river with no killing whatsoever, or a trophy-fishing river where one or two trout above fifteen inches are permitted, would probably make its fishing even better. The sulphur content of its water makes most Firehole fish ordinary table-fare anyway.

Similar regulations will probably be necessary on all wadable, easily fished streams in the future, if Americans want to enjoy decent trout-fishing on their public waters under population pressures, and the Firehole is a graphic example of management techniques for that future.

The last time I fished above Biscuit Basin, there was a twenty-inch brown rising regularly in a shallow lava pocket. It was a difficult place to approach without frightening the trout, and I spent almost fifteen minutes circling around below his position and working stealthily up the ledge-rock riffles on hands-and-knees. Finally I was in position for a delicate presentation and dragless float, and started false-casting when some tourists from Nebraska came down the path to the river. The man was wearing a white shirt and his wife had a bright yellow dress.

Catching anything? they asked innocently.

The big brown had spooked long before they reached me. Their children began running up and down the bank, throwing rocks into the water and splashing in the shallows with sticks. The smaller trout stopped rising in terror. There was no point in fishing after such bedlam, and I reeled-in unhappily to look for a quieter reach of water.

Riverside Geyser erupted as I reached the car, putting on the sporadic show that dwarfs even Old Faithful. Tourist cars began stopping everywhere, until crowds of people were milling around me. Cameras were clicking furiously as I put my rod away. The geyser reached its peak and began to subside, and torrents of scalding water cascaded down the banks. The morning was filled with the acrid choking odors of sulphur. Clouds of steam towered into the crisp September air, and billowed across the landscape until it was impossible to drive or see the river. Such experiences are typical, and make the Firehole the strangest trout stream on earth.

Legend and the Letort

Tᴴᴇ remarkable literature and tradition of fishing for trout is unmatched by any other sport. From its treasury we can draw a single conclusion: anglers are thoughtful men and angling is a contemplative art, and many anglers have been the kind of men who have placed their thoughts and experiences on paper to share them with others. From their books has come literature, and from the literature of fly-fishing have come its legends.

Legend is a nebulous sometime thing, born in the mist-shrouded half-world between reality and romanticism. Legends are spawned in the spinning of tales and thrive in the middleground between things as they are and things as we would like them, and angling legend is no exception. The contemplative men who have fished and loved our rivers have left a rich legacy of their thoughts and experiences, their triumphs and failures.

Many have written of their sport in language as lithe and bright-colored as the fish themselves, and for this we are grateful. Through their books we can return through time and relive their experiences, seeking the source of our own fascination in fly-fishing with the legendary authors themselves as guides to the best water.

Knowledgeable modern anglers are familiar with the substance of fly-fishing legend. There is telling and retelling over campfires on the dark tea-colored rivers of our north country, over sour-mash whisky after the evening rise at storied Catskill fishing inns, and over leisurely midweek lunches in Manhattan.

Legend and tradition and a passion for bright water are the essence of angling. The foundations of angling legend are mostly European, but not all of the well-springs are there. The sparkling rivers of the Catskills and Poconos are the classic landscapes of our American tradition. Our legend has its genesis on the big beautiful pools of the Beaverkill and Willowemoc, the legendary water of the Neversink, and the laurel-hung pools of the lovely Brodheads.

There is a legion of legendary names. It begins with Dame Juliana Berners in the fifteenth century, the unknown author of *The Arte of Angling* in 1577, and Walton seventy-six years later. The parade continues through the Cottons and Halfords and Marryats of England, down to the classic Americans like Gordon and Hewitt and LaBranche.

The more knowledgeable know their writings as well as their names, and their accomplishments are part of our American heritage. Angling legend is already more than a century old in America. Few legends are fully formed in such brief time, since most are shaped slowly with strata-like telling and retelling until their origins in fact are all but lost in the embellishments of fancy. Legends are difficult to recognize in embryonic form, and it is rare that we are permitted to participate in their beginnings, rare that we are able to observe their birth and evolution.

There is such a legend forming now, and that new legend might be called the Legend of Letort Spring Run, for it was conceived on the quiet weed-channelled currents of that small limestone stream in Pennsylvania. Hewitt wrote in his *Trout and Salmon Fisherman for Seventy-Five Years* that there are no American rivers like the English Test. Hewitt is wrong: there are several from Pennsylvania to the Sierra Nevadas, and the lovely cress-bordered Letort is queen of them all. The Letort is somewhat smaller than the Test, but its trout and its character are much like that of the upper Test on its Oakeley or Whitchurch beats.

Anglers are shaped by their rivers, and difficult rivers like the Test and the Letort have evolved accomplished anglers in the past. Their shy trout are the supreme challenge and their skilled practitioners are drawn Mecca-like to their quiet currents year after year.

The historic challenge of the British chalkstreams caused the classic twelve patterns of Berners and the dry-fly innovations of Halford in the nineteenth century. Selective brown trout are the pleasant enigma of both the Test and the Letort. The men who fish and love both rivers are an unusual breed content with a modicum of hard-won success, and accept the challenge.

Letort regulars comprise a veritable round table of great anglers who fish according to a strict code of chivalry. Charles Fox is the author of books like *Rising Trout* and the acknowledged leader of the clan. Vincent Marinaro is a perfectionist best-known for the contemporary angling classic, *A Modern Dry-Fly Code,* and is certainly the Merlin of the Letort. Ross Trimmer, tobacco-chewing retired police officer, is undisputed court jester. There are many others, and the court has no Guinevere except the little river herself. The regulars may be found paying her homage each evening in the water meadows above Carlisle.

The love they have for the river is incredible. They scorn the too-easy supermarket scramble for stocked fish that occurs on most waters, because the truck-dazed hatchery trout are robbed of their fear during a pampered hand-fed existence, and their resemblance to wild fish is only superficial.

Letort regulars fish solely with flies and kill *none* of the trout they take. The native wariness and selectivity of these fish is honed to perfection with each successive capture and release. Each trout becomes both an old friend and an old adversary, and its holding and feeding lies are familiar as soon as mid-season.

These men do not post their water, but permit access restricted to fly-fishing and prohibit the killing of trout under fifteen inches. Violation of these rules constitutes trespass. Since these rules went into effect, the regulars have noticed a singular increase in natural spawning and average size of fish, since female brown trout are seldom fully mature until they reach twelve inches.

The character of the river is worth comment. Like other limestone rivers in Pennsylvania, it bubbles out cold and complete from cavern-fed springs of remarkable volume. British chalkstreams are spawned in the cretaceous chalk downs of southern England, while the eastern limestone streams emerge from the cretaceous caverns of the Appalachians. Each results in lime-rich water capable of supporting unusually heavy populations of fish and fly-life. These Appalachian rivers are relatively small, leading brief lives in their pastoral warmwater valleys. Limestone trout are fat with crustacea, and are seldom taken on dry-flies unless they are already feeding on the surface.

Fishing the water at random, in the classic American fastwater manner, is fruitless unless one knows exactly where the fish lie when not rising. Fishing over known holding-lies is possible in grasshopper season, but on the whole, limestone experts have learned to watch the water and fish only to rising trout, like their counterparts on the chalkstreams of Hampshire.

The unique character of the Letort has played a major role in the legendary innovations conceived on its weedy currents. There are no calendar-picture falls or boulder-broken runs or dark pools hung with rhododendron. The little river is born in two large springs that flow strong and full into a gentle landscape of manicured fields and brick-patterned barns and dairy cattle.

The headwaters are cavern-cold and flow smoothly over the pale gravel. Watercress and beds of elodea divide the quiet current tongues. Cress is cultivated on one tributary, and the other has long been defended by a remarkably belligerent bull. Fishing is not feasible on either stretch. Such protection results in undisturbed spawning grounds, blessed with a constant volume and temperature of flow. The trout population is a fine stock of native fish.

Gentle hills protect the Letort from the prevailing winds. Heavy rains are quickly absorbed into the limestone aquifers beneath the valley floor, and seldom affect the color or volume of flow except for a slight limesalt milkiness and a barely imperceptible rise in level. It is like the chalkstreams of England or the lava-field rivers of Iceland.

Hewitt described the freshet-free Test in *Telling on the Trout*, and writes of a fine large house near Stockbridge with flat lawn reaching to the river. The house has glass doors opening out to the grass less than twelve inches above the water, yet no freshets ever threaten to enter the house. Hewitt believed this condition was unique with the Hampshire chalkstreams, but on the little Letort there was once a small fishing-hut on concrete piers less than ten feet from the stream and about ten inches above the water. None of the Letort regulars can recall water rising under the fishing-hut floor.

Constant water temperatures are a major factor in Letort fishing. The midsummer temperatures are extremely cold when compared with other eastern trout streams. Early morning usually finds the water a chill fifty degrees. During hot weather it warms steadily at about two degrees per hour, until it reaches a mid-afternoon peak of sixty-five. The fish begin rising sporadically as the river reaches fifty-six degrees in later morning. Rises increase as the temperature increases, both in the number of fish and the frequency of rises. Peak feeding begins with peak water temperatures, and the momentum of feeding activity continues until darkness reverses the temperature cycle.

The cold water both limits and benefits the aquatic fly-hatches on the Letort. Only those species adapted to low temperatures and slow water are present, and they are limited to a few species and are relatively small in size. The constant volume of flow insures their survival, while on other streams subject to extremes of temperature and water level, the fly-hatches suffer badly. The limited number of aquatic species has a surprising result too, because it has focused the attention of the trout on the minute terrestrial insects in the Letort meadows.

These two factors: the limited number of aquatic hatches and the importance of the tiny land insects, have had a major role in the Letort story. Letort regulars have been forced to solve the complexities of imitating minute aquatic and terrestrial flies. Like their predecessors on the Test, the Letort fishermen have mastered a difficult river and its selective trout. The importance of terrestrial hatches throughout the season was unknown, although writers like Ronalds and Halford and Moseley discussed them, until the unusual conditions on the Letort have forced an unusually talented group of fishermen to perfect a complete terrestrial theory and technique of imitation for such insects.

Grasshoppers and flying ants have long been observed in the trout diet, and the many fishing writers have discussed their importance. Ronalds was famous for his *Fly-Fisher's Entomology*, which included caterpillars, beetles, ants, and leafhoppers among its imitative fly-patterns. However, their importance throughout the season, rather than merely during peak seasons or mating flights, was never emphasized in past angling books. Ants are continuously on the water in great numbers as the season progresses, but their important place in the trout diet has been virtually ignored; and the daily role of the miniscule leafhopper, one of the major foods on meadow streams, was almost unknown.

Here is the source of the Letort legend. The evolution of workable terrestrial imitations is an angling breakthrough that make the Fox-Marinaro studies on the Letort the modern equal of the Halford-Marryat collaboration that perfected dry-fly theory on the Test.

Modern terrestrial imitations are an angling event of near-legendary stature. The frustration of casting to terrestrial-smutting trout has been ended. Classic patterns for smutting fish were merely tiny conventional dry flies. Anglers call them midges. Yet such adult *Chironomus* midge imitations are consistently refused by selective trout when they are taking terrestrials, since the silhouette of conventional midge flies does not suggest the opaque shapes and light patterns made in the surface film by such insect-forms as ants and leafhoppers and beetles.

The day of discovery is eloquently recorded in Marinaro's *Modern Dry-Fly Code*, which describes fishing the meadows with Charles Fox near the little fishing hut. There were no visible insects on the water, but the fish were busily working. Conventional methods had failed miserably in the past and were no better that afternoon. The rise forms were the familiar bulges so frustrating in the Letort meadows. Fox and Marinaro tried fish after fish, resting one and casting to another, exchanging helpless shrugs as they passed.

Marinaro writes that his frustration finally proved too much. He stopped fishing to study the current. Prone in the warm grass, Marinaro watched the slow current-pattern slide hypnotically past. Some time elapsed in pleasant reverie before he was suddenly aware of minute insects on the water.

He rubbed his eyes but they were really there: miniscule mayflies struggling with their diaphanous nymphal skins, tiny beetles like minute bubbles, ants awash in the surface film, and countless minutiae pinioned in the smooth current.

His mind stirred with excitement as he hurried toward the fishing hut. There he quickly fashioned a fine-mesh seine with sticks and mosquito netting. Its meshes were not long in the water before his suspicions were confirmed by the thin residue of tiny insects that collected at the waterline. There were mayflies with wings less than an eighth-inch in length, beetles less than three thirty-seconds of an inch in diameter, tiny reddish-gold and black ants an eighth-inch in length, and leafhoppers of minute dimensions in astonishing numbers.

It was the moment of discovery. Charlie Fox came downstream and examined the tiny insects. Both men searched their boxes for flies of proper color and size. Several good fish were quickly caught, and autopsies of stomach contents confirmed a diet of minute forms. The frustration of the bulge-rises was over.

But modified conventional flies were often rejected in the days that followed. New patterns were needed. Many experiments were tried before a workable fly-dressing formula was perfected. The basic concept was slow in coming, and the early attempts were less than fruitful. Beetle imitations are typical of the problems. Small coffee beans were tried first, filed and mounted on the hooks with cement like tiny bass bugs. They floated too low and landed too hard and the trout wanted none of them. Cork and balsa wood were no better. Clipped and folded deer-hair beetles were too water absorbent. Black sponge rubber worked sometimes, but tended to twist on the hooks and made it difficult to hook the fish. All worked fairly well on other streams, while the Letort fish remained skeptical.

The full shape and thickness of beetles was ultimately forgotten, and a fresh theory of fly-dressing evolved. Silhouette and light-pattern in the surface film were its essence.

Marinaro used large jungle-cock eyes first. Their opacity was good and the fish came well to imitations with wings tied flat, but jungle-cock feathers were fragile and tended to split after a few trout were taken. They are now prohibited from entry into the United States and stocks are dwindling.

Ross Trimmer and I were sitting in the Turnaround Meadow one August afternoon. I was tying flies and noticed some pheasant-skin pieces in a hackle cannister. There were a few dark greenish throat-feathers on one fragment. We tried them instead of jungle-cock, soaking several feathers together with lacquer to get toughness and opacity. The lacquered feathers were trimmed to proper ovoid shape and tied flat over trimmed hackles. Success was remarkable and immediate. We tried them in the meadows above the trestle and took twenty-one fish. Such a score on the beetle-feeders was unbelievable.

Although the jungle-cock beetles often proved too fragile, the jungle-cock wing proved marvelously successful in another context. It is the key to imitating the ubiquitous leafhoppers with a remarkable series of patterns called Jassids. These diminutive flies are one of the great all-season solutions for difficult, dimpling trout. Much of the surface feeding in the hot low-water months of summer is concentrated on leafhoppers. Alfred Ronalds mentions leafhoppers in his *Fly-Fisher's Entomology*, but his imitations are poor for selective fish. Jassids have proved excellent, and their development will make Marinaro an angling legend wherever big midsummer browns feed quietly in flat water.

Both the ringneck-feathered beetle and the minute Jassid are proof of the same theory: that the fish cannot sense the thickness of small insects drifting above them, and that proper opacity and silhouette and light pattern in the surface film are the critical elements in successful terrestrial imitations.

Their success led the Letort regulars to reappraise their traditional Mayfly patterns. Letort trout were refusing dry-fly imitations of the conventional style. Such flies have primarily evolved from the classic Halford formula, with wings and hackles at the hook-eye. Body materials occupied the remaining hook shank. Wings were fashioned with fragile wing-quill or duck breast feathers. Hackles and tail-fibers support the fly-weight in the surface film.

Halford chose his colors in the following manner: hackles suggested mayfly legs, wings imitated natural wing-color and configuration, bodies simulated the sternite or belly-segment colors, and tail fibers were chosen to match the color and length of the *setae*.

Letort observations convinced Marinaro that two basic errors flawed the Halford system of imitation: that leg-color hackles distorted the percentages of overall color distribution and tended to obscure the all-important silhouette and color of the wing, and that the silhouette of the thorax structure ahead of both legs and wings had been forgotten entirely as a component of English fly-dressing configuration.

Experiments on the Letort confirmed that hackles should be chosen to reinforce wing color, ignoring the color of the legs, and that fly-configuration should be changed to suggest the mayfly thorax silhouette. Although there were several preludes to such thinking in the writings of Burke and Harding and Dunne, it was the Letort School that perfected a fully workable thorax-fly theory of mayfly imitation.

The system is revolutionary: hackle-point wings and hackles were placed near the middle of the hook, and body material was used on both sides of the hackle, simulating both the abdomen and the thorax. The bodies were shortened proportionally, since the upward curving posture of mayfly bodies tends to foreshorten length when viewed from below. The thorax style is designed to float the fly on the hackle and body structure, making a light pattern of thorax, abdomen, and legs in the surface film. Tails were cocked upward, just as the mayflies hold their *setae* high. The thorax-style concept was thoroughly proved on the selective browns of the Letort, and has been adapted into daily practice.

Critics who argue that wings are unnecessary may be right on most rivers, but they are wrong on smooth water like the Letort. The remarkable experiments that settled this argument among its regulars were conceived and performed. The regulars reasoned that wing-clipped natural mayflies might be floated over a hyper-selective trout that was rising steadily to the hatch. They were particularly interested in watching the reactions of the fish to wingless naturals. The experiment caught their imagination and was quickly tested on the stream.

The test subject was chosen with great care. There was a good brown so legendary for his choosiness that the regulars called him the Trout-without-a-Mouth, because most of them had gotten him to rise without hooking him. The line of drift that carried his food to his feeding position was precise. The little sulphur mayflies were hatching, and the current tongues came together above the fish to concentrate all the naturals in a single, weedy channel. The trout was rising methodically.

Naturals were carefully gathered. Their wings were scissor-clipped and they were placed back on the water, alive and wriggling. The fully-winged mayflies came down and were taken in sipping, confident rises. Thirty-seven wingless naturals were drifted over the trout and each was refused. The trout continued to take the winged naturals without hesitation. Letort regulars have not questioned the importance of wings since that afternoon, except in the smallest imitations.

Original experiments in fish culture were also tried. Letort regulars were among the first to use personal fish tags and fin-clipping to study the trout caught and released. These methods were used to keep track of the feeding and migratory and growth characteristics of the individual fish they caught.

The early data seemed to indicate that three distinct behavior strains were present in the Letort fish population: fish that were easily fooled and seldom survived the fishing pressures of early season, surface-feeding trout that proved difficult and selective, and fish that were never seen except by several skillful old-time bait fishermen who have special permission to frequent the river.

Certain handsomely colored fish of good proportions were taken regularly on dry flies. The regulars thought that such exceptional fish might breed a special strain of trout, with good configuration and a pronounced tendency to seek food at the surface of the stream.

They reasoned that such fish could be artificially isolated to breed together. The theory led to the next project: restoration of an old millrace in the Barnyard meadows for an isolation spawning channel. The millrace was carefully prepared. Sluices were constructed to control current speed over spawning beds. The beds were laid with carefully selected gravel. Cover was placed to provide shelter for the beds, and grilles were constructed to contain the isolated brood stock while letting their progeny escape back into the Letort.

Freeway construction ended the millrace experiments before conclusive results could be observed, but all agreed that a noticeable increase in free-rising trout had been achieved. Frequent rises were also recorded earlier in the day than before, and the selective-breeding experiment appeared successful to the regulars on the river.

Consistent Letort water temperatures and volumes of flow and ice-free winters resulted in another experiment: the build-up theory of fish stocking. The regulars believed that fingerlings would have a better rate of survival when planted in the headwaters of a limestone stream than on other waters. Fingerling hatchery trout commonly sustain nearly one-hundred percent mortality from a combination of birds, high temperatures, predator fish, low water, anchor ice, collapsing snowbanks, and other natural causes. Several experiments were tried. One thousand fingerling browns from three to four inches were planted in the spring-head meadows. Their ventral fins were clipped to mark them, and the stocking was made in November. The baby trout began to show themselves in April. They were two miles downstream and averaged six inches in length. These fin-clipped fish were present along the entire stream in September. Several were taken on the last evening of the season, and had reached twelve inches in ten months.

The wild trout of the Letort are legendary for their choosiness. The catalogue of their basic rise-forms is a mixture of chagrin mixed with humor: the simple rise which has the fish coming back under the fly to take it quietly, the compound rise that follows several moments of nervous inspection, and the complex rise, which passes through both simple and compound stages and ends in a rapier-quick rise after several feet of vacillating inspection and refusal. The three-rise catalogue of fish behavior is recorded in *Modern Dry-Fly Code*, and has become a standard part of Letort dialogue and practice. Several years have passed since the three-rise pattern was described and diagrammed. My experience on the Letort leads me to add another exasperating rise-form common with its trout: the compound-complex rise which proceeds through the entire nerve-shattering sequence and ends in complete rejection.

My own Letort odysseys follow the typical pattern of limestone addiction. The fishing intrigued me first because of the writing born on its waters. The first pilgrimage was made to satisfy my curiosity and pay homage to the river and its circle of fishermen.

The sulphur mayflies were hatching on that first trip and my second trip introduced me to the subtle orgy of the Japanese beetles. The third occurred early in the late summer Bacchanalia of the grasshoppers. Letort regulars still laugh about that summer: not wanting to purchase a full-season license on the first trip, I took a tourist permit. The pull of the river proved so strong that I finished that summer with a total of seven five-day tourist buttons on my fishing jacket.

The limestone lessons of that summer have helped my strategy and technique on many rivers, and the difficult trout of the Letort have been fascinating tutors for many years.

Their lessons have taught me much, and might best be characterized in describing two hot afternoons when I raised my biggest Letort browns.

The first happened in beetle season. Japanese beetles were clustered on the wild grapevines and rose bushes like crawling bronze-colored berries. Beetles droned like bees in the sycamores. They were active at midday, flying across the stream and getting into the water, and the trout were getting many of them.

Below the limestone quarries, the current was divided into two deep channels in the watercress. The larger channel was on the near side of the stream, where the current flowed over gravel and marl. The smaller channel was across the stream, little more than twelve inches wide and bordered by cress and beds of elodea. It was sheltered by wild grapevines. The heat was oppressive and I stopped to rest.

Wetting my face and neck felt good, and sitting in the grass was pleasant. My lassitude was broken by a quiet, sucking rise upstream. The rise-form was not visible as I searched the narrow channel for its disturbance. The sound came again. There was no disturbance again, but my eyes were ready as the fish came up a third time along the cress. The rise was gentle. It bulged out imperceptibly against the current and its after-rise was quickly absorbed against the weeds. The rises were small, but the sound spelled a heavy trout, and it was feeding steadily. Beetles were active in the vines above its station and it seemed likely they were getting into its line of drift.

There were plenty of beetle imitations in my fly-box and I waded stealthily into position. The thick beds of elodea cushioned the waves of my cautious chest-deep wading. The fish continued to rise. Checking the leader for wind-knots, I tied a beetle to the tippet. Then I waited and watched several minutes before trying the fish. The leader was all right, the beetle was oiled with silicone paste, and I was ready.

The trout came up again, and the cast dropped nicely

above his feeding station against the cress. The beetle came down flat and dark on the water. It flirted with the weeds and a shadow-like bulk appeared and evaporated under the fly. The fish had inspected my beetle and rejected it. My leader tippet was reduced a diameter to .0047. The fly dropped softly and drifted back along the cress. It disappeared in a quiet rise. The fish bolted along the watercress channel and wallowed angrily at the surface. Then it jumped twice, stitching the leader neatly through the weeds on both sides of the channel, and was quickly gone.

Four pounds, I estimated unhappily.

This was a typical Letort tragi-comedy, since heavy trout on gossamer leaders are difficult to handle in weeds, but the real challenge and accomplishment lay in getting such a trout to rise in the first place, and since that hot afternoon the channel patterns have changed, and no one has seen that particular fish again.

Things went better with the second trout. It was a windy afternoon in August, and the water meadows were filled with ducks from the barnyard. Ross Trimmer had lost a good fish below Otto's Meadow and we went to try it. The trout occupied a deep hole under a brush-pile corner. Ross herded the tame ducks away from the place and we waited. Twenty minutes passed before a quiet rise bulged out from the brush. We waited until the feeding rhythm was finally steady.

Finally, I dropped my grasshopper above the brushy corner and watched it drift over the trout. The rise was splashily audible and I struck gently. The fish jumped and bored deep under the brush. Ross made pungent comments and kept the ducks away and stained the backwater with tobacco while I forced the trout away from deadfalls and weeds. We were lucky. It was a fat nineteen-inch female and we released the handsome henfish to spawn again that fall.

Letort regulars are philosophical about their little river, and seem almost unaware of their own legendary exploits. They gather to celebrate the closing of each fishing season under the buttonwoods. There is always a picnic table heavy with ham and fresh baked bread and beer, and the regulars crouch around the fire telling and retelling the Letort stories that are becoming legends.

There are many such stories. The talk goes on into the darkness and the river is black beyond the firelight. There is good-natured laughter about the fishless sessions Hewitt experienced on his several Letort visits, and speculation about the sinister monster-fish that engulfed Marinaro's grasshopper and fought him for hours while helpless friends offered their fruitless advice. There was the fifteen-pound brown captured in the mill dam that is drained now, and the eight-and-a-half pounder taken with a dry-fly in the upper meadows. The regulars laugh about the free-rising rainbow where newcomers were led for frustration with their Cahills and Coachmen, and the supercilious Trout-without-a-Mouth that once lived in the Barnyard.

There is regret for those who will never fish the little river again, and regret for the wasteful pollution that stains the entire watershed and threatens to erase it forever. The pollution is both an enigma and a tragedy. The once-classic lower mileage has long been polluted in spite of assurances from the factories and a new sewage treatment plant at Carlisle. The river below its final effluent remains unfit for trout. Septic tanks along the entire watershed have polluted the subterranean springs and aquifers with detergents, and the thoughtless use of fertilizers has threatened to choke the stream with weeds. There is tragedy in the dead mileage below the town and its knitting mills, and in the continuing denigration of the richest trout stream in America. Letort fishing could equal the great British chalkstreams if its entire length were rehabilitated and protected in the future, since the brief mileage from its headwater springs to the warmer Conodiguinet has incredible capacity to support large numbers of trout and heavy flyhatches. The continuing loss of such a unique fishery would be a tragedy.

Firelight flickers on the regulars, and they dream of restoring the river. There is speculation about the fame of its past and the sporting potential of its future if proper steps were taken. Carlisle could become a midsummer Mecca for light tackle and minute flies.

There is talk of transplanting fly-species and the nonmigratory strain of rainbows from Falling Spring Run. Talk aways turns to the slow decimation of other limestone waters. There is laughter as someone suggests that rosebushes and grapevines should be planted instead of trout to attract more Japanese beetles. The fire dies slowly, there are only scraps of talk as the men sit looking into the coals, and then finally the talk dies too. Now there is only the soft whisper of the river under its buttonwoods. Water is spilled on the ashes of the fire. The season is finally over and the regulars file up the meadow path to leave. There is always some sadness that last summer evening along the Letort.

See you in the spring! somebody is saying. *See you in the spring when the sulphurs are back!*

The little river is alone for another year. The moon is high and there is mist rising from the current, and the cool September night stirs in the Cumberland Valley. It will not be long until there are yellow leaves sailboating on the surface of the river, and later its black currents will flow through the ice-covered reeds.

Some believe the old-time limestone fishermen are on the river again that last evening, working their ring-and-keeper rods of Greenheart and hickory, and complaining about fewer brook trout. The grass is full of ghosts in the meadows. Their spectral lines whisper through the rising mist and fall without disturbing the moon-bright current. Hewitt and LaBranche are still arguing in the Barnyard meadows, while the spectre-trout of the Letort continue to rise softly and ignore their collective fame.

Act of Mercy

STILES Brook is a tumbling little tributary that flows into the Ausable between Upper Jay and Keene. The brook is colder than the river. It was unseasonably hot that summer. The river was low and warm enough for swimming. We drove down the steep road into the meadows behind the abandoned farmhouse. The tractor lane wound into the waist-high grass until it reached the deep ledgerock pool below the birches.

We jointed our rods and threaded our lines. Our waders smelled hot in the sun, and we shouldered into our tackle vests. The gravelly beach was bright beyond the trees, and the river pushed against my legs. The thermometer throbbed deep in the current.

What's the reading? yelled Mac Talley.

Water dripped from the thermometer. *Seventy-six!* I shook my head. *We can forget the fishing!*

Last one in is a smallmouth! he laughed.

Seventy-six degrees will drive most fish into spring holes for cooler water or lethargic half-sleep on the bottom. Sometimes I have seen them in the weepholes of bridge abutments for the cooler flow of such man-made springs. Talley was already rummaging for his bathing suit.

Just right for a swim! he said. *See you!*

It was noon when we reached the Keene highway and started back upriver toward Keene Valley. Haze paled the high timbered ridges of the Adirondacks to the color of woodsmoke, and we stopped on the road above the spring hole at Stiles Brook.

Is that a fish? I pointed.

The little tributary sparkled through the trees, reaching the river in a tiny pool like an oversized bathtub. Its current eddied briefly in the pool, swelling up in a smooth glide over the pale stones before spilling its cold flow into the river. There was a long fish-like shadow lying in the little pool. It was so large it was visible from the highway above.

It can't be a trout! I shook my head.

Probably not, Talley agreed. *It's probably a big sucker looking for colder water.*

Why would a sucker need colder water?

You're right! he said.

We suited-up and waded across the river, approaching the pool infantry-style. There were willows above the mouth of the tributary, and we crawled along the rocks and cautiously peered through. The dark shape hung in the smooth current under a driftwood stump.

My God! we breathed.

It was a big brown with dime-sized spots. *That fish will go five pounds!* whispered Talley. *Nymphs?*

Good! I said. *We'll try them!*

The trout moved upstream slowly until its head was lost

in the tumbling whitewater of the little brook. It worked its head in the foaming current, rolling weakly in the flow.

Something's wrong, I said.

The big fish drifted back on the current, its eye white in its dark socket. *It's blind!* gasped Talley.

You're right! I said.

We moved cautiously below the pool to the tiny gravel bar on the other side of the fish. *Both eyes!* said Talley softly. *Poor fish is completely blind!*

It seems a pity to let it die slowly, said Talley. *What do you think we should do?*

It'll probably die soon, I agreed.

Can you net it? he asked.

I waded carefully beside the trout without disturbing the stones and held the net-bag above its head like a sling-shot, hoping to sweep it headfirst into the meshes. It worked perfectly. The big trout fought pathetically until we killed it with a quick blow from the priest-knife.

That was an act of mercy, Talley said sadly.

We drove back to Keene Valley and stopped outside the Spreadeagle. *How about a drink?* Talley suggested.

He carried the big trout inside after we weighed it. *Want to see a five-pound brown?* He laid it on the bar and ordered two Gibsons.

Several summer people gathered around the fish. It lay gleaming on the bar, its twenty-six inches covered with rich patterns of spots. Our audience admired the trophy and we accepted their applause without comment. The bartender dressed the fish and wiped the bar. Our audience drifted back to the tables.

They think it's a celebration, Talley speared the onion in his glass, *but we know it's a wake.*

The Rainbow of
Rosh-Ha-Shanah

THERE was mist rising from the Yellowstone just after daylight. The current flowed swiftly through the timber abutments of the bridge where we crossed from the island into Livingston. There were two cowboys and a brakeman in the railroad cafe, and an old dog was sleeping behind the stove. The first cold nights had colored the aspens high on the mountains, and the cottonwoods were beginning to turn. The clouds were burning off the highest peaks of the Gallatins, and in the north the sun was already bright on the barren foothills of Crazy Mountain. Two days earlier on the Firehole, we had heard a bull elk trumpet his challenges.

Sounds like a shofar! said David Rose.

Trout dimpled selectively in the weedy channels. *Maybe we should try a ram's horn on these fish,* I laughed. *We could use a little help!*

Remember us unto life, O King, he intoned solemnly, *and inscribe us in the Book of Life.* He missed a rise and watched the big brown spook-upstream, leaving a frightened wake in the shallows.

Sorry about that, I grinned and changed flies.

David shook his head. *These fish sure have no respect for us!* He sighed unhappily.

Those Firehole browns were impossible that day, and we drove north into the Yellowstone country. Three nights of hard frost had colored the high ridges, and there was new snow on the peaks. The fall is beautiful in Montana. The sun is soft on the mountains and the cottonwoods turn yellow. Wind rises in late morning and scatters their bright leaves into the rivers, and at daybreak the mountains are dark against the high windless skies. The cold nights start the pintails and mallards migrating downriver, and the brown trout moving upstream toward the spawning gravel in the headwaters.

Mule deer were grazing beyond the loading pens when we reached the lane of poplars that led to the ranch. They melted into the creek bottom. The red corrugated roofs of the main house and its outbuildings were ahead in the cottonwoods. We parked the station wagon and rigged our tackle. The trail led down into the watercress bottoms toward the Spring Creek meadows.

There are many chalkstreams in Montana. They are spring creeks that rise in geyser basins and limestone hills and hot-spring bogs. Rich in weeds and fly-hatches, they are not unlike the storied chalkstreams of Normandy and Hampshire where the dry-fly method was born.

We crossed the shallows and waded an irrigation ditch. The meadows were straw-colored, filled with cattle and reaching down toward the cottonwood channels that marked the river. Behind us the hills were still deep in shadows, but beyond the river and its hay-meadow bottoms, the morning sun was warm on the foothills across the valley and the smoke-colored mountains beyond.

These spring creeks are principal spawning grounds on the upper Yellowstone. The actual spawning takes place in late fall and early winter, but the fish begin arriving in the deep pools downstream at the end of September. We reached the first river pools below the creek and prospected for trophy-size browns.

Fall spawners are known for their moodiness. That morning they were uncooperative, and we fished two pools carefully with big nymphs and bucktails without moving anything over eighteen inches.

Let's give the creek itself a try, yelled David.

We moved upstream along the creek, stalking its shallow pools and studying them for the long, dark shapes of the spawners. We located a twenty-inch fish in the second pool and took him easily on a big stonefly nymph. The trout was butter-fat with an orangish yellow belly and bright spots the color of poppies. Most of the pools were empty, and we explored upstream along the creek carefully.

Below the ranch, the stream slowed and spread into a watercress slough. Its currents gathered in a deep channel at the bottom of the slough. The bottom was covered with moss and pale gravel, and we crouched in the meadow to watch for rises. The wind stirred in the cottonwoods and riffled across the main channels of the slough.

There! I pointed to a soft rise-form.

The dark shape moved out from the cress-bed shadows and dimpled softly in the quiet current. *My God!* whispered David. *That fish is six or eight pounds!* The fish rose again.

It's a rainbow, I said quietly.

There were two of them. They were lying tight against the cress, dark-spotted and olive with the rich rainbow stripes down their sides. The rise-forms were unobtrusive, sipping and porpoise-rolling in the surface film. The quiet current moved with the disturbance of their bulk under water, swirling down the narrow cress channels below their rises.

They're too big for me! said David.

The still current and soft rises spelled a fine tippet and minute flies. My leader was lengthened to 6x and I chose a tiny spentwing. It was not even inspected on several floats. Midge pupa imitations were examined and rejected. Jassids were a failure, but a tiny ant got a long heart-stopping look and refusal. The floats seemed perfect, and it had to be the fly-pattern.

The wind gusted again and scattered leaves across the slough, and the big rainbows were working again.

Terrestrials! I thought aloud.

But you tried the ants and Jassids, reminded David.

The rises stopped when the wind died in the trees. *Maybe its something like tiny bark beetles,* I said.

There was a minute beetle imitation in my fly-boxes. I trimmed its wings into a smaller oval and oiled it in silicone paste. The modified fly was clinch-knotted to my leader. The wind moved in the cottonwoods and the big rainbows began working again.

The cast dropped perfectly, with the leader slack and the tiny beetle in the current tongue. One rainbow ghosted out from the cress shadows and drifted into position, waiting for the fly, and as it reached his position he eased up and inhaled it quietly.

I paused and tightened, hoping to seat the tiny hook. The smooth current bellied the leader downstream until the fish sensed the pressure, and exploded full-length into the air and fell heavily and jumped again.

My God! shouted David.

The rainbow jumped six times. Each time I watched him jump against the belly in the line, expecting him to shear the fragile tippet. Then he bolted downstream, shaking his head angrily and raking the line across the weeds. The fragile leader still held.

Should have lost him a dozen times already, I said.

The reel chattered and stopped when the rainbow worked deep under the cress beds. *He's gone!*

But I could still feel the fish quivering in the smooth current. Working out into the weeds, I held the rod at a low angle and applied a slight pressure. It seemed like hours. Finally the fish edged out grudgingly into the channel, and hung sullenly in the smooth current. Suddenly he exploded into the sun again and fell down into the weeds. His tail stood high in the air, out of the cress and moving weakly.

Solve that! laughed David.

I waded out waist deep and worked him free, and he promptly bolted deep across the channel into another weed bed. The channel was chest deep, and the cold water trickled down into my waders.

He's probably off, I thought aloud.

My arm went deep into the weeds, expecting to find the fly fouled in the cress. It was a surprise when I felt the fish. I worked it free gently, and it moved into the channel again. Weeds trailed from the fragile leader and I followed him slowly downstream. He tried to burrow deep under a deadfall. My gentle pressure held him short, but I felt the tippet catch twice on the snags. It held again. Then the rainbow made a long run into a riffle, running the reel into the backing. I extricated myself from the weeds and muck, and ran splashing down the riffles. Finally the fish stopped, and David reached me just as I had recovered most of the line. It was an open pool now, free of snags and weeds. The rainbow seemed weaker, and I worked him into the shallows. I shook my head and laughed.

It's a miracle! I said. *This fish should have broken off an hour ago!*

It's Rosh-Ha-Shanah! yelled David. *It's no miracle!*

Sure! I laughed. *Sure!*

The big rainbow porpoised and rolled weakly, its spotted length half out of the water. The sun flashed on its silver sides and it looked huge.

Eight pounds! I thought. *Easy!*

The leader splice slipped through the tip guide, and I was reaching with the net when the fly came out. The great fish drifted free.

Rosh-Ha-Shanah! I said angrily.

David filled his pipe. *God is punishing you,* he smiled.

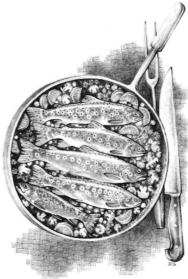

Charity on
the Little South

THE cooking smells of eggs and fresh trout
and coffee drifted through the tent. There is a half-hour in the
morning when a sleeping bag has an almost delicious warmth.
It ends when the sun gets hotter, playing its leafy patterns of
light on the canvas.

You awake! asked my father.

Yes, I answered deep in the goose down. *You fish the
early hatch this morning?* I yawned sleepily.

It was pretty good, he said. *Smell them?*

I laughed and yawned again. *The best fish went about
fifteen inches,* he said.

Good fish, I said. *Where'd he take?*

Forks Pool, he answered.

We were camped on the Little South two hundred yards
above its junction with the Pere Marquette. It was our annual

trip to Michigan when school sessions were over, and it was our first morning on the river that summer. The breakfast utensils were washed and scoured in the current, and we rigged our tackle.

We walked down the road along the river.

Who's fishing? said my father.

There was an old Plymouth parked near the bridge.

Damn! I said. *They're fishing the water we wanted!*

There was a man in working clothes fishing a night-crawler in the run above a tangle of logs. His two sons were fishing worms downstream, working their bait under the bushes.

They would be in our favorite water, I grumbled.

Maybe we can Tom Sawyer them, said my father.

You really think so? I grinned. *Talk them into fishing another piece of water?* My father laughed softly.

Let's give it a try, he said.

We walked down to where they were fishing. *Had any luck?* we asked. *Nothing,* the man answered.

It's not good worming water, my father said.

No? He looked puzzled.

You have to stand right over them to fish bait here, father explained. *It spooks the fish to get too close.*

That so? he reeled in his nightcrawler.

It's good dry-fly water, my father continued, *but there's better worming over at Baldwin.*

Where at Baldwin? The man waved to his sons.

Try the fish-hatchery stretch, I suggested. *There's a deep concrete channel between the spillways.*

That's right, added my father.

Those fish are used to seeing people, I continued, *and there're some big browns there.* That part was true because we had seen them ourselves, and once I had hooked a heavy fish and played it for an hour before the fly suddenly pulled out.

We'll try it, said the workman. *We're obliged!*

They started the battered Plymouth and drove north into town, and the boys waved. *It worked!* We grinned guiltily at each other and walked down toward the river.

It was a good morning. There was a fine hatch of caddis-flies, and the trout were already rising well. We both took several good fish, and were fishing the still tree-sheltered stretch of the Little South where the man and his sons had fished when a car stopped on the road. It was the same battered Plymouth.

Hey mister! yelled the boys.

Their father came around the car. *Sure want to thank you folks!* he grinned. *Can't thank you enough!*

My father looked at me, and we stood in the river with the current sliding past our waders. *What do you suppose they want now?*

Are they serious? I whispered.

The workman went to his trunk. *Yessir!* he raised it and dragged out a thirty-inch brown. *Caught this eight-pounder right where you said!* he laughed. *Can't thank you enough!*

Grasshopper Wind

MANY trout-water summers ago, my fishing apprenticeship began with live grasshoppers in Michigan. Getting bait was sport in itself, and we gathered the grasshoppers in the mornings when they were cold and clambered stiff-legged in meadows still beaded with dew. The grass was wet against our boots, and we picked them like berries.

My first trout was caught below a timber-sluice culvert above the farmhouse. Its pool was sheltered under a huge elm, with the trout lying tight in the run along its roots. Our rods were stiff in three pieces of pale split-cane popular in those days. They were well-suited to dapping the live, wriggling grasshoppers over the trout. The first trout came on a windy afternoon in August. Our stalk was made on hands and knees through the alfalfa until we sprawled belly-flat under the elm, its roots pressing up into our ribcages. My father crawled close and outlined tactics with whispers and gestures.

The grasshopper dangled five feet below the agate tip of the rod and I lowered it slowly between the tree and the fence that crossed below the culvert. The action was eager and immediate. There was a splash and the stiff rod dipped down and I reacted. The trout was derricked violently up into the elm and it hung there, struggling feebly in the breeze. Somehow we extricated it from the branches and sat in the meadow admiring its beauty. Wild twelve-inch brook trout are still treasured in the world of adults, but to my boyhood eyes that fish seemed bigger and more beautiful than any other I have ever caught.

The next summer saw my introduction to the dry fly. June was a good month and the mayfly hatches were heavy, and I caught my first dry-fly trout with a spentwing Adams in the Little Manistee. But that first dry-fly trout was only nine inches long, and in August there was grasshopper feeding in the meadows. My father gave me several Michigan Hoppers and told me to try them when it got hot in the middle of the day. They worked and along a sweeping bend in the river where the coarse grasses trailed in the current I caught my first big trout.

My casts with the grasshopper imitations came down along the undercut bank or ticked into the grass until I coaxed them loose. One cast came free and dropped nicely along the bank and the fly floated past the trailing grass. After three feet of float the fly was suddenly intercepted by a shadow-like trout and the rise was vicious, and I was into a fat seventeen-inch brown.

This meadow water was open and undercut along the deep grassy side and I fought the fish down over a pale rippled-sand bottom. There were no visible snags or deadfalls and I was able to handle such a trout in spite of my tremble-fingered excitement and the errors of my inexperience. After this grasshopper triumph came a week of doldrums. The trout became sluggish and fed little. One could see them lying on the pale bottom against the sand and gill-panting weakly as they waited for cooler water.

We gathered in the local tackle store and talked of fishing. *You be nice to your boy,* they told my father, still twinkle-eyed about the big grasshopper trout. *You be nice to your boy,* they laughed, *and maybe he'll tell you how he did it.*

My father always smiled. *Maybe he will!* he was pleased and generous about the trout. *I've never caught one any larger,* he said, *even during the caddis hatch!*

Talk always returned to the late August doldrums. *No decent rise of fish for two weeks,* observed the town doctor and the others nodded in agreement.

What we need is a mackerel sky, said the ice-cream proprietor, *and then some good windstorms and rain to clear the weather.*

We sure do, agreed the old logger who fished at night in the marl swamps, *that and a grasshopper wind.*

The season ended in doldrums that lasted until after Labor Day and I did not see the grasshopper wind that summer. That winter was spent learning to tie flies. My father bought some Michigan Hoppers tied by the late Art Kade and I used them as models. The copies were less than elegant, but the originals were exquisite: scarlet hackle tail-fibers cocked down under a tufted yellow-floss body palmered with brown multicolor hackle. Brown turkey-feather wings lacquered with feather glazer held the body hackles flat along the sides. Stiff multicolor hackles completed the flies. The hooks were elegant long-shank English up-eyes. These patterns were so classic in proportions that they still influence the style of my flies.

Several summers later I saw my first grasshopper wind. The incident occurred on the upper meadows of the Arkansas in Colorado during the late-August haying. Rock Creek was low and clear and the trout had not been rising well for several days. Then the haying started and the irrigation ditches were closed off to dry the fields for the mowing. The irrigation water was diverted back into the stream, and it came up several inches and the water was measurably colder. The trout became active again and the men began working in the fields. Grasshoppers rose up in front of the mowing machines and the hay rakes, and the warm wind moved up the valley and carried them in shaky, precarious flight patterns over the water.

The lower reaches of the creek were once damned by beavers, and their leavings consist of two long chest-deep flats divided by a shallow gravelly riffle. Both flats are deeply undercut along the banks and their bottoms are soft and pincushion thick with old beaver sticks. Approach from the haymeadow side was easy and that bank was well worn with the boots of fishermen. Everyone fished from there. But this approach was in plain view of the trout, and I never saw any there except small fish.

On the morning of the grasshopper wind I came down through the willows and brush on the other side, keeping some distance below the stream. The evening before I had been reading my fishing bible of those years, Ray Bergman's now-mellow classic *Trout*, and had covered several passages about fishing difficult pools from their less-travelled sides. I was absorbed with this idea and the ranch was quiet when I put the book down and turned out the lights in the bunkhouse.

It worked on the beaver-dam flats. The brush was thick where the creek riffled out into the wide Lake Creek shallows, and I was sweating heavily when I finally stumbled out and sat down on the bank. I checked my clothes for cattle ticks and washed my face and wetted my hat while I watched the mowing machine pass in the meadow. Grasshoppers rose up ahead of the sickle bar and the warm wind carried them over the creek. Several faltered and came down like mallards in the lower flat. Wakes appeared in the smooth water, and the unfortunate grasshoppers were collected swiftly in a series of calm showy rises that spelled size.

I was spellbound. The trout were large, larger than any I had seen before except for hatchery breeders or mounted fish on tackle-shop walls, and I watched them cruise the flat like hungry alley cats. There were no more grasshoppers on the water and the big trout vanished. The mowing machine chattered back toward the creek and I hastily got ready. The fragile 4x gut tippet was clipped off and I searched frantically for a grasshopper in my fly boxes. One battered split-winged hopper crouched forlorn and neglected in a compartment full of Hendricksons. Hooking it out of the box with my index finger, I clinch-knotted it firmly to the tippet. I tested the leader and crawled up the riffle to wait for the mowing machine and the grasshopper wind.

Three grasshoppers settled into the quiet current and started kicking toward shore. There was a heavy boil and the fish were feeding again, and my artificial flicked over the pool to drop near the undercut bank. Two big browns came cruising down the flat and each took a grasshopper as he came. I held my breath. One came toward my floating grasshopper and then detoured swiftly to take a kicking natural. I twitched the slowly drifting artificial, and the trout turned like a shark and came ten feet with his dorsal fin showing.

The fish wallowed clumsily when I struck, and bulldogged deep into the beaver sticks under the bank. I felt the leader pluck and catch as it slipped over the sunken branches, but it did not foul and the trout turned out into the open water of the channel. Then the fish made its mistake. It bolted down over the shallows where I crouched, its spotted back showing as it came, and I followed the trout with much splashing into the open water below.

The rest was easy. The fish finally recognized its danger and tried to get back into the pool again, but I splashed and kicked and frightened it back. It was tired now when it circled close, but pumped out again when it saw me waiting with the net in the shallows. It measured an even twenty-six inches, heavy and hook-jawed with maturity, and I ran back up through the meadows to the house with its strong-muscled bulk threshing convulsively in the net.

That was my biggest dry-fly trout for several years, and he held the title until my second encounter with a grasshopper wind. It occurred in the Cooper meadows of the Gunnison in Colorado. There are high-water side channels of the big river in these meadows, and there are big trout under the brush piles, trapped in the side channels by the receding water of summer.

On this afternoon I hooked and lost two dry-fly fish, both brutes, and returned talking to myself. The first was grasshopper feeding under a high bank. I changed to a big wool-bodied hopper and clinch-knotted it hastily. The trout saw the fly land above it and came upstream and splashed water wildly as it felt the hook. It bored up the pool, rolled deep along the bottom and turned. It came back strong and I stripped line clumsily and it wallowed in the shallows, smashing the leader at my feet.

Five pounds, I whispered.

The second fish was slashing at grasshoppers above a log tangle that bridged the narrow channel. It took my imitation on the first float and spurted upstream in a series of bucking rolls. Then it hung high in the current above the logs and reconsidered. It turned and bored brazenly through the log tangle. The fish was below me now, below the jumbled logs and brush, rolling feebly on the leader in the quiet water downstream. Several seconds passed. It was too big to force back through the brush.

Then I remembered the brush-pile trout Charlie Fox once hooked on Cedar Run in Pennsylvania and passed the rod carefully through the logs to continue the fight below. The trout shifted gears as I tightened up and he tore back through the brush. This time he broke off and hung in the current above the jam, shaking his head at the annoying fly and leader before he drifted back into the logs trailing five feet of nylon.

There had been only two grasshoppers in my jacket and both were lost in trout, and I went downstream toward the ranch and the fly vise. Just above the junction of the side channel with the main river was a deep log-lined pocket, and Frank Klune crouched beside the water. He was studying the water and not casting. I yelled and he waved me away and continued to watch the water. I circled through the meadow well away from the stream and I could not see the water, but Frank was casting again. Then he yelled and stood up to handle his flailing rod. The fish was running now, and I was running too and the reel was going. The trout was high and rolling in the deadfalls before Frank finally turned it. Then the fish writhed and turned and flashed silver deep at our feet, and bored back upstream. It seemed confused and I watched its big rose-colored gills working slowly.

What did he take? I asked.

Grasshopper, said Frank. *The one you tied yesterday.* He gained some line and had the big rainbow back on the reel.

Took right up there in the brush!

Can't see the fly, I said. *He must have taken it deep.*

Then the fish exploded. *He's got it deep alright,* yelled Frank and we were running again.

The trout porpoised down the side channel toward the big-water Gunnison. The reel was going again and we were running down the high meadow bank. Thirty yards downstream was a narrow gully. I was running ahead with the net and broad-jumped the gully, but Frank was busy playing the fish and missed. The fish was still on and Frank was trying to scramble out of the gully and handle the rod. The rod was bucking dangerously and suddenly the fish was gone.

Good one! he said sadly. *You get a good look?*

Yes! I said. *At least six pounds!*

The artificial grasshoppers I was tying now were still similar to the Kade patterns I had used for prototypes as a boy. The yellow-silk floss had been abandoned. Floss turned dark when it was wet, and floss bodies were too delicate and slim for bulky grasshopper bodies. Dubbed yellow wool was the best we could do, and it achieved a fat hopper-like body silhouette and did not change color when wet. Between the wings was an underwing of fox squirrel to achieve more buoyancy and counteract the absorption of the wool.

This version seemed good for several years, particularly on the less-selective trout of the big western rivers. But the hyper-selective brown trout of the small Pennsylvania limestone streams were another matter. The old patterns worked much of the time, but there were also many refusals, particularly from the larger wild trout. Anglers on limestone water had long experimented with hopper patterns: many used the traditional Michigan and Joe's Hopper flies, and some even tried the more radical fore-and-aft-dressings. Charlie Fox had used fore-and-aft grasshoppers for years on the difficult fish of his Letort Spring Run, and these flies had been tied for him by the late Ray Bergman. But the selective Letort trout seem to become more difficult every year, and they were refusing these old-time imitations with nose-thumbing frequency. New variations seemed necessary.

The first attempt was created in the Turnaround meadow on Charlie Fox's Letort water. Western experiments with deer hair had worked well on the big Jackson Hole cutthroats, and many anglers had reported good luck with the Muddler Minnow fished dry during sessions of grasshopper feeding. Using this information as a beginning, we concocted some lightly-dressed wingless hoppers with deer hair and yellow nylon wool. They seemed to work better than the earlier patterns, but it was July and the grasshoppers were still small and not many fish were looking for them yet.

Subsequent refusals and successes caused us to restore the old-time turkey wings to the new hoppers and alter the deer-hair dressing. The silhouette of the wings and the trailing deer hair proved important. The absence of hackle permitted the bulk of the fly and its yellow-dubbed body to float flush in the surface film. The light pattern created by the dressing in the surface film looked hopper-like and promising.

Looks good, observed Ross Trimmer. *Maybe we'll name it the Letort Hopper.*

The trout liked it fine. We used it with good success on the Letort and pulled up trout that were not feeding on many occasions. But there were some refusal rises too, and that was disconcerting. We experimented some more and the final improvement came near the end of the season when the grasshoppers were at full growth. Tying bigger imitations resulted in the change: when the deer hair was looped and pulled tight it flared out like thick stubby hackles tightly bunched, and these butts were scissor-trimmed in the blocky configuration of the grasshopper head and thorax. The earlier versions had these deer-hair butts trimmed close and covered with the head silk. The bulky version was better. We tried the following pattern that next morning on the Letort and it worked wonders on demanding fish:

Tails—none

Body—yellow nylon wool dubbed on yellow silk

Wings—brown-mottled turkey glazed with lacquer

Legs—brown deer-body hair

Head—trimmed deer body-hair butts

Silk—oo yellow

Hook—sizes six thru sixteen 2x long down-eye.

We found our final proving ground on a small privately-owned limestone stream in central Pennsylvania. The browns were big and stream-spawned, and they were trout that had been caught and released many times during the season. Charlie Fox and our host walked down through the meadows with me to the stream in the early afternoon. Five hundred yards below the deep sapphire-colored spring, where the stream comes up full-size from limestone caverns, is a long marl-bottomed flat. The flat is smooth and clear and colder than sixty degrees through the heat of August. One side is bordered by limestone ledges and sheltered with trees. The shallow side is bordered by a marl shelf and a sizeable hay meadow. Charlie Fox decided to try the water above the flat where he had spotted a big brown that morning. Our host walked with me where the meadow was alive with grasshoppers.

We reached the flat and moved cautiously down the path toward the water. The sun was high and the hot wind moved down across the valley and its hay meadows. We stopped short when we saw the water: big wild browns were cruising the flat in twos and threes.

We crouched low along the flat and studied the rise-forms to see what they were taking. The rises were quiet and we decided the Jassid was the probable answer, since it had produced several fine trout that morning. The little Jassid was already on my leader when we felt the hot wind and saw the grasshoppers. They rose up as the hot wind crossed the meadow and were parachuted out over the flat. The water was quiet, too wide for them to cross once they were committed to the wind, and they came down hard. Their shallow, faltering trajectory was futile and the big trout stalked them when they fell. The trout had learned that the grasshoppers were helpless, and their rises were quiet and calm, completely lacking the splashy eagerness characteristic of most grasshopper feeding. We watched the quick demise of several grasshoppers. *It's the wind,* I said, *it's a grasshopper wind!*

Five of the new 'hoppers were in my fly box, tied the night before at my inn on the Letort. I changed to a grasshopper pattern, but neglected to change the fragile Jassid-sized tippet to something heavier. It was a mistake. Two big fish came up above us over the marl shelf and I placed the imitation between them. One turned and took the 'hopper without hesitation and bolted thirty yards into a brush pile. The delicate leader sheared like wet tissue-paper.

I replaced the grasshopper after cutting the leader back to a heavier calibration. Under the trees a big muskie-sized trout took another natural. The roll cast dropped the fly in the sun, but the trout had disappeared somewhere in the shadows along the bank. The float was good and it flirted with the bank shadows and I was already picking up the cast when he slashed at the fly. The big mouth closed and I tried to set the hook, but the fly came back in a loose leader tangle at my feet. The heavy trout rolled in panic and bolted up the length of the flat, brush-pile black and leaving a frightened wake.

My shout of disappointment died. *My fault,* I said.

Five pounds, consoled our host.

The other fish were still feeding, and the first cast with the fresh grasshopper produced a fat reddish-bronze two pounder. The fish was released after a strong fight. The fish were so intent on their grasshopper prey that they ignored the heavier nylon tippet. The new grasshopper patterns worked beautifully, and none of these big selective browns refused to rise after a brief inspection.

Three casts later I was into another. *Should have brought my rod!* said our host.

The fish went eighteen inches and had the reddish tail and adipose coloring of wild limestone-stream browns. It was released and I promptly hooked and lost another.

You have an extra 'hopper? asked my host.

Sure, I laughed and he disappeared to get his rod.

The fishing was fast and Charlie Fox appeared at the head of the flat fifteen minutes later. The best fish of the afternoon was recovering its strength on the marl shelf at my feet, hook-jawed and heavy at twenty-three inches.

Grasshoppers! I yelled.

He was already casting over a good brown. His rod doubled over and there was a heavy splash under the trees at the head of the flat. We took twelve browns between us from fifteen to twenty-three inches, releasing them all.

Our host arrived late in the rise and promptly left my last grasshopper in a heavy fish. Light rain misted down the valley and the wind turned cool and the grasshopper activity was over. There were no rises when the rain finally stopped, and five big suckers were the only fish in sight.

Good score for the new 'hopper, said Charlie. *These big wild browns were a really perfect test.*

No refusals mean something, I agreed.

Our host was amazed at the grasshopper feeding. *They haven't come that fast all year,* he said.

We stopped to feed a fat brook trout from the suspension bridge over the big spring. *Had some refusals on the fore-and-aft 'hoppers,* said Charlie, *so it was a good comparison.*

How do you tie the legs and head? Our host was examining the tie.

Like a bass bug, I said. *Bunched and clipped.*

Charlie and I drove back down to the Letort that night, and we had a final day with the grasshoppers before the end of the season. Ross Trimmer met us in the Turnabout Meadow early that afternoon and went upstream with me above the Barnyard. We were in high spirits and Ross periodically stained the stream with tobacco. We were paying an end-of-season visit to the logjam.

We ought to try the Bolter, Ross had suggested at the Buttonwood corner.

The Bolter was a heavy brown trout several of us had hooked and lost when he bolted and broke off. The fish was an estimated twenty-two inches. It was feeding quietly along a cressbed cover when we approached under the trees. The rises were methodical and gentle, but several ugly white ducks squatted on the logs just below the trout. The ducks were notorious on the Letort for swimming ahead of an angler and spooking his fish.

Ross crouched and moved above the ducks. *I'll drive 'em downstream away from the fish,* he said.

The ducks waddled along the logs and dropped clumsily into the current. The trout continued to feed. The ducks drifted downstream, protesting noisily. When they were twenty yards below the fish I slipped into the stream and edged slowly into casting position. Ross sat on the logs and we waited. Five minutes later the trout came up again.

There he is! said Ross. *How's that for gillying?*

You make a good gillie, I grinned.

Well, my part's done and I'm waiting. The heavy trout came up noisily again and its rise was impressive.

Okay, I said.

The cast was difficult and the first two attempts failed, and finally the grasshopper fell right. I could not see its line of drift down the face of the watercress, but I heard the soft rise and saw the rings push gently into the current as I set the hook. There was a heavy splash instead of the usual rapier-quick bolt and the trout wallowed under the cress. It probed deep up the channel and I turned it short of the tree. The fish was under the cressbed again and I forced it out into the open water with my rod tip deep in the current. It was getting tired now and I kept the fish high in the water and out of the elodea. The light was wrong and we could not see the fish. Then it rolled head down and the broad tail fanned weakly at the surface. I turned the light rod over for the strain of the in-fighting and it turned slowly headfirst into the net.

Looks better than twenty, said Ross.

I pushed the hook free carefully. *Henfish,* I said. *She's really perfectly shaped and colored.*

Well, Ross said, *let her go.*

We crossed the current and walked back along the railroad. That evening we gathered at the Buttonwoods and celebrated the end of the season. The old stories were recounted again about Hewitt and LaBranche going fishless on the Letort, and the heavy sulphur hatches on Cedar Run in the old days, and the record fifteen-pound brown taken on a fly from the Upper Mill Pond on Big Spring.

For big trout I'll take the shadflies anytime, somebody was talking about Penns Creek.

They only last a week, said Charlie Fox, *but the grasshopper season lasts over a month.*

Right, said Ross. *I'll take the 'hoppers.*

I'll take the 'hoppers too, I agreed happily. *'Hoppers and meadow water and a grasshopper wind.*

The others murmured agreement. We fell silent and the little Letort whispered past the bench in the moonlight. The year was over again. Somewhere above the buttonwoods a trout came up in the darkness and we turned to listen.

A Duck Is Better
Than Nothing

THE plane shuddered past the ragged serrations of basalt behind Akureyri, and settled in the smooth air above its harbor and deep-water fjord. The overcast hung just above the mountains. We slipped the Cessna between the clouds and the smooth granite face of the pass, sliding across its snowfields on the wind. Farmsteads flashed under the plane and children waved from the hayfields.

We turned and banked with the valley, completing the bad-weather route between the fjord and the valley beyond. The clouds hung low, scudding past the canopy of the plane, and we crossed the glacier-melt river at three hundred feet. There was another river ahead.

That's your river! yelled the pilot.

The other rivers had run milky with glacier-melt, but the Laxámyri ran clear over its bottom of lava ledges and black volcanic sand. *Husavik!* the pilot pointed to the fishing village on the seacoast ahead.

The airstrip was ahead on the moor. It was three thousand feet of crushed chocolate-colored lava. Orange-painted petrol drums marked the runway. Its radio shack is seldom manned except when the weekly Fokker arrives at noon from Reykjavík.

We were meeting Bob and Jimmie Graham for a week of salmon fishing on the best-known river in Iceland. Their twin-engine Apache had already arrived on the airstrip, surrounded by jeeps from the farmstead at Neskirkju. The fishing rights on salmon water must be leased, like the salmon rivers of Europe, and each fisherman is rotated twice daily to fish different beats, specific reaches of water that are assigned him exclusively for fixed morning and evening periods.

Our engines stopped and we opened the hatch. *Heimir Sigurdsson,* the head gillie introduced himself.

Vurli Hermadursson, said the other gillie.

Since the first sportsmen who fished in Iceland were British fly-fishermen, their word for the combination fish wardens and guides in Scotland is used. The men who guide visiting anglers are called gillies.

We drove slowly up the barren valley floor past the thickets of bracken and volcanic cinder-cones. Ptarmigan were dusting in the road. Finally we reached the Neskirkju farmstead and wound in toward the fishing house. The cook had a lunch of cauliflower soup and smoked salmon and richly roasted lamb waiting when we arrived.

The gillies like my two-handed rod, said an old Belgian fisherman after lunch, *but they don't think much of my tube-flies.*

Don't worry, Bob laughed. *Guides are always suspicious of things they've never seen before.*

We'll be the opposite, added Jimmie. *Our flies are okay but our rods are probably too small.*

You're right! I laughed.

We all drew good beats at four o'clock. The Belgian had the smooth-flowing pools above Neskirkju, Bob and Jimmie got the famous water below the churchyard, and I was assigned Presthylur and Thvottastrengur. They were the pools fished successfully that morning.

Petri heil! said the Belgian.

Petri dank! We exchanged the ancient German greeting between fishermen.

We drove through the river bottoms with Heimir in his Russian-built jeep. The morning sun was warm and we opened and closed cattle gates where the road wound toward the smooth Wyoming-looking hills. There were geese on the river. Its marshy bottoms were filled with plovers and snipe, flushing ahead of the jeep as we drove.

Heimir stopped in the meadows above a vast chalkstream pool that flowed smoothly in a gentle bend. Weeds trailed in its silken currents, waving sinuously with their patterns of flow. *Presthylur,* Heimir said.

It looks like an English chalkstream, I thought. *It really doesn't look like an arctic river.*

Laxámyri is not an arctic river like those found in Lapland or the Labrador. Like the Yellowstone in Montana, it rises in a vast mountain lake rimmed with geysers and hot springs, and its rich fly-life supports an impressive population of fish. Its warm currents are a pleasant surprise. Arctic char and brown trout rise softly in the channels in its weeds, and its big salmon are particularly prized in Iceland.

Heimir rowed the boat carefully in the smooth current. Our casts worked back and forth, dropping the flies along a dark bed of weeds that marked the best holding water. There was nothing after several casts, and we fished the weedy channels below the island, where goats grazed and mossy springs trickle and cool the river. Once a salmon rolled and pulled at the fly, taking a short length of line, but it was not hooked.

Two fish jumped downstream, but none came to my flies. We worked the boat back into the grassy shallows and drove farther downstream.

Thvottastrengur is a great pool. Hundreds of pintails and buffleheads and scaup feed in its still currents. Its bottom is lava and black sand from its volcanic headwaters. There is a long dark-bottomed channel between the weeds where the salmon lie, and we fished it carefully without luck. Below the channel there are lava ledges that check the current in a series of eddies and glassy flows. The fish lie above the ledges, in a crevice in the lava below the weedy channel, and in the smooth chute between the outcropping of ledges and the footpath along the bank.

Good place, grunted Heimir happily.

The line worked out into the sunlight, gathered speed in a slow series of left-hand hauls, and dropped the cast far across the current. The fly came back in a long teasing swing, swimming around against the belly in the line. Suddenly there was a boil behind the fly.

Salmon! I said. *Didn't take!*

The fly was still swinging through the lava shallows, and I pumped the rod-tip enticingly. There was another boil and I felt the weight of a salmon, and the rod bent heavily.

He followed it! yelled Heimir.

The fish pirouetted high into the air and writhed back slowly into the river, and its splash echoed in the cliffs across the pool. The salmon worked powerfully up the channel in the weeds, shaking its head angrily and stripping line from the reel in great rasping lengths. It sulked and I recovered some of the line, until it turned and bolted down the pool. Line dwindled off the reel, and it shrieked and rattled in protest.

Laxá fish are strong! Heimir laughed. *You should really have a two-handed rod for them!*

My rod will handle them, I grinned.

Perhaps, he said grudgingly.

The powerful Orvis parabolic turned the fish well short of the ledges, and I pumped it firmly back to the shallows. Heimir finally tailed it cleanly and carried it ashore.

Your first Laxá salmon! he smiled.

The scale dipped and shuddered at sixteen pounds. *Thanks,* we shook hands. *It's a good beginning.*

Your rod worked, Heimir admitted.

Yes, I nodded. *But a longer rod would help work the fly in these currents and hold the line free of the weeds.*

But not for our salmon? Heimir laughed.

They're strong, I agreed, *but a smaller rod than mine could beat them except for these weeds.*

Weeds and wind! Heimir added.

The warm sun glittered on the smooth-flowing current. *Wind?* I laughed. *There isn't any wind.*

Heimir laughed. *We have a saying in Iceland,* he continued. *When you don't like the weather—wait a minute.*

The old gillie was right. During the night the weather changed abruptly. The clouds darkened and a cold wind came in from the Arctic, scattering hail against the windows. My morning beat lay in the meadows below the Nupafoss waterfall. It was raining softly where the pool at Breidengi farmstead bulges and slides over smooth volcanic ledges in its holding shallows.

Sometimes they follow the fly, explained Heimir, *and they look like sharks in the shallow water.*

It's hard to wait until they take like that! I smiled.

Já! agreed Heimir.

We fished the pool without moving a salmon. Heimir pointed downstream to the Stráumall beat and we walked down through the water meadows, startling a pair of nesting mallards. Stráumall is a narrowing of grassy banks where the current gathers and flows swiftly. We fished it for an hour, casting across and working the fly back through the deep holding currents until it nearly touched the bank. Then we moved two steps and cast again. Deep in the pool there was a strong pull that spelled salmon, but the fish was not hooked. It was time for lunch and we stopped.

Weather! suggested Heimir.

Maybe this evening will go better, I said.

My evening beat included the great pools at Graustraumur and Vitadsgnafi. We started in the smooth run above the Graustraumur outcroppings, and on the second cast I moved a salmon.

Change flies! whispered Heimir.

He picked a small Orange Charm I had tied the night before. The old man knotted it firmly to the tippet and I cast again to the fish, carefully repeating the cast. The fish came almost wildly and engulfed the fly in the shallows at our feet. It jumped in a threshing series of cartwheels that carried it across the river.

Watch the lava! warned Heimir.

We clambered high on the lava shelf above the pool to hold the line free of the lava ledges. The salmon jumped again and again, down the long Mori shallows that spread into the waterfowl bottoms below the pool. Swans rose flapping from the river as I followed the fish. It was a long fight that carried deep into the backing behind the fly-line, but we finally worked it back and carried it ashore.

Twenty-three pounds, scaled Heimir.

It was a good week of sport. We took salmon regularly from each beat, although the most productive pools were Graustraumur and the beautiful Skriduflud, where the strangely serrated ledges of lava broke and sharpened the current. There were so many fish coming up from the sea that we took them in the best pools, the meadows at Breidengi, the tumbling shallows at Simastrengur, and even in the tiny island pockets below the farm. But salmon are legendary for their fickle moods. Bob and Jimmie Graham had excellent fishing and the old Belgian had several fine salmon, but late that week my luck went strangely sour.

You have to understand salmon, they kidded.

Their luck held at better than a fish-a-day per rod, while I took only occasional salmon from the best pools. Somehow they even caught them regularly on the poorest beats, and their mealtime dialogue became unbearable.

These fish can't read English, explained Bob.

American either! Jimmie laughed and shrugged. *They don't know you're supposed to be an expert!*

They haven't read your books! Bob choked.

The last morning Jimmie drew the beat below Oddahylur, and I had the water above. It includes the famous Skriduflud and the long, silken currents of Kirkjuholmakvisl, where the fish lie tight against the wildflowers. The pool is justly famous and is mentioned in the work of the late Steingrimur Baldvinsson, the poet who lived and worked as the riverkeeper on the Laxámyri.

Here where the Laxá is
Playing the tunes of her lyre,
It is easy to forget my sorrows and
I feel I can never find
Another home.

It seemed like a good pool to change my score. Graham wished me better luck and walked down the meadows to his beat. The fish lie in pockets and crevices in the first gathering currents of the pool, and then gather deep in the eddies between grassy banks. The lower reaches are a narrowing throat with wildflowers on the opposite bank. The cast must drop the flies tight against the flowers to take salmon there. There was a deep swirl in the current and a fish was hooked briefly, but it suddenly fell free on the second jump. No fish were moved in the rest of the pool.

Jim has one! Heimir pointed downstream.

Sunlight was dancing on his rod as Graham fought a heavy salmon into the shallows and his gillie tailed it. *Maybe Skriduflud will finally give us another fish,* I said sourly.

Perhaps, Heimir smiled.

Several flocks of eider ducks passed, moving swiftly downstream on the wind. Their rapid *whew-whew* wingbeats were audible above the river sounds, and we watched them pass. *We should be careful,* I laughed. *There are so many ducks flying we might hook one!*

Heimir grinned and shook his head. We finally reached the pool and the old man pointed out the best holding lies. The cast worked out, gathering speed quickly with the left-hand haul, and the impossible happened. The line whistled out and snapped over above the current, and a passing eider hooked itself solidly.

My God! I shouted. *It happened!*

Heimir was laughing hysterically, and the reel screamed as the duck stripped line and lost altitude like a kite with too much tail. The dragging line finally pulled it back into the river. It fell with a heavy splash, floundering and stunned for a moment, and then it threshed across the current trying to take off. We ran down the banks in pursuit with the eider still splashing wildly. It had taken two hundred yards of backing, and I held the rod high over my head to clear the line from the rocky shallows.

Finally I worked it back to our bank, and Heimir waded out into the river to retrieve it. The duck fought hard, trying to take off and showering him with water. He almost fell gathering the frightened bird against his stomach and stumbled back ashore.

Tail it! I laughed. *Tail it!*

Heimir pinned it against the grass with a body press while I carefully worked the hook out of its wing. The eider waddled unhappily down the bank, shook its tangled feathers and glared angrily, and took off again in a long foot-slapping run across the river.

It was a good fight, I laughed.

Heimir nodded and washed his hands in the shallows.

Graham and his gillie arrived fifteen minutes later carrying a twelve-pound salmon.

See you finally got a fish! he said.

That was no fish, I said sadly. *It was only a duck.*

They laughed derisively and I shook my head in mock despair. *Well,* Heimir filled his pipe and smiled, *a duck is better than nothing!*

Raspberries
in the Rain

IT rained softly through the night. The mountains were covered with clouds just after daylight, and the street was wet when I crossed the gardens of the Lindström Hotel for breakfast. There were gulls working and wheeling over the tidal shallows below the river.

The breakfast room was empty but the cold table was already laid and waiting. Breakfast was soft-boiled eggs and goat cheese and brislings in dill sauce, and when the coffee was finished I returned to my rooms to dress for the river. It was chilly and the radio promised overcast weather and more rain. There was an extra pullover in my duffle, and I rummaged for the rain jacket and scarf. The fresh Ackroyds and Orange Charms I had dressed after dinner were lying on the table beside the vise.

The ferry from Kaupanger arrived while I was loading

the Mercedes, and its horn sounded along the valley and echoed from the cliffs above the river.

It looks like a good morning, said Andreas when I reached his house.

Raining like this? I smiled.

Yes, said the riverkeeper. *The river goes down when it is raining.* It seemed strange.

Down when it rains? I laughed.

The old man smiled. *Rain stops the snow-melt in the mountains,* he explained, *and when there's no snow-water the river gets low and clear.*

Sounds good! I said.

Andreas Olsen knows the river like no one else in the valley. His father was riverkeeper on the Laerdal for Lord Henry Portman, and most of his years on the river were spent gillying and fly-making for the late Prince Axel of Denmark. His equally famous son Olav is a great fly-tier and has often gillied for Crown Prince Harald of Norway. Andreas has the seasoning of sixty-five years on the river, and is acknowledged as its Dean Emeritus.

The road winds south from Laerdalsøyri, past the tiny clapboard houses and the churchyard and the farmhouses above the town. The windshield wipers danced rhythmically when we passed the hayfields at Hunderi. The fields were wet and there was no one working and raking and building hay-fences that morning.

Farmers were loading milk cans on the timber truck-platform at the Tonjüm crossroads, and we left the car at the bridge above the Kvellehølen Pool.

What pool did we draw? I asked.

Wallhølen, said Andreas.

Thomas Falck was fishing the sweeping currents of the Kvellehølen above the bridge. He waved and shook his head to tell us there was no luck there, and we clambered over the stiles and stone fences along the path toward the Wallhølen

Pool. It was the water we had drawn in the lottery for morning beats at Rikheim.

The path winds along fields of potatoes and cabbages, through thickets of wild raspberries. The berries glistened with drops of rain. We crossed the raspberry fields and followed the path into some silver birches, and I could hear the river tumbling beyond the trees.

The river comes down through the Gammleboll meadows and sweeps against the huge granite walls that form the highway. Its currents churn along the rough moss-covered masonry and dance into the Wallhølen Pool.

Salmon lie down the first hundred yards of current. They hold in the main currents where the river is oily smooth, and below the river shallows and slows over fine gravel. There are sea-trout in those quieter places later in the summer, but we were after bigger game.

Andreas shook his head over my light rod. *We're fishing small flies now*, I explained again.

Pray for grilse, smiled the old man.

We selected one of my fresh Ackroyds and he carefully knotted it to my leader. Andreas led the way up the rocky beach toward the head of the pool, stopped thoughtfully and studied the river for several minutes.

Start casting here, he pointed finally.

They're lying this high in the main current? I asked. *Seems like pretty heavy water.*

Sometimes even higher, Andreas answered.

The casts switched out and began working back and forth in the rain as I lengthened line and dropped the fly tight against the masonry. The fly started working and I lowered the rod and pumped the fly rhythmically back across the current. Each cast sliced out through the rain, dropping across the river and swimming enticingly with the steady working of the rod.

The first heady anticipation of fishing a strange pool had

almost passed when I had fished halfway down the best holding water.

It seems dead, I said sourly.

Patience, smiled Andreas. *There is still another thirty meters of good water left.*

Suddenly the current changed, and two huge swirls boiled up behind the swinging fly. Andreas smiled and refilled his pipe and cupped his hands around the match.

Cast again, he said softly.

The salmon came back, sliding out of the heavy water like a dark pewter-colored shadow, and the rod bent suddenly when it turned back with the fly in its jaws. It shook itself angrily, writhing and bolting down the main currents, and cartwheeled explosively into the rain.

How big? I yelled.

It's no grilse! laughed the old man.

The salmon was better than thirty-five pounds. Cars were stopping on the road to watch, and the daily bus to Fagernes and Oslo joined them. People crowded along the huge monoliths of granite that form the guard-rail, shouting encouragement in the rain. The fish jumped wildly again and the crowd gasped at its power and size. The salmon turned and bored down the pool again, shaking itself sullenly along the bottom. It surfaced and threshed clumsily, forcing me to surrender more and more line. We ran awkwardly along the rocky beach, and the salmon stopped before it reached the swift, riffling shallows that left the pool. Slowly I worked it back into deeper water until it turned and came up the pool itself. There was another jump and it surfaced weakly.

He's getting tired! I yelled happily.

The fish was almost finished. Its huge tail fanned weakly in the current, and we walked upstream, stealthily recovering line. The salmon was out of the heavy currents now, rolling helplessly against the pressure of the rod.

Get ready! I said prayerfully.

Andreas waited in a half-crouch with the gaff, and the salmon rolled on its side, working its gills weakly as I forced it toward him. Its dark shoulders and bright spotted flanks were clearly visible in the shallows.

The old riverkeeper reached cautiously with the gaff, stretching toward the salmon as it rolled over. It was almost in reach when the fly came out suddenly and the huge fish drifted into deep water. The crowd groaned and turned back to the bus.

Damn! I said angrily.

The old riverkeeper came ashore slowly and said nothing as we walked back through the birches. We climbed the stiles and stone fences, stopping to eat raspberries in the rain. The berries were cold and sweet. Sometimes the best skill a gillie has is his silence.

The River of the Spirits

Six weeks after Christmas we climbed slowly through the Caleufu foothills into the heat of the barren Cordoba Pass. Condors circled lazily on the wind. The hills shimmered in the heat ahead of the truck, and the driver geared back to wind slowly up the narrow switchbacks toward the twisted wind-pines at the summit.

There is a small arroyo three hundred yards below the trees where the water trickles through the stones across the road. Several partridges were dusting and drinking. The birds flushed as we reached the crossing, and dropped into the canyon in a long side-slipping glide before they set their wings and settled into the brush. There were no other signs of life. The driver finally shifted into second gear and the truck growled toward the river. Clouds of volcanic ash billowed high on the wind.

Hot! I wiped my face unhappily.

The driver grunted and I soaked my handkerchief in water from the canteen, wrapping it across my neck. It felt cold and the water trickled down under my shirt, tracing delicious rivulets of coolness until it reached and gathered wetly above my belt.

The road wound down into a strange valley of lunar monoliths and high rock chimneys. The hot wind eddied in the draws and washes, and the road picked its way carefully along the alkali shoulders above the Arroyo Cordoba. The truck strained down against its engine, geared back and whining as we worked the switchbacks carefully. There was a strange purple light in the valley floor below, where the river looped in the shadows.

Traful? I yelled over the protesting gear-box.

The driver nodded and shifted gears as we crossed a fence-line and reached the bottom of the pass.

What does it mean? I asked.

It's Araucan, he said. *Something about spirits.*

The River of the Spirits, I thought.

The road follows the base of the mountains, winding east along the river until it meets the steep-walled gorge of the Limay. The trestle bridge crosses the Traful at Confluencia, three-hundred yards above its meeting with the huge river that drains Lago Nahuel-Huapi. Confluencia lies in a stand of slender poplars at the bottom of the Valle Encantada, its hosteria and gas station lights twinkling in the darkness.

The rude bed was hard and the room smelled of fly-spray, but it was cooler and the wind eddied in the poplars and I slept. Breakfast was an omelette and a rare *bife* and a pot of tea with milk. The jeep from the Estancia came down at noon and we loaded my gear in the back. The road winds along the south bank of the Traful, crosses the small Cuyin Manzano on a timber bridge, and rises high across the shoulder of the mountain on a cribbing of logs jammed along the precipice.

Finally it climbs through a natural entrance in the rocks, with a huge log portico.

Estancia la Primavera! read the driver.

Springtime, I thought. *It means springtime.*

The main ranch buildings lie in a dense stand of *alamos*, with a formal avenue of willows leading down toward the river. The house is a rambling mass of stone and heavy timbers and tiles with an extensive English garden. It was built almost fifty years ago, the dream of an Australian named Guy Dawson, who came to Patagonia with a shipment of Corriedale sheep, liked the strange valleys above San Carlos de Bariloche, and decided to remain in the Argentine.

Dawson lost his dream to the Thirties depression, and his Estancia la Primavera was sold to a former French officer who had served as a military attaché in various French embassies around South America. Phillipe Larivière also loved the half-European cities and the sweeping landscapes of the Argentine frontier, loved its fishing and its shooting, and when the beautiful region on the Rio Traful was available he bought it.

Its fishing was so good and its reputation for beauty was so great that the ranch was confiscated under General Juan Peron as a sporting retreat for the Argentine dictator and his circle of friends. It was restored to the Larivières after the fall of the Peron government, under the revolutionary *junta* headed by the late General Pedro Aramburu.

The ranch controls the entire valley from the outlet of Lago Traful to the lower reaches of the river at Confluencia. The river flows smooth and incredibly clear from its fjord-like lake, sliding into the upper pools under giant monoliths of basalt. The first pools are closed to fishing, including the famous currents of the Campamento, to preserve the prime spawning beds of the best landlocked salmon river in the world.

There are other great pools below the famous Cipreses and Nellie Blood. The Pool of Plenty and the Leonora lie at the base of pale ledges of basalt, and the Piedra del Viente is a huge pool under a towering monolith pierced by the wind with a huge hole. Cordoba lies where the tributary from Paso Cordoba reaches the river, but the best fishing usually lies in the first mile below the lake.

The river and its fishing are a happy accident. It happened early in this century, when a shipment of fertile salmon eggs was being carried overland to Bariloche and a temporary hatchery. The fisheries experts with the pack train became concerned that the landlock eggs from Sebago Lake in Maine would spoil, so they left the party to hatch them in a makeshift trough above Confluencia. The decisive battles for control of the Argentine frontier had just been fought with the Araucan tribes less than a hundred miles above the Traful. Scattered war parties remained in these Andean foothills, and leaving the government pack-train still held some risk.

The biologist built a shallow spawning channel in the Cuyin Manzano, narrowing his crude coffer dams to control the current speed and settling the eggs in gravel roughly culled for size in the riffles. It worked and finally the tiny alevins wriggled up through the gravel. The fisheries expert and his cavalry escort stayed briefly to protect the baby salmon from the birds until the small fish dropped downstream into the river and their work was finished. The finest landlocked salmon river in the world began with those few tiny fingerlings, hatched six thousand miles from Maine in a small tributary draining the opposite side of the earth.

Phillipe Larivière came out to meet the jeep. *Pim Larivière!* he introduced himself warmly. *Come and meet my sons!* We shook hands and went inside the house.

The older son was tall with an oval face like his father. *Maurice,* he said softly and shook hands.

Felipe! said the lean younger son.

Their wives joined us for a lunch of roast lamb and fresh tomatoes from the gardens in the valley and slender French bread baked in the Estancia ovens. There was a perfectly chilled Santo Huberto vintage from Mendoza, and coffee and Cuban cigars followed in the library.

Come see our fishing log, said Maurice.

It was the record of the river over the years, and included a fishless session President Eisenhower entered into its pages in his handwriting. It also included a half-dozen fish better than the current landlock record of 22½ pounds, potential world record fish that were never certified.

You want to camp on the river? asked Pim.

That's right, I said. *I'd hoped to camp to catch the mood of the river that way if it's alright with you.*

Anchorena is camped at the Pool of Plenty, Pim shook his head thoughtfully. *We must find Ernesto another campsite.*

Felipe brought cognac and more cigars.

Below the Nellie Blood? suggested Maurice.

Perfect! Pim agreed.

We went down to the Anchorena campsite after lunch and found Bébé and his family resting in the warm grass. Anchorena is one of the great Argentine fly-fishermen, and held the world fly-record for brown trout for several years.

Any luck? I greeted them.

The pool is full of salmon, grinned Bébé, *but they're as moody as usual.*

Carolina caught one! said Carola Anchorena.

Yes, Bébé shrugged philosophically. *Carolina had a fish of six pounds in the Leonora pool yesterday.*

It was late afternoon and the siesta was over. Pim and Maurice went down to the Nellie Blood and scouted the pools up toward the outlet of the lake while I made a simple camp in the cypresses. The Nellie Blood is a classic reach of salmon water. It has almost a hundred yards of taking current, beginning with a dark channel along some boulders and deadfalls at the top of the pool. Its main water is a long, chest-deep glide over smooth gravel. There are beds of weeds trailing in the current and a backwater of reeds across the pool. The tail of the pool is the best lie, where the channel narrows against the house-sized boulders and a sheer precipice of basalt that rises from the water.

The salmon lie scattered from the swift, upper currents of the pool to the deep slow-moving channel at the tail. *Sometimes they're in there like a flotilla of submarines!* pointed Pim excitedly.

You can see when the light is right, added Maurice.

We walked upstream along the river and talked about its fishing and its history. *Guy Dawson caught a twenty-six-pound salmon on a spoon about forty years ago,* said Pim Larivière, *so he really holds the world record as far as we're concerned.*

We have the photographs, said Maurice.

There have been several between twenty-three and twenty-five pounds on flies over the years, added Pim.

How do they run now? I asked.

The average has dropped these last few years, Pim answered, *but most fish are between six and nine pounds.*

There was a towering monolith of rock upstream, rising high above the shadows of the river into the evening sun. The river came down in a sweeping curve, the light warm beyond the copper beeches and cypresses, and turned past the precipice of basalt into the depths of the pool. Slowly the current gathered again, sliding over the weeds and waist-deep gravel past a clump of gnarled and twisted cypresses.

Cipreses, announced Maurice.

It's not as good as the Nellie Blood, said Pim, *but there are usually a half-dozen fish lying on the other side.*

Too bad we can't see them in this light, I said.

Let's try them! suggested Pim.

Both men insisted that I fish the Cipreses before we walked back to the Nellie Blood. Its current is surprisingly strong, deceptive under its sliding mirror-smooth surface, and the river is so clear that the waist-deep run looked almost shallow above its bed of pebbles.

It looks like easy wading, I groaned in surprise.

You should be careful on the Traful, they said. *It's always much deeper than it looks.* It has proved good advice on many rivers around the world.

The salmon were uncooperative that evening, rolling and jumping in the Nellie Blood, and refusing our flies until it was dark and I returned to camp. There was a pile of wood gathered by the gauchos for my cookfire and I laid it quickly. Firelight flickered in the cypresses around the tent and I grilled a steak with a pan of fried potatoes and a can of *palmitos* from Brazil. The half bottle of *tinto* and strong coffee completed dinner, and I sat watching the firelight die as the moon came up across the strange volcanic landscape beyond the river. It whispered past the campsite and the stars seemed terribly bright as I crawled into my sleeping bag.

God, I thought, *it's beautiful here!*

The river glittered through the trees, and across from my camp, several springs trickled down the cliffs through beds of flowers and ferns. The currents were crystalline and smooth, with long beds of weeds trailing silkily downstream. The mountains towered above the river.

Maurice and Felipe arrived in their jeep. *Come upstream with us,* they said. *We want to show you the reserve.*

We drove along the river past the water posted against fishing to protect the river and its salmon stocks. The sun was high above the outlet pool where the river gathers and flows smoothly from the lake. Big salmon were lying everywhere in the sun, and several big fish porpoised lazily in the shadows of the sheer cliff across the pool.

The riverkeeper rowed us out to the huge rock that lies above the outlet in about fifteen feet of water. He moored the skiff in the slack currents behind the rock, and we watched the outlet channel while the salmon drifted back into position in the current. The tumbling little rivers that feed Lago Traful are usually too cold for landlocked salmon, and the fish drop back into the outlet river to spawn in the middle of February.

Look at them! I said. *Look at them!*

The big fish settled back into position, hovering above the bottom like pewter-colored torpedoes in the gathering currents. There was one lying above the school that looked better than twenty pounds.

It was too much. Let's fish! I said.

Maurice went down with me to the Nellie Blood, and searched his fly-books. *Try this one!* He handed me a small streamer dressed with olive-dyed grizzly hackles.

What is it called? I asked.

Matona, said Maurice. *It imitates a baitfish we have.*

Looks good! I tied it to the leader.

The line worked briskly in the sun and dropped the streamer above the fish in Cipreses. There were six salmon lying over the pale gravel in full sight. The little streamer worked enticingly across the fish, passed their holding position slightly, and two fish suddenly turned to follow its swing. The lead salmon took the fly with a heavy swirl, ripped off twenty yards of line, jumped quickly and fell free. The swift cartwheeling fight was over in thirty seconds.

That was quick! I laughed sheepishly.

The two days that followed were all like that. Fish sheared the leader on deadfalls and ledgerock and boulders. Flies came out on the first jump or just when the salmon seemed ready to surrender. One fish bored deep into a bed of weeds and tore itself loose. The number of fish that came to the fly wildly and were missed by striking too soon is embarrassing to remember. It was exquisite torture.

The last morning was beautiful, but the salmon seemed dour and sullen. *We'll have a picnic at the Campamento,* said Maurice. *It's to celebrate your last day on the Traful.*

I'll be there! I said. *See you at noon!*

The rich cooking smells drifted downstream on the wind from Campamento, and finally I reeled in and walked to the picnic. The Anchorena family arrived with the Larivière wives and the celebration started. It was hardly the simple picnic lunch promised under the cypresses.

Any luck? I asked.

Maurice had one at the Leonora, said Felipe, *and Bébé took a six-kilo fish on the Pool of Plenty!*

Better than twelve pounds! I said.

Fourteen! corrected Maurice.

The picnic lunch was a relevation. The gauchos had built a big fire that morning and its pit was a glowing circle of coals. There were partridges and whole lambs and baby goats roasting on steel spits. The wine was chilling in the river. There was a fine Chilean *blanco* and a heavier red Argentine vintage from Mendoza. The gauchos were basting the partridges and when they were ready, each of us was served a bird. *Perdiz?* they asked politely.

The birds were deliciously roasted and served with the river-chilled Riesling. The roast lamb was the next course, dripping with *salsa criolla* and cooked to perfection, and the baby goats followed.

Cabrito? asked Felipe.

It was delicious and we gorged ourselves.

The salad was fresh lettuce and sliced tomatoes and artichokes and peppers from the Estancia gardens. Its dressing was Spanish olive oil and vinegar mixed with a dark, coarsely ground ingredient.

Truffles? I gasped in surprise.

Maurice laughed. *Truffles!* he nodded.

The children were gathering berries from the *michay* thickets along the river, and we had them for dessert with heavy fresh cream. They were a little like tiny blueberries. *There's a legend about michay,* Filipe poured the cognac. *The Indians believe that anyone who eats the michay will come back again to Patagonia.* We raised our cognacs to his toast.

It's like the legend of yerba maté, I said.

Exactly, Felipe nodded.

There was still an hour or two of fishing before time to leave for Bariloche. Maurice and I walked down to Cipreses and I waded out to cover the fish on the far side, where the cypresses twisted above the current. The big bucktail worked across the salmon and started its swing into the tail of the pool. Suddenly there was a huge bow-wave and wake behind my bucktail, and the fly was engulfed in a sailfish-sized strike. It was a huge salmon, bulldogging past me into the depths of the pool. Three times it cartwheeled at close range, showering me twice with water until my sunglasses were covered, and I tried to counter its moves half-blind. It jumped again and ripped the bucktail free with a fierce, wrenching pirouette in the sun.

Six or seven kilos! sighed Maurice.

That's the seventh fish I've lost in three days, I waded ashore unhappily. *Nothing like a perfect score!*

The michay will bring you back, he said.

Several years passed before the legend worked its magic, and memories of that week of failure on the Traful still haunted me. It is one of the most beautiful rivers in the world, and its salmon continued to elude me even in my dreams. Douglas Reid was waiting when the flight from Buenos Aires reached Bariloche. It was a bright autumn morning in April and the poplars were turning orange along the river. The rooftops and houses of San Carlos de Bariloche were bright across the lake, and behind the brown foothills the Tronador volcano towered into the sky.

Tronador has fresh snow today, I pointed to the volcano. *It's been cold,* said Douglas, *and it should start the salmon coming down from the lake.*

They expect us at Cipreses? I asked.

Yes, Douglas answered, *and we're expected for dinner at the Estancia too.*

The road crosses the Limay where the river gathers its currents above the half-mile ledge of lava that blocks its outlet. It leaves the lake along a hundred yards of spillway-like ledges. Estancia Nahuel Huapi guards the crossing, almost hidden in its windbreak of poplars, and the road climbs beyond the ranch into the bare Wyoming-looking hills. We wound through the basin of the Anfiteatro, where the river loops into a series of channels and islands, winding back on itself in a tangle of sun-bright riffles and pools. Following the river downstream, the river winds through the strange chimneys and lunar outcroppings and honeycombed cliffs of the Valle Encantada.

Confluencia was ahead where the Traful meets the Limay at the base of a strange salmon-colored mountain. We took rooms in its familiar little *hosteria* and drove upstream along the river to fish. The river was just as I had remembered it, winding lazily across the valley floor. We reached the ranch and wound past the main house down its lane of willows into the pale grazing land that drops toward the river. Douglas forded the jeep expertly across the swift shallows of the little Minero, wound across the volcanic-ash bottoms, and followed the trail into the cypress thickets that conceal the winding course of the river.

Maurice was already into a six-pound salmon in the swift holding water at the top of the Nellie Blood. We clambered out of the jeep just as he worked the fish out of the strongest current. It fought stubbornly without jumping until Maurice parried its bulldogging runs, and forced it slowly into the shallows, where it finally began to fight.

Look out! I yelled.

The salmon turned and gathered speed quickly and threshed into a churning half-hearted jump. Its second jump was a clean, cartwheeling splash so close it showered us with water, and then the fish leapfrogged down the shallows. It jumped again twice under the big cypress half-way down the pool, almost fouling itself in its overhanging branches. Finally the salmon came grudgingly back up the current.

He's coming now, grunted Maurice.

Felipe arrived carrying a bigger fish. *¡Hola!* we shook hands heartily.

Maurice worked the fish close and tailed it expertly and waded ashore. *¡Hola Pescador!* laughed Maurice as we shook

hands. *The michay worked and you've come back to our river!*
Yes, I smiled.

We weighed their salmon on the scales. *We're running out of time,* said Maurice, *and we've saved Cipreses for you.*
The light was warm on the monoliths above the Cipreses. We walked upstream along the path through the cypresses, looked at the weeds undulating in the current.
What have they been taking? I asked.
The river is low this year, said Felipe. *You should fish something small and dark like a Black Fairy.*
And a floating line, added Douglas.
There was a Silver Monkey in my box, dressed low-water style on a slender eight hook. Its hairwing was silver monkey over a dark herl body and a collar of grizzly hackle.
Well, I laughed, *the last time I fished the Traful my performance was less than triumphant.*
Buena suerte! said Douglas.
The cast worked out into the twilight, gathering distance and speed, and settled the fly above the fish. The water was down that summer and the salmon-lie was about five yards lower in the gathering tail-currents of the pool. The fly began working around past the lie in its lazy, teasing rhythm and suddenly a fish porpoised. The line bellied and tightened against its weight, and I raised the rod.
Salmon! I yelled. *Salmon!*
The rod was bucking now as the fish frog-walked upstream, showering water wildly the length of the pool. It jumped again and turned to fight me angrily where the smooth flow broke into the swift current downstream. Finally I forced it back into quieter water. It stubbornly refused to surrender, and when I worked it close for tailing, it writhed and churned in the current. The river eddied past my waiting fingers. The fish was quiet now and drifted back on the surface, working its gill covers weakly, and I carefully seated my fingers in the wrist of its tail.
Olé! shouted Douglas. *Olé!*

My luck had changed and I waded happily ashore with a nine-pound salmon. We drove back through the darkness for dinner at the main house. *News of your luck already reached us!* said Pim. *Welcome back!*

Mil gracias! we shook hands.

The family gathered in the library for cocktails, and the talk ranged from salmon to thoroughbred horses and truffles. We studied the fresh entries in the fishing log while the family changed for dinner and drifted into the dining room. They were wearing dinner jackets and pale brocade pant-suits, and the servants were dressed in white-gloved livery.

My black-tie is five thousand miles away! I groaned.

It's a family custom, explained Felipe.

Pim Larivière took the head of the table. *Welcome back!* he raised his glass. *We hope our river and its salmon treat you better this time!*

It was a dinner that surpassed the picnic beside the Campamento pool six years before. Smoked salmon from the river was followed with broiled quail. The main course was roast *ciervo*, and the incredible menu reached its climax with *crepes suzette* served a thousand wilderness miles below Buenos Aires.

That night the *pampero* wind rose in the mountains, and the next morning the wind was still fierce. It lashed the cypresses below the lake and raised huge waves on the Limay below Confluencia. Leaves scurried and scuttled across the road, and clouds of dust and volcanic ash and pumice towered in the gusts that ripped the valley floor. It was a strange morning best suited to fishing the sheltered places on the lower river. *It's crazy,* laughed the owner of the hosteria. *No salmon will venture out today!*

We'll see, I answered.

It proved a remarkable morning. The jeep shuddered and bucked in the wind as we crossed the bottoms above the Cordoba Pool. Pebbles rattled across the windshield and the hood. It was difficult to string the rod in the wind, even in the shelter of the willow thickets and the jeep. It gusted down the river, tossing the eucalyptus trees violently, and forcing white-caps down the length of the pool. The small creek from the Cordoba Pass trickles through the willows into the head of the pool, and a heavy chute boils in past the trees into the slower currents, sliding deep and green past the rocks.

There were a half-dozen big marabous in my fly-book, dressed on 1/0 hooks with bright blue feathers above their white body and wings. Their heads were painted a similar blue on the back with yellow eyes and silver mylar sides. It is a deadly imitation of the smelt-like *pejerrey* baitfish. The first cast rolled out to avoid the willows, caught the gusting wind and sailed high across the pool. It was a lucky cast and the big streamer dropped tight under the trees. The current snatched the fly past the willow roots, working its glittering mylar swiftly in the sun, and it disappeared in a slashing rise that showered water.

Salmon! I shouted to Douglas.

The reel screamed above the shrieking wind. The salmon jumped again and again, vaulting high and losing its balance in the gusts, falling back clumsily into the whitecaps. It was a long fight in the surf-like waves, difficult because it was impossible to see and anticipate the fish. Finally it surrendered and I tailed it cleanly and waded ashore, and sighed happily when the scale touched fourteen pounds.

The rest was an incredible hour when each cast seemed to find a salmon, and the river eagerly surrendered its riches. More than a dozen were hooked and lost. Fish rolled behind the fly and leapfrogged its swing without taking, and six were hooked and landed in the Cordoba alone. The best was a fifteen-pound cockfish that assaulted my streamer in the Piedra del Viento, where the huge monolith of igneous rock marks the primary holding water. When it finally gasped and beached itself, the wind suddenly died and the salmon stopped taking completely.

The river was generous all that week. There were fresh-run salmon in all the pools, falling all over themselves to attack our flies. It was a strange week in which everything went right. *There was even a fish at Confluencia!* I told Maurice at the Nellie Blood. *This year there was even a fish for me where there are no fish!*

You've been lucky, he agreed.

The pool flowed smooth and silken against the boulders and ledges. Two salmon porpoised like lazy cats. The sun was behind the trees and shadows covered the pool, and it was time to fish again. Two casts and there was a heavy strike against the rocks. The fish made a strong run upstream and jumped in the sun.

He's huge! I yelled.

The salmon looked like fifteen or twenty pounds. *Your luck is still good!* Maurice came running along the river. *That's the biggest fish we've hooked all year!*

It jumped again and turned back into the current, bolting wildly downstream along the bottom. The line hung dangerously slack and I reeled frantically until the fish showered me with a final jump and threw the shiny marabou high into the twilight.

There's always another year, Douglas smiled. Downstream another salmon jumped, and fell heavily in the gathering darkness.

The Time of
the Hendricksons

IT is still winter outside the farmhouse. There were several whitetail does foraging in the snow along the woodlot this morning. Their coats are almost as gray as the winter woods, and it has been a lean year. My fly-tying table is littered with lemon woodduck feathers and a pair of fine Andalusian gamecock necks. There is a delicate Hendrickson half-finished in the vise and a flock of crows just settled in the oaks outside, showering a dust of snow through their rattling limbs. It is a time for daydreams.

Each angler has a favorite hatch of flies on his home river, and each favorite echoes his experience with its timeless cycle of the seasons. Each river is unique too, with its own fingerprint of fly-hatches.

Some fishermen like the early *Paraleptophlebia* hatches. Others prefer the larger Gordon Quills that emerge on April afternoons, perhaps because they are the harbingers of another season astream. Others prefer the later *Stenonema* drakes, and fly fishermen on the classic limestone streams anxiously await the Pale Sulphur hatches. Some anglers still give their allegiance to the Green Drakes, although these big *Ephemera* flies are sadly in decline on most rivers. Fishermen who live on the larger eastern rivers happily await the slate-winged *Isonychias*, perhaps because they are large enough to coax big trout to the surface. There are still others on the storied eastern rivers who like the pale hatches of late spring and early summer—the straw-colored duns best imitated by their delicate Gray Foxes and Cahills.

There are many hatches worth the notice of the serious fly fisherman. Men who frequent the Raritan and Musconetcong have learned to love the Blue-winged Olives common on their waters. Skilled fishermen are becoming aware of ants and leafhoppers and beetles in the cycle of the season, particularly since we have mishandled and damaged our familiar aquatic hatches in past years, with the careless lumbering and tanneries and highway construction and pesticides typical of our technological myopia. The decline of the Green Drake has been partly compensated for by the ultimate heresy of the summer leafrollers—the apple-green worms that emerge a few weeks later to perform their acrobatics above the river on silken threads, tempting the bigger trout.

Each fisherman has his favorites, and those favorites may change with his rivers and the layers of experience he accumulates across the years. Mine follow a similar pattern of experiment and continual change. The early summers were spent in Michigan, where I learned to like the egg-laden *Ephemerella* spinners that swarmed over favorite boyhood riffles on the Pere Marquette. There were giant *Hexagenia* drakes in the midsummer darkness on Michigan rivers like the Boardman and the Manistee. Other favorites have followed in later years, and each of these hatches triggers memories of many rivers; but on this winter evening I would probably choose the hardy

Ephemerella hatches of late April—the ubiquitous Hendricksons familiar to most eastern fishermen.

There are many memories of Hendricksons from these past few seasons. Such memories include an April float on the familiar Au Sable in Michigan, with weak sunlight and fresh snow in the swamp birches along the river, and the wonderful hatch of *Ephemerella* flies that came off the river in the sweeping bends below Grayling.

Hendrickson memories tumble down the years, like a reach of broken water between favorite pools. There was a heavy hatch one afternoon on the Yellow Breeches, when the warm winds of the Shenandoah country eddied north and transformed winter into spring, and the dark ridges above the Cumberland valley became touched with green overnight. Memory returns to the excellent hatch that emerged one April on the classic Ferdon's Pool, that shrine on the Beaverkill where Albert Hendrickson himself first tried the Steenrod flies that would later carry his name. There have been Hendricksons on many rivers over the years, and sometimes they have rescued me from the misfortunes of April, like the hatch that triggered an impressive rise of trout on a bitter day of snow squalls along the Schoharie.

There are many memories and reasons for loving the time of the Hendricksons. The trout are already conscious of dry flies, and have been conditioned to surface food by the smaller stoneflies and mayflies that usher in the season. Hendricksons appear when the first brave leaves are budding in the trees, touching the branches with yellow and rose. The first real warmth is found in the midday sun, and there are violets in the sheltered places. Bloodroot is often blooming when the Hendricksons are hatching on the Raritan and Nissequogue, and there are dogwoods in blossom when the hatch reaches the Neversink and Battenkill farther north.

Some signals are found elsewhere, like the barometer of forsythias and magnolias. Commuters on my morning train pass the richly flowering magnolias along Blair Walk, which leads down from the Princeton campus to the railroad station, without realizing the significance behind the blossoms—the anglers among us try to forget them, hiding our disappointment in the *Journal* and *Times* because we are deskbound on a day that promises Hendricksons.

These familiar hatches are typically composed of three closely-related species. Perhaps the best known is *Ephemerella invaria*, first described for anglers by Preston Jennings in his classic *Book of Trout Flies*, and perfectly imitated with a properly-dressed Hendrickson. Almost as familiar is *Ephemerella subvaria*, its abdominal segments flushed with the rusty pinkish markings described by Art Flick in his little *Streamside Guide*. His book has helped a generation of Catskill fishermen to know their fly hatches, and his version of the Hendrickson is tied with the pinkish belly fur of a red fox vixen to suggest the pinkish abdominal cast of the *subvaria* hatches on the Schoharie. Sometimes I tie Hendricksons with dun hacklepoint wings, and bodies with rusty pink dubbing ribbed over a base of cream fox when the browns are particularly choosy. *Ephemerella rotunda* is the third insect of the Hendrickson group, and has its abdomen ringed with rusty brown tergite and sternite markings. Its nymphs are fast-water dwellers, perhaps requiring more oxygen than its *invaria* and *subvaria* cousins, and its activity is concentrated in the more broken reaches of river. The familiar Red Quill developed by Art Flick is an excellent imitation on rivers which have good hatches of *Ephemerella rotunda*.

Some mayflies are temperamental, emerging sporadically throughout the day, and often failing to appear when conditions seem absolutely perfect. Hendricksons are usually punctual and predictable. There is nothing timid about them once their hatching is started, and they often last from mid-April until the third week in May. Hendrickson hatches are still relatively heavy, perhaps because these hardy *Ephemerellas* have survived the damage we have inflicted on the ecology of our eastern rivers. Perhaps because of their hardiness, the

Hendricksons will continue as a major hatch, and eastern anglers can enjoy them in the future—as much as our fathers have loved them in seasons past. There is something civilized and particularly charming about Hendricksons. City anglers can rise late when they are hatching, spend a leisurely breakfast, fuss with their equipment, and lazily reach the river after eleven o'clock—secure in the knowledge that an angler with little interest in flogging the water with early-morning bucktails has missed nothing of importance.

The nymphs of these *Ephemerellas* clamber about the bottom in all types of water, although most specimens are found in moderate riffles and currents. The nymphs of the *invaria* species are medium to dark brownish, with darker mottlings and light markings of buff and olive. The nymphal forms of *subvaria* are generally dark brown, with pale tergite markings and a rather olive-colored cast. The thorax and wing cases are almost black before emergence. The back segments of the abdomen are dark brown near the thorax and the tails, with the gills and gill segments a somewhat paler brown. The belly segments are brown, darkening toward the tail filaments. The legs are olive with dark brown mottlings. The tails are light olive and banded with brown. The nymphs of the *rotunda* species are yellowish brown mottled with darker markings on the thorax, wing cases and tergites. Both legs and tails are tan mottled with brown. These three species are remarkably abundant in the richer streams, and thrive in all types of water from tumbling runs to gravel-bottomed riffles and the silt of quiet backwaters and eddies. Particularly fertile rivers support as many as a thousand *Ephemerella* nymphs in a square yard of bottom.

The spinner stage is also important, but few anglers are familiar with it except to imitate the egg-filled females during the evening mating swarms. These spinner flights occur after the duns have hatched from the river and molted, and the mating swarms in good seasons can resemble a winged blizzard. Male spinners are also important trout foods.

The spinners of these Hendrickson flies are surprisingly different in color. The *invaria* species is perhaps the most familiar to anglers, since it was described in Jennings' *Book of Trout Flies* more than thirty years ago. It has clear wings, a reddish-brown thorax, yellowish legs, light brown tergite mottlings on a pale yellow body, and three pale tails ringed with brown. The spinners of the *subvaria* flies are somewhat darker in colorings, having clear wings, a dark reddish-brown thorax, olive legs flushed with brown, a dark reddish-brown abdomen ringed with pale amber markings, and olive tails ringed with brown. The mating swarms of *rotunda* flies have clear wings, a yellowish-brown thorax, pale yellow legs, amber ringed with yellowish brown, and pale tails marked with brown. Each of these spinner species has bright yellow egg-sacs extruding from the mating females, and a rather pale version of the Female Beaverkill has long been a favorite with fishermen during these spinner flights.

These spinners are usually as punctual as the Hendrickson duns, and appear over the river between five and six o'clock in the late afternoon. The swarms rise and fall over the river, moving gradually upstream until the females oviposit over the riffles. Once the eggs are extruded, the females fall exhausted to the surface with their wings askew. Later their wings lie spent in the surface film, and both spentwing males and females are sometimes still available the following morning. During the mating swarms, the trout often rise eagerly to the egg-laying spinners, since the heaviest insect activity lasts little more than an hour. The feeding activity is rather splashy. The rise-forms encountered with spent spinners the following mornings are soft and deliberate. Fishing during these *Ephemerella* spinner flights is rather more at the mercy of the weather than it is for the Hendricksons, and relatively warm spring evenings are typically best.

But enough stream entomology, because the memory is filled with Hendrickson fishing, and a typical April day on a familiar reach of the Brodheads is taking shape in the mind. The morning was dark and squally before breakfast, but the rain had stopped at daybreak. There was nothing to entice me outside, and I spent two hours dressing fresh Hendricksons and Red Quills before wandering upstream to look for rises. There were no rises evident in either pool where sporadic morning hatches are often good. I wandered upstream toward a deep run under slate ledges, its current tongue spilling from a heavy riffle where I have often collected nymphs. The riffle typically holds hundreds of *subvaria* and *rotunda* specimens, and it seemed a good place for nymph activity.

There were no rises, but I was sure the nymphs were restlessly anticipating their afternoon hatch. The morning seemed less cold when I changed reels and strung a sinking line through the guides. The first cast reached out and dropped the weighted imitation above the ledge, where the riffling currents slowed in deeper water. The nymph drifted deep and tightened on the sinking line, swimming over the bottom gravel where it was stopped by an unseen trout. It was a twelve-inch brown, his gills dark with unswallowed Hendrickson nymphs, and I released him gently. Several more were taken on the deep nymph, fished tight against the bottom of the ledge. There were still no rises when I left the river for lunch.

Lunch was leisurely and pleasurable, and filled with anticipation as the weather improved. Patchy clouds and half-warm sunlight were welcome as I reached the river at one o'clock. The improving weather was still blustery, and a chill wind gusted downstream. There were already a few fluttering duns coming off, and twice I saw trout chase mayflies sail-boating with the wind.

There was still an hour before the regular afternoon hatching period, and I did not want to disturb the pool I had chosen for the main hatch. I ignored the occasional splashy rises and fished the nymph instead, casting both to the rise-forms and known holding-lies where I had taken fish before. Several more trout were taken in the hour that followed, and I killed a fifteen-inch brown to check its stomach contents— there were three adult mayflies and twenty-six *Ephemerella* nymphs in his gullet.

Two o'clock arrived and I walked back to the pool I had chosen for the afternoon. The wind had dropped and I waited in a sheltered pocket of sunlight until there were mayflies coming off everywhere. I watched patiently until the trout had settled into good feeding rhythms, determined that the insects were *subvaria,* and moved stealthily into position with the proper imitation. Fifteen trout were working, including one heavy fish at the head of the pool. Sometimes there are days when everything goes predictably and well. This was one of these rare days when the main hatch came at precisely two o'clock and the imitation worked perfectly, and each decent float over a rising fish equalled a rise. The trout were so busy with the naturals that bad casts and poor floats did not disturb them. The final count was thirty-seven browns, including the fat two-pounder working at the head of the pool, and I re-leased them gently.

Fly-hatches are seldom that predictable. Some mysteries and moods of the river are impossible to explain. Sometimes the hatches simply fail to appear, and sometimes the fish ignore a current covered with flies. April and its hatches share moodiness and many pleasant enigmas, and I think of them both when late-winter snow is sifting through the trees.

River of Regeneration

IT was getting dark and the lakes under our floatplane looked like inkwells. The river forced its steep-walled gorge through the Labrador highlands. The dying light was warm on the caribou-moss plateau and we flew the river looking for the Eskimo encampment.

We'll have to turn back if we don't find it soon, yelled Bob Bryan over the engine. *We can overnight back at Indian House Lake!*

We crossed the four-mile chute of rapids at Helen Falls and spotted cookfires downstream. The entire village came down to the rocky beach when they heard the plane, and we flashed low over its waving population to check the river for floating debris.

Looks okay! I shouted.

The river narrowed above the freight landing, gathering

in a vast glass-smooth current across a giant outcropping of granite. The wild chute of water below slowed in a mile-long pool. The village sprawled along the morraine above the river, its radio shack and white Eskimo tents like giant mushrooms in the gathering darkness.

Judging from the waves on the slack water currents above the camp, the wind was downstream. We pulled back into a climb, past the steep escarpments and spiraled for radio altitude.

Unreel the aerial, Bryan pointed.

Lac Rapide answered immediately. *Hello six-nine-easy!* Static crackled inside the cockpit. *What is your position?*

Six-nine-easy, we answered. *Estimate May's Landing in five minutes—estimate five days here.*

Roger, they answered. *Understand!*

Looks like good salmon water, we said.

Good fishing! Lac Rapide signed off. *We'll expect your next contact in five days.*

Six-nine-easy! We reeled in the aerial.

Bob Bryan is not yet forty and a legend in the Labrador. His career already includes hockey at Yale, completion of its Divinity School, and service as chaplain at the Choate School in Wallingford. His father-in-law is New York lawyer Dana Lamb, one of the best known American salmon writers, and his interest in fishing first made him aware of the opportunities for missionary work in the Labrador. It occurred to Bryan that a modern circuit-riding parish was possible with a floatplane Cessna, and Bryan has since spent ten years as a flying clergyman.

Ted Rogowski was buckled into the jumpseat, sandwiched behind our equipment. Rogowski is a former Wall Street lawyer, served as founding president of the Theodore Gordon Flyfishers, and is a legal officer on water pollution in Washington, D.C. for the Department of the Interior.

Let's set her down! yelled Bryan.

Our final turn dropped into the steep-walled canyon and

throttled back lazily past its granite cliffs on full flaps. The village was ahead. The broken rapids flashed under the floats as we sideslipped into the mile-long pool, taxiing in toward its rocky beaches. The people walked down to the plane and I stepped down on the starboard float to wave them back from the propeller. The floats touched and Bryan cut the throttle. I waded ashore with the anchor line.

We turned the plane around and rooted the anchor shovels deep in the rocks. The twilight was filled with the sounds of the river as we unloaded the plane with help from the village. The factor came down and introduced himself.

We shook hands. *Bob May*, he said.

How's fishing, we asked.

We get a lot of arctic char in our nets, said May, *but the salmon are starting to come now.*

Can we try them? Bryan asked.

Tomorrow morning, he answered. *Let's find you an empty tent and something for supper.*

We ate a supper of fresh salmon, potato soup, and cabbage. The canvas-roof dining hall was filled with the roar of the river, and the mountains were black against the stars. When we finished, we followed the cookboys along the trail to our tent. Eskimo summer tents are spacious ovals of white canvas with wooden door-frames and a single Hudson's Bay stove at the center. Our tent was warm and filled with our gear. The cookboys had cut fresh spruce boughs and laid them ankle deep on the floor, filling the tent with their sweet odor. Our sleeping bags were deep in a mattress of spruce needles, and after the long flight from Lac Rapide in the Cessna we were tired.

The salmon fishery on the George River was virtually unknown as little as fifteen years ago. Ichthyologists long believed that Cape Chidley and the east-flowing rivers of the Labrador plateau were the northern limit of the Atlantic salmon in Canadian waters. But the development of mineral deposits in the subarctic and the deployment of military radar-systems across those barren latitudes has led to considerable exploration in recent years. Helicopter and floatplane prospectors discovered rich lodes of nickel and iron, and the fly-fishermen among them found a half-dozen major salmon rivers. Rumors began to reach the fishing world through word-of-mouth and the reports of fishery biologists in obscure journals on the subarctic. Our trip had started with such rumors.

Some stories came from the ironfields of the Labrador interior. Others were traced to a helicopter sales-executive who had caught salmon on the George. There was a crew-cut PBY-pilot who had bought them from Eskimos at Fort Chimo. The Norseman pilot from Lac Rapide confirmed stories about the River of Whales, first heard from a radar officer at Goose Bay. There was a halfbreed skin-trader at Nain who believed all the Ungava rivers from Cape Chidley to Sugluk held salmon.

The Labrador is changing rapidly. Its past was virtually a mystery except for the ill-fated Hubbard expeditions and the Grenfell missions among the coastal fisherfolk. There are still great solitudes, inhabited only by Eskimos and Nas-caupee Indians, but the subarctic wastes are gradually being settled. Miners crowd new towns carved from the wilderness. Soldiers crowd bases and radar stations on remote escarpments and islands. Geologists and engineers continue to search the caribou barrens in their bright-lacquered floatplanes and chattering helicopters.

Discovery of new salmon rivers is a major event in a world seemingly determined to eradicate the species. There are five vast watersheds in the Ungava wilderness that hold Atlantic salmon—the storied George, Payne, Koksoak, Leaf, and Whale.

These rivers have major tributaries like the Larch, Wheeler, Kaniapiskau, Pas, and Ford. And there are almost a hundred lesser rivers that remain virtually unexplored. Their fishing seems to be holding its own in spite of the deep-water netting off Greenland, and their fish apparently remain primarily in coastal waters, but decimation has occurred.

Summer in these latitudes is ephemeral, often lasting a few weeks. Winter ravages the subarctic latitudes. Its cruelty is obvious in the stunted trees and high-water channels of the June snow-melt and the faces of the people. The pale caribou-moss barrens are bright with tiny flowers in midsummer. Salmon enter the George on the first high tides in August, riding the rising muddy waters that arrive with churning, quick-silver speed across the tidal flats. Ungava tides are fierce against the spreading river, mingling and mixing their silty currents.

The salmon hold in the brackish shallows, impatient to complete their homeward journey and spawn in the shallows where they were hatched. They porpoise and roll restlessly, waiting in currents rich with the memories of their parr-life in the riffles upstream. The gulls wheel above the tides and their peevish melancholia echoes across the flats. August is a month of bright water and salmon, and the fish travel eagerly against the currents once they have entered the rivers. Salmon still have sea-lice fifty miles above tidewater on the George.

The next morning we moved upriver to camp below the falls, where the tumbling rapids eddy and slow into a lake-sized pool a mile in diameter. The Eskimos carried our equipment upstream in freight canoes, portaging the great chute of water above May's Landing. We leapfrogged the plane upstream with our fishing gear, fly-rods stowed in the float-strut cannisters and a full load of fuel. The engine caught and Bryan studied the gauges while I crouched on the float, waiting to push off with the paddle.

Push her off! Bryan yelled.

The current caught the floats, and we turned and taxied down toward the spreading tail of the pool. *Full flaps!*

Flaps down! I set the lever as we turned back into the current. *Rudders secure!* I hooked the ring between our seats.

Throttle open and spray flying, we roared up the pool past the village and its waving Eskimos. The shadow of the plane flashed across the rapids and we skimmed the river, passing low above the party of freight canoes.

The lake below the rapids looked good. It was deep enough that no shoals or ledges showed anywhere, there were no deadfalls and floating debris, and there was a sheltered beach. Bryan finished his approach and settled the Cessna carefully on the smooth expanse of river.

The floats touched and streamed, and we settled and powered-in toward the beach. Bryan cut the engine and I climbed down on the float and waited until we touched. We turned the Cessna around until its rudders creased the sand. Rogowski tossed the anchor far up the smooth unmarked beach, and tugged at its line until the shovels rooted and held. Gulls wheeled in the morning sun, crying above the roar of the falls.

The old sense of anticipation and excitement welled up as we rigged our tackle. The Eskimos would make our camp when they reached the plane so we hiked upriver to prospect for salmon.

The trail wound through stands of bracken and spruce, crossing meadows of caribou-moss and flowers. Jays quarreled over roots and berries. Two weeks without rain had left the moss dry and brittle underfoot, and it held our footprints like fresh snow.

We stopped and unshouldered our packboards on the ledges. Slicks and runs flowed smooth among the rocks.

It sure smells like a salmon river! said Rogowski.

Let's try it, I grinned.

We squirmed into our waders and checked our gear. Salmon fishermen cannot be careless with their tackle. Missed guides, poorly-mounted reels, or faulty knots can spell failure on fish that reach forty pounds and strip a hundred yards of line in seconds. While we selected our flies, two salmon vaulted into the sun.

They're here! Bryan pointed happily.

Our casts switched out and lengthened across the oil-smooth currents where the fish had rolled. The current was deceptive and I mended the swing twice before the impossible happened: there was a bright flash and swirl, and the tightening line bellied downstream.

Salmon! I yelled happily.

The current exploded and the fish somersaulted wildly. The reel shrieked as it stripped line. It jumped again and line still burned off the spool, threatening to reach the rapids.

You'll have to follow! Rogowski shouted.

Shed-sized boulders and ledges blocked our pursuit. I held the rod high and leapfrogged downriver over the rocks. The reel protested in its shrill aria. Rogowski scrambled along behind, yelling advice and opening his salmon tailer. It proved a bit premature.

The rod was dancing dangerously when the salmon jumped again and the line fell slack. *Damn!* I croaked unhappily.

The salmon was gone. We had covered two hundred yards over a glacier-smooth obstacle course of ledges and rocks. We had lost and I reeled to recover line. My breath rasped and my leg muscles ached, and my mouth was filled with the bitter taste of pennies.

Rogowski collapsed the tailer.

How big? yelled Bryan two pools upstream.

I was too tired to answer. *Fifteen pounds!* shouted Rogowski. *Maybe as much as twenty!*

The backing almost filled the reel and my hairwing Minktail inched toward us in the current. Rogowski sighed and sprawled on a sunny ledge. *We're getting soft!* he said.

Our lungs and legs still ached. The fly was almost back, trailing in the current when we rested. Gulls passed downriver and my breathing was almost normal when it happened. The fly disappeared in a huge swirl, and the rod wrenched down and the reel rasped angrily.

No! I groaned. *Not yet!*

Twelve pounds of salmon somersaulted, showering us with water as I scrambled to follow. It was running the reel and I chased it helplessly over the rocks. Rogowski waved the tailer and shouted advice I could no longer hear above the river. Our pursuit reached a dead end at a building-size boulder. The fish was still running. Rogowski clambered on the rocks and lifted my line clear while I circled around, hurdling from boulder to boulder. Fatigue was forgotten in the running fight.

We tailed the salmon exuberantly two-hundred yards downstream. *Paydirt!* yelled Rogowski.

We carried it ashore, laid it on the pale river-smooth ledges, and collapsed with happiness. Our fatigue seeped back and we sprawled on the rocks until a line squall forced us to find shelter. We took cover beneath a rain-dripping ledge while the rain misted along the river. The mountains disappeared as the squall reached Bryan.

Salmon! he yelled as his rod doubled into a tight circle and another twelve-pounder jumped.

It broke off on its seventh somersault and Bryan took shelter from the rain. *That's some holding-place you found!* he laughed.

Three fish hooked in fifteen minutes!

Found? Rogowski grimaced. *He didn't know they were there until they attacked him!*

What do we call this pool? I said.

Tyro's triumph?

Bryan grinned. *Duffer's delight?*

Okay! I laughed.

The squall passed and the rocks were shining in the sun. The mountains were black behind a ragged rainbow, and another salmon jumped in our nameless pool. *We've hit the mother lode!* I sighed.

The Eskimos had completed our camp when we hiked back for lunch, and were busily racking a cord of firewood between two trees. When our lunch was finished, they ferried us across the lake to the other side, and hiked upstream to show us the pools. It was sweaty work crossing the glacier fields of boulders, and our senses were filled with the roar of white water. Finally the Eskimos stopped.

Johnny-the-Boatman pointed to the gathering current slick above some boulders. *Salmon!* he spoke almost no English and the single word sounded like French. *Salmon!* The Eskimos grinned and waited.

They seem to believe that's a good salmon-lie out there, Rogowski smiled. *Let's see!*

Rapids tumbled and chuted down great gaps in the ledgerock, and lost their ferocity in a huge half-mile pool. Its currents looked perfect. Salmon had to stop in those oily-smooth slicks over the bedrock and boulders, but the light was wrong to see them. We happily readied our tackle to fish the run. Bryan chose a hairwing Black Fairy in the deeper places with a conventional wet-fly swing, and Rogowski tried the Portland Creek hitch with a small Silver Rat. My choice was the greased-line method with a delicate hairwing Orange Charm.

We fished out several casts without moving a salmon, *You sure these Eskimos are right?* I laughed.

We'll see, Rogowski answered.

Suddenly Bryan hooked a fish and bolted over the rocks to follow the jump-crazy salmon downstream in a run that threatened to reach the rapids. Then my fly-swing throbbed taut in the current. The fish held for several seconds, and then porpoised slowly in the rolling half-jump that spells size. It looked like a fresh henfish of twenty-odd pounds, bright and flashing sunlight as it sulked along the ledges.

Look out! Rogowski shouted.

He was into a quicksilver ten-pounder that cartwheeled past me miraculously without tangling lines. *That's three hooked fish at once!* I laughed as he scrambled downstream.

Excuse us! he passed under my rod.

Suddenly my fish broached, working its jaws weakly until the hook pulled out, and Bryan returned without his fish. *Broke my hook on the rocks,* he shook his head unhappily.

Rogowski was still into his jumping ten-pounder. *Nine!* he was counting its pole-vaulting leaps. *Ten!*

Eleven! I laughed.

Finally it tired and he tailed it, wrestling it up the rocky beach and the small Silver Rat dropped out. *Good Lord!* He shook his head. *Both hook-points are gone!*

Both barbs of the double hook were broken. Its blunt ends had taken a fleshy hold and somehow held through the eleven jumps. Rogowski shrugged and replaced his fly.

Some luck! we laughed.

Skill! he smiled.

We walked back upstream to the giant pool after the Eskimos had returned downstream to May's Landing. The sun was higher now and the rain had passed. Suddenly the vast pewter-colored bottom was revealed like a rising second-act curtain.

My God! we goggled at the sight.

The pool was filled with a flotilla of salmon, phalanx after phalanx hovering in the current. The river was filled with fresh-run fish, flashing in their wilderness aquarium.

The George was generous that afternoon. Sixteen fish were landed between ten and eighteen pounds. Many others were lost when the fish fought into the rapids and broke off. The fishing averaged four salmon an hour, incredible sport in a time when salmon rivers are in decline, and shadows were reaching across the river as we started downstream.

The freight canoe returned to the bottom of the rapids and the Eskimos shouted and waved. Salmon rolled and jumped as we hiked downstream. Rain rattled sporadically on our shoulders. We reached the canoe in a driving rain, and they ferried us happily across to our new camp.

It was high on a morraine above the river, half-hidden in a grove of stunted conifers. It was warm with a fire already roaring in the stove. We hung our rods and fishing gear on the peeled spruce poles inside. Supper was a housewarming of fresh-baked bangbelly, canned butter, salmon, and a grilse chowder rich with vegetables and canned milk. We chewed happily on the hot bread.

You know, Bryan grinned, *you could coat bangbelly with varnish and keep it forever!*

The fishing was exceptional that week, and on Saturday we travelled downriver to a party at May's Landing. Eskimo families had travelled sixty miles from the mouth of the river for the celebration, and the main shack was filled with people. The radio room was warm with cooking smells, and tobacco smoke was layered in the lamplight. Children crowded outside, their wide-eyed faces pressed against the windows.

Music tumbled happily from an old accordion in the hands of a grinning Eskimo boatman. The men rose and danced first—hopping around the tiny room, stomping the floorboards, and singing wordlessly—while their women clapped time with their hands.

The men shook the floor and the house with their dancing and stomping. Their faces were bright with sweat. Finally the women and young girls joined them, and the accordion turned to more familiar tunes. Skirts swirled and soft sealskin boots drummed the floor. Two old women joined the dancers, their bright toothless laughter the lustiest of all.

When the dances ended, we traded tobacco and dollars for Eskimo art and goods. There were sealskin slippers and soapstone animal carvings and wooden kayaks, and finally the village chief presented Bryan with the huge pelt of a white arctic wolf. *From our people to the flying preacher,* the Hudson's Bay factor translated the Eskimo words. *The pelt of One-Who-Steals-the-Caribou-in-Winter.*

Some days later we sprawled in our encampment making flies. Bryan had still not shaken his long run of bad luck with the salmon, although he had caught an impressive number of grilse.

Teach me to tie flies, he said finally.

Change your luck, we agreed.

We sat crosslegged in our tent making hairwing Charms and Minktails and Fitchtails. Like most beginners, Bryan decided to tie his own patterns, and searched our field kits for exotic materials. *How about using the wolf?* he suggested and smiled.

We shrugged and grinned, helping while he struggled through a pair of hair flies using the wolf-skin. *You think they'll work?*

Maybe on wilderness fish, Rogowski laughed.

They really worked that next morning.

Bryan stopped to fish an enormous, churning pool and was into a heavy fish in only two casts. We stopped to watch while he parried and played it faultlessly until an Eskimo grabbed the leader, and it was lost in a shower of water.

Bryan shook his head and said something angrily that was lost in the roar of the river. *Can we quote you?* we laughed.

Bryan grinned and knotted his second wolf-fly to his nylon. Five casts later he was into another fish. The fifteen-pound salmon pirouetted wildly across the rapids, showering spray on the gusting wind. The line melted off the reel, until the white backing disappeared in a streaking blur. The fish leaped again and again.

Damn! Bryan growled. *He's gone!*

But the fish was still on. It turned back up the pool while he fought to recover the long belly of line that throbbed in the current. Fighting both the river and the rod soon took its toll of the fish. Bryan trailed it expertly, and the Eskimos grinned while we cheered wildly.

Twenty-five pound? said Johnny-the-Boatman, trying to recoup some standing with the exaggeration.

Fifteen! Rogowski corrected.

That wolf sure changed your luck! We shook hands.

It's about time, Bryan smiled.

The Eskimos asked him for Anglican services the following night, since they would not see another clergyman until they migrated back to Fort Chimo in the fall. Bryan speaks no Eskimo, since his usual parish lies in the English-speaking islands and coastal villages on the Labrador coast. The son of the skin-trader volunteered to translate his sermon.

The congregation gathered in the radio shack, the women wearing plaids bartered from the Hudson's Bay Company at Chimo. Rifles were racked behind the radio that linked the village with the outside world each evening. The women and children gathered first, and finally the men entered with their older sons. The men settled on the front bench, whispered together and chose a hymn.

Abide with me, the faces were grave and the familiar melody had a high-pitched oriental singsong in the Eskimo. *Fast falls the eventide—the darkness deepens Lord with me abide!*

The sermon was short and simple. *Your river is for us a river of regeneration,* Bryan began, *and we have come to these solitudes to find the salmon and ourselves.* The boy translated into the Eskimo as the wind rose in the darkness outside.

Bryan explained that we had used the primordial flyways of the geese to come to their village. He told them we came from a giant village called New York, where people lived together in great flocks like the geese on the River of the Whales. The people listened gravely and nodded and murmured that they had heard of this village.

His sermon ended with the thought that men have not yet learned in their hearts what the geese have always known: *The world is small and we are brothers.*

There was a final hymn. *Rock of Ages,* the shrill voices of the women soared in the tiny room. *Cleft for me—let me hide myself in thee.* The older women behind the cookstove sang with their wrinkled faces raised and their eyes closed, their nasal voices reed-like and high pitched. We opened the Anglican prayerbooks and kneeled on the rough-sawed boards.

Bryan dropped to his knees to lead the final prayer, his black coat bunched tight across broad-muscled shoulders. It worked above his hips to reveal the huge knife that hung from his belt.

When the services were over we walked high above the

river along the morraine. The tents were almost eerily irides-cent in the darkness, and the northern lights seethed and shimmered overhead, signaling the end of our brief subarctic summer. Our tent was warm and we sat crosslegged in the fresh balsam cuttings for a broiled grilse and bangbelly.

It was getting cold and the glowing tent-canvas snapped like sails in the darkness. Finally we zippered into our sleeping bags and turned down the lamps. Bryan stoked the fire and added more wood. The northern lights were visible through the pale canvas. The mountains loomed in the darkness, and our sleeping bags grew deliciously warm. The fatigue of the river filled our bodies and the sound of its rapids filled the darkness. We were soon asleep under the glittering silence of the stars.

The next morning we fueled the plane from the stacked cache of gasoline drums on the beach. Our equipment was gathered on the mossy ledges below the falls. Gulls and camp-robbers gathered on the rocky shore, and salmon were por-poising in the shallows upstream.

It was difficult to leave a river filled with fish. Finally I succumbed and waded out to cover a small reach of water above the plane. *The only way to handle temptation,* I smiled to myself, *is yield to it!*

There was a break in the underwater ledges where I had moved fish several times before. Just as I reached casting position, the holding-lie was disturbed with wild gyrations and two salmon showed. Then the dance-like disturbance sub-sided and the fish slipped back beneath the surface. It was a strange performance. The salmon rolled and threshed again, repeating their restless choreography. Then the light changed and revealed the bottom. There was a female with the male, a bright hen salmon of sixteen pounds poised in the swift current.

Rogowski had followed me along the rocks. *Those two seem paired off for spawning,* he suggested. *Sometimes you can take them both if you get one and rest the other.*

The fish seemed settled now.

I selected a small Orange Charm and knotted it to my leader. It was an easy cast, and the current was good and I mended twice to get a dragless swing over the salmon. Ten casts teased over them without apparent interest until the little low-water pattern came down current again, and I lost sight of the salmon when the wind riffled across the pool.

The drift stopped softly. *Salmon!*

The line tightened and bellied downstream. *Salmon!* I raised the rod and it came alive.

The twelve-pound cockfish writhed into the air and windmilled wildly down the current. The reel protested as the salmon stripped into the backing. Six jumps later I worked him into the shallows and snapped the tailer, and carried him ashore in triumph. Rogowski held him gently on the tailer, working his gills in the current while we rested the pool.

Maybe the henfish is ready, said Rogowski.

The male salmon had fully recovered his equilibrium, and Rogowski restrained him gently in the shallows while I waded carefully into position to try the female. The suspense was overpowering.

The henfish took the third heart-stopping cast and slashed out across the current into the white water. I worked her cautiously out of the rapids, pumping and reeling to regain the precious line. Twice she reached the rapids and twice I worked her back again. We were both exhausted when I hand-tailed her sixteen pounds in the shallows. Then we carried them back to the pool, stroking and coddling them both in a quiet backwater until they recovered. Finally they forced themselves free and slipped back into the current.

The salmon paused over the pale gravel. We watched them until they moved out into the deep water and disappeared beyond the algae-mottled ledges. Our salmon expedition was over. Below the rapids, where the white water lost its force in the dark boulder-broken currents of the pool, a salmon leaped sea-bright and silver in the sun.

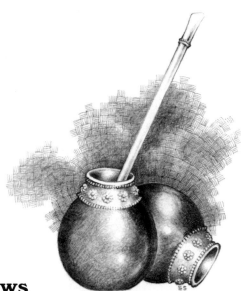

The Rainbows
of Pichi Traful

THE river dropped through the steep jungle-looking mountains, pausing in pools that were deep and emerald green. Its currents eddied and tumbled through pale moss-covered boulders and strange looking pines. Scissortails and parakeets darted through the tree-fern thickets. Our *campamento* was in a sheltered meadow of copper beeches and cypresses, where the river slowed and large trout dimpled softly in the twilight.

It was a strange and exotic landscape. Flocks of *bandurrias* rose shrilly from the river when I waded out into the current. It was my first experience on a Patagonian river, and the cane-thickets and exotic conifers seemed strange and eerily unfamiliar.

Dinosaurs would love it! I thought.

The rainbows averaged eighteen inches until I reached

the deep run in the bamboo tree-ferns. It was getting dark and only the fish seemed familiar.

The narrow pool was smooth-flowing and dark under the trailing vines. Pale caddisflies fluttered off the water and into the brush. Deep in the gathering shadows a big fish porpoised and his rise disturbed the entire pool. There was a big Donnelly Variant in my fly-boxes. The cast fell right and the trout took it softly, and it stripped line angrily when the leader tightened and it felt the hook.

It jumped six times. It was infighting after that, all writhing and bright-silver rolling on the bottom. The jumps and reel-stuttering runs were finished. It bored stubbornly in the shallows until its muscled six pounds surrendered in a violent net-splash that showered me with water.

Rainbow! my shout echoed downstream.

Parakeets protested from the *coihue* thickets. Flocks of geese and flamingoes were startled and rose flapping from the shallows. Exultation exploded in another wild shout, half in triumph and half in tribute to Patagonia and its swift little Pichi Traful.

It was a beautiful fish, its sides and gill-covers pink and sheathed in silver. Its strong fight had frightened the others. The rises in the tree-fern shadows had stopped. The rainbow lay gleaming on the gravel. Flocks of parakeets and *checau* birds threaded and wheeled through the twilight, and I filled my pipe to smoke and rest the pool. It was twenty minutes before the rises began again.

Two fish were working softly under the vines. The big straw-colored caddisflies were still hatching. It was almost dark when the first cast settled the variant over the bottom fish, and it disappeared in a heavy swirl. The rainbow jumped and bolted into the swift shallows below the pool, cartwheeling water in showers of spray.

The fight lasted two hundred yards. It threatened to break off several times in brush-piles and deadfalls, and twice the rainbow almost beached itself. It lasted thirty minutes. The fight threshed and churned in a shallow flat below the *campamento* meadows. Finally it was over and the second fish hung writhing in the meshes. It was exactly like the first, deep-bellied and silver in the darkness. The cookfire of the *campamento* flickered through the cypresses.

It seemed a shame to kill the second fish. *No puedo esta trucha matar!* I thought happily.

The fish gasped and shuddered in the net, and I stroked its sides until the ragged gill-workings steadied and slowed. The big rainbow held exhausted in my hands. Finally it shook itself and torpedoed back into the river, spreading a huge wake across the gravel shallows.

Guy Dawson was waiting in the firelight. *Any luck?* he said. *That was a pretty good hatch!*

Fantastico! I agreed.

The cookfires of the gaucho encampment upriver glowed in the darkness, and the smell of their herb tea drifted on the wind. Dawson admired the six-pound rainbow and gutted it for grilling over the fire.

Fish course, he explained.

Took two rainbows just like that one! I grinned and sighed happily. *Just like peas in a pod!*

It was a good beginning, nodded Dawson.

Perfect! I agreed.

There's a bottle of wine chilling under the big cypress, Dawson pointed. *Quiere tinto?*

Siempre! I hung my waders on the tent.

It was already cold along the river, and the stars glittered behind the mountains. The starlight danced on the bottle as I pulled it dripping from the shallows. The wind was cool and the fire was welcome.

Dawson pulled the cork and filled my cup. *Ah!* I sipped the wine and sighed. *It's perfect!*

It's a good Argentine tinto, he agreed.

The bright-red slabs of trout were ready and Dawson forked huge pieces on my plate. *That's great fish!* I said. *That's the best trout I've ever eaten!*

It's not trout you're eating, he laughed. *It's crabmeat.*

Crabs? I said. *You're putting me on!*

Dawson shook his head. *It's true!* he said. *That red meat comes from eating the cangrejos.*

What are cangrejos? I asked.

Dawson explained that Patagonian trout feed primarily on the plentiful freshwater crabs that inhabit the cold watersheds of the Andes. *They're called pancora on the Chilean side,* he added.

Taste good too! I took another helping.

Thick steaks grilled over the coals finished our supper, with fresh bread and sliced sweet Rio Negro onions. It was cold now and moonlight glittered on the river. We threw more wood on the coals and the fire caught quickly. My baptism on the rivers of Patagonia had been perfect.

It felt a little strange tonight, I lit my pipe with a glowing stick. *The bamboo thickets and trees were a little unsettling.*

You expect cobras and crocodiles?

It seemed possible, I admitted sheepishly. *Dinosaurs could take a bath in that river and feel at home!*

Dawson smiled. *You're right!*

He poured the last of the wine into our cups. *Let's drink to the Pichi Traful!* I said. *My favorite river!*

You haven't seen anything yet!

I'll drink to that too, I laughed. *Patagonia!*

Several gauchos came down through the cypresses into our firelight. They were carrying herb-tea gourds and silver *bombillas* that caught the moonlight, and the headman carried a sack of herb tea. *They watched you fish,* Dawson explained, *and they're offering us their maté.*

Maté? I asked.

It's an herb tea the gauchos drink, he said. *Its legend says anyone who drinks maté will return to Patagonia.*

I'll drink to that! I said.

Dawson rummaged in his cooking gear and produced a *maté* gourd and a silver drinking-tube. He filled the gourd with the dark mossy-green herbs, tamping them carefully with his thumb. The gourd was steeped in sugar and river water and then he added boiling water from the tea-kettle. The rich odor of the dried herbs filled the darkness, and he handed me the ritual *maté* that would bring me back to Patagonia.

Gracias, I said gratefully.

Night Comes to the Namekagon

It's musky fever, she said.

The old woman was washing glasses behind the huge mahogany bar. There were worn places in the floor from the boot-caulks of lumberjacks, and there were mounted white-tails with a lever-action rifle across one rack of antlers. The place was empty.

Musky fever? I sipped a beer slowly.

You see this town? she asked. *You see any menfolk between twelve and eighty-five?*

No, I laughed.

They've all got the fever, she continued. *They're all crazy for muskies in this town.* She placed the glasses in a careful pyramid behind the bar.

Sounds like a sickness, I said.

Happens every year about this time, she sighed and rinsed the sink. *They're all crazy!*

What about the river above town? I asked.

Namekagon? she asked.

Yes, I said. *Smallmouths?*

Some smallmouths, but mostly trout, she wiped the bar. *Nobody pays much attention to them in musky season.*

Big trout? I asked.

Guess so, she poured herself a beer. *They catch some five or six pounds every spring above the railroad trestle.*

Browns? I finished my beer and paid.

Don't know, she shook her head and frowned. *All they ever talk about 'round here is muskies!*

Musky fever! I laughed.

Some of the best wild-trout fisheries left in America are neglected because they flow through the muskellunge country of northern Wisconsin, and the largest is the Namekagon. Between the once-thriving timber center at Hayward and its junction with the Saint Croix, its sweeping pools are prime smallmouth bass fishing, but above the town and the sawmill impoundment that warms the lower river, it is prime brown-trout water.

Although I spent many boyhood summers on the better-known trout streams of the country above Chicago, the Namekagon was a stranger. My introduction to the river and its almost unknown limestone sister-river, the little East Fork of the Iron, was a happy accident.

Several summers ago I was selected to represent Princeton University in a think-tank conference held at Grindstone Lake near Hayward, and three weeks before the conference a letter arrived from a fisherman who had read my book *Matching the Hatch*. The letter thanked me for writing the book and the help it had been in identifying and imitating the fly-hatches on the rivers between Ashland and Duluth. It closed with an invitation: whenever travel carried me back to northern Wisconsin, there was a willing guide in Ashland to show

me his rivers. *You might be surprised at the fishing,* read the teasing sentence at the close, *on our Wisconsin chalkstreams.*
Chalkstreams! I thought. *That's something new!*

Chalkstream fishing in the jackpine hills of Wisconsin was a puzzle that nagged me for days after the letter arrived. Finally I telephoned Ashland and announced that I was coming to the conference.

Grindstone Lake? said my host.

Yes, I said, *staying at the Grindstone Lodge.*

I'll call you there, he agreed.

After the opening session of the conference, I wandered down through the trees to the boathouse. Several boats were out and I watched one cover the shoreline below the camp, one man rowing and his partner standing in the bow, heaving a huge lure along the weeds. It hissed out and landed with an horrendous splash.

Musky fever, I thought disparagingly.

Wisconsin hospitality is first-rate and my new friend called during lunch. We agreed to meet at a diner near Ashland. *I'll show you my secret chalkstream,* he laughed.

Art Besse, he introduced himself the next morning.

We drove down the county roads while Besse explained that his real estate business dovetailed neatly with trout fishing, and that his tackle was always in the trunk. Besse parked the car along the road with no river in sight. We slipped into our waders and shouldered into our wading vests, and I followed him into the trees.

We'll cut cross-country, he explained, *and fish the river back almost to where we leave the car.*

It was hot and the forced march through the brush, carrying the rod butt-first to protect it and worrying about snagging its guides in the branches, was getting uncomfortable when we reached the river.

East Fork of the Iron, he announced.

The river flowed smooth and deep between the alders, its current slipping past an occasional deadfall. *It's a little milky,* I said. *You have a rainstorm last night?*

Besse laughed. *That's the chalk,* he said. *The river comes out of a marl swamp and that chalkiness is limestone.*

Just like the British chalkstreams, I shook my head.

Exactly, he grinned.

His fly-books were filled with juicy-looking wet flies and nymphs, and he selected one carefully. *Try this,* he said.

It was a grub-like pattern with a rough muskrat-fur body and a trimmed brown hackle dressed palmer-style on a long-shank hook. *I thought you read my book,* I laughed, *What's this thing?*

Don't laugh until you've tried it, he smiled.

He explained that boyhood fish taken on bait had always been filled with grayish-brown beetle larvae that were thick in the river, and that he had worked out the pattern as an imitation. It was clinch-knotted to my tippet and Besse pointed to a deep run under the adlers.

It landed with a plop and I laughed. *That thing has got the glideangle of a brick!*

It's weighted with fuse wire, Besse explained.

The cast worked back deep under the bushes and stopped with a soft pull that spelled trout. The fish bored upstream when I tightened and it jumped at the head of the run. It finally surrendered to the net and we admired its color and condition.

It's really fat, I said. *It's only sixteen inches but it must go at least two pounds.* Its scarlet spots were bright against pale ochre-colored sides.

It's the marl swamp, said Besse.

Alkalinity from the lime deposits, I nodded.

My secret chalkstream, he smiled.

Art Besse was killed in a tragic automobile accident later that summer, and no longer fishes his secret stretches of the

Iron and the Namekagon and the Brule, but I will never forget his hospitality and streamside companionship that week. We fished until evening on his secret chalkstream, catching fifty-odd trout on his beetle larva until a hatch of pale *Epeorus* flies made us switch to a small Light Cahill to match the fluttering naturals.

The next evening we met at the railroad trestle on the Namekagon above Hayward and rigged our tackle. The river looked shallow, flowing through a hundred weedy channels in the elodea, and there were cottages on both banks. Just above the bridge was a deeper-looking run under a thick clump of flowers.

Those look like irises, it seemed strange to find a flower bed in the middle of the river. *Are they wild?*

No, he laughed. *Probably washed out upriver.*

While we watched, a fish rose tight against the roots.

Try him, Besse suggested.

We waded carefully into position below the fish and I dropped the beetle larva above the flowers. There was a heavy boil and a good three-pound fish hooked itself. The quarter mile upstream produced a half-dozen twelve- to sixteen-inch browns between us.

It's some river, I admitted.

Wait until twilight, smiled Besse. *We've been due for a hatch of big Isonychia drakes about now.*

Hate people who read my stuff carefully!

We drove upriver to fish another stretch. *Gooseneck Bend,* said Besse. *The big drakes should be hatching there.*

Sounds good, I said.

The river comes down from a tamarack swamp, flowing strong and deep into Gooseneck Bend. The huge pool eddies and slows against a steep earth bank, gathering its currents again in swift tail shallows past a logjam of deadfalls. The current sucked and slipped along the logs before it broke into a quarter mile of tumbling waist-deep riffles.

We fished the riffles indifferently until the *Isonychia* hatch began coming off. Big drakes fluttered down the current. Three good fish started working in the fast slick along the logs.

Those are big trout! I whispered.

Besse picked two mayflies off the current and studied them in his palm. *Isonychia sadler!* he announced.

That's not in Matching the Hatch! I grinned.

You're right! he said proudly.

The hatch is practically identical to the eastern Leadwing Drakes, and I selected a big imitation from my fly-boxes. *Works on the Neversink,* I said. *Now for the Namekagon!*

The first fish was rising methodically against the logs. The cast cocked the fly nicely and it disappeared in a quiet self-satisfied swirl. The trout was well hooked.

How big? yelled Besse.

The fish hung stubbornly for several minutes until I forced back the logs. *It's a good fish,* I guessed. *Might go three pounds!*

Suddenly it porpoised and revealed a shark-sized dorsal and tail. It shook its head sullenly, turned and bolted into the fast water. It splashed wildly two hundred feet downstream. *Only three?* Besse laughed.

The reel rasped grindingly. *Maybe four!*

We coaxed the trout into the tamarack backwater and finally netted it in the shallows. *That trout could go as much as six pounds!* Besse gasped when he saw its bulk.

The others were still rising steadily. The first was working tight against the jam, and it lunged sideways to engulf the fly. The second fight echoed the first, except for a clumsy jump that ended in a heavy splash. Finally it surrendered, threshing heavily in the meshes.

This one will go four! I laughed.

The third fish splashed for a fluttering drake. *That one would be an anti-climax!* smiled Besse.

These two are fantastic! I agreed.

We walked back through the meadows to the car as the

moon rose huge and yellow through the pines. *Let's get them weighed and dressed at the tackle shop,* suggested Besse.

The tackle shop was busy with fishermen buying baitfish for fishing walleyes, and jointed plugs and huge bucktail spinner-rigs and sucker minnows for muskellunge. The smallest brown measured twenty-one inches and weighed better than three pounds. The second went a fat twenty-four inches and weighed more than five. The largest dropped the store scales solidly to almost seven pounds.

Those are some fish! I said.

The clerk seem unimpressed. *Those trout were caught on flies!* said Besse. *The big ones took dries!* The tackle-shop clerk looked bored as he dressed the trout for the freezer.

Aren't they something! Besse pressed.

They're okay, said the clerk, *but you should've seen the thirty-pound musky they caught this morning!*

The Fickle River of
Giant Salmon

BRUNO Jensen has fished Norwegian salmon rivers all his life, and has represented his native Denmark in the world casting championships.

Salmon fishing isn't really a sport, Jansen smiles wryly. *It's more like a religion.*

Salmon anglers travel the world, searching compulsively for rivers of greatness. Their pilgrimages can lead from the Spanish rivers of Galicia deep into arctic Lapland, and from Maine to the caribou barrens of the Labrador. Such pilgrimages can also include rivers that flow past ruined abbeys and storied castles in the British Isles to remote rivers in the wastes of Iceland. Atlantic salmon are a vanishing species, and fishing them has become as risk-filled and expensive as roulette. Salmon addicts spend their lives and fortunes chasing

179

fish, neglecting both families and their professions—men who carry pictures of salmon instead of wives in their wallets.

Their discussions range across the salmon rivers of the world. Talk covers halcyon years on the Restigouche and the Cascapedia. Tradition-minded anglers are drawn to the castle beats of the Ballynahinch, and pools below the ruined abbeys on the Wharfe. Fishing the weedy shallows and volcanic ledges of Iceland also has its regulars, and some wilderness fishermen argue for the tumbling rivers of the Labrador.

Salmon fishermen who search for trophies are fascinated with the rivers of Norway. Few anglers have been privileged to fish its storied beats, and rivers like the Alta and Årøy are the Himalayas of salmon fishing. Talk of Norwegian rivers inevitably turns to the Vossa, which drains a region of picturesque lakes and mountain villages and forests fifty miles east of Bergen.

Vossa is a moody river of greatness, much praised and much maligned. Its discussions are always heated, because the reputation of the river is mixed. Fishermen who know its generous moods argue that its salmon have the highest average weight in the world. Others have found its pools barren of salmon, and have dismissed the river as a fishless fraud.

Both arguments are correct. Its salmon average thirty-odd pounds and are extremely unpredictable, even for a species known for its moodiness, and the Vossa is a fickle river of giant salmon.

Bruno Jensen introduced me to the river. We were fishing from the charming Hotel Lilands in Bulken, where generations of anglers have stopped. There is a huge portrait of Jensen in its sitting rooms, holding a brace of forty-pounders killed in a single morning at Tokjelda, and I looked forward to fishing the famous Vossa beats in the morning with an angler of his reputation.

Early light gathered across the lake while we breakfasted with Sigurd Liland on the hotel balcony. Liland is another expert salmon-fisherman. His family has fished the Vossa for generations. Breakfast was typically Norwegian with its hot cereal and blueberries, boiled eggs, sweet goat-cheese on fresh rolls, brislings in tomato sauce, milk from the herds that grazed in the hotel meadows, and pots of strong English tea. Two small boys were rowing and trolling for trout across the still water, and mountain snow-fields were bright in the early morning sun.

Sigurd looks worried, laughed Bruno. *The weather looks too good for salmon-fishing.*

Clouds and rain are better, said Sigurd.

Norwegians are so serious about fishing that they won't wish each other luck, said Bruno puckishly, *so they always wish each other bad fishing or worse!*

Sigurd shook his head in gloomy agreement. *Danes are never serious about anything!* he said.

Both men laughed like some old ritual between them had been completed. *Maybe the salmon will be perverse,* I grinned. *Maybe they'll take in this weather.*

Careful! Bruno protested, *That's optimism!*

The road downriver wound through the village of Bulken and climbed steeply into the timbered hills beyond. Woodcutters were already working in the forests, and farmers were readying their wagons for haying. Bruno stopped the car high above the river where it tumbled over a series of granite ledges in the morning sun.

The pool below those falls is excellent, he said. *It's called the Flagefossen.*

The river record was caught there almost fifty years ago, Sigurd added. *The fight lasted five hours and the fish weighed seventy pounds.*

Five pounds under the world record, said Bruno.

Johannes Horveid was waiting on the Evangervatn lake when we arrived at the sod-roofed farmstead. Bruno and Sigurd shook hands warmly and introduced me to the most famous fly-fishing gillie on the river. The water was still calm and wind-riffled down the narrow fjord-like lake, and we passed hundreds of nets.

Are they legal in freshwater? I asked.

Sigurd shook his head sadly. *Norwegians think salmon are inexhaustible,* he said, *and believe they'll always appear no matter how much they exploit them.*

Bruno agreed unhappily. *Fishing here is the best in the world in spite of the netting and trapping,* he added. *Think how good it might be if the Norwegians thought about the future, and took better care of their rivers.*

The offshore drift-netting is serious too, Sigurd continued. *We're hoping for better laws.*

People never learn, said Bruno gloomily.

Americans are the same, I said. *We thought our buffalo were inexhaustible too.*

Exactly, they shook their heads.

Johannes maneuvered the boat expertly where the river flowed smoothly from the lake, and we moored off the moss-covered rocks of the boat-landing. Johann Bolstad and his nephew Kjell were waiting. Both men removed their hats in the ancient ritual between fishermen and gillies, and we shook hands all around.

Bruno questioned the gillies and decided our strategy. *Sigurd will fish Osen and Prawn with Johann, and I'll fish Mehrhølen with Kjell.* He turned to me, *You'll fish Kjeilo with Johannes, since he saw several fresh-run fish there this morning—and he thinks it's the best chance for your first salmon from the Vossa.*

Sigurd looked unhappily at the bright weather. *Good morning for tourists,* he grumbled.

Bad for salmon? I grinned.

Maybe, winked Bruno.

It's always maybe with salmon-fishing, Johannes smiled, and we started down through the meadow from his farmhouse to the storied Kjeilo Pool. Bruno and Kjell walked down the road toward Mehrhølen.

Bad fishing! shouted Bruno happily.

You too! I answered.

Johannes handled the boat faultlessly, rowing easily to hold us parallel with the current while I punched out casts into the downstream wind. Salmon-fishing is mostly discipline and patience. Each cast is placed about two feet farther downstream so the fish are covered with a precise series of concentric current-swings. Expert boatmen are priceless in such fishing, and adjust their rowing to the fishing rhythms of each fisherman, bringing the boat parallel to the current as each successive cast is readied and swinging it smoothly to extend the current-swing as the fly comes around. Johannes rowed tirelessly, with a stamina that ignored his seventy-odd years.

Sometimes the mind drifts in fishing. The senses are lulled in river sounds, and the creaking oarlocks and the patient repetition of each cast. The sun was fierce and the river seemed fishless. Hundreds of casts had covered most of the pool, and the enthusiasm of fishing a strange river had begun to wane. Johannes grunted his approval and grinned when a long cast reached out toward the tail-shallows. *Beste plass!* Johannes pointed downstream.

Bruno had pointed there earlier. *The best holding-lie is just above the rapids,* he advised, *particularly off that pine that leans out over the river.*

Johannes was working harder now where the gathering currents sucked at the boat. We had just about covered the last of the holding-water when the current erupted just above the rapids and the rod dipped savagely.

Salmon! I shouted happily.

The reel growled as the salmon bored deep across the current-tongue. Johannes was rowing hard, fighting the boat back into the quieter water, while I grudgingly surrendered line to the fish. The salmon was still below us and I was worried. It bulldogged and shook its head along the bottom, and we could not maneuver below it or follow a strong downstream run without risking the tail-current—which could take us into the Mehrhølen rapids.

The salmon started upstream, gathering speed past the boat until the line vibrated like a guitar-string in the heavy current. Finally it stopped a hundred yards upstream, fighting both the river and the rod-pressure. Our optimism lasted until the reel suddenly screamed and the fish exploded into the sun—cartwheeling down the pool in a run that melted backing from the reel and almost reached the rapids.

Pray! I thought grimly. *Pray!*

Johannes worked the boat downstream, holding us carefully in the quieter currents near the bank, while I anxiously regained a hundred yards of line. Fifteen minutes passed while the salmon held stubbornly below the boat.

Suddenly the fish exploded again, rasping line off the protesting reel until it wallowed just above the rapids. Johannes groaned and tried to hold the boat while I worked to hold the fish. The swift tail-shallows pulled us inexorably toward the rapids, and Johannes pulled hard without gaining ground, sweat soaking his shirt.

Slowly the salmon came upstream. *The fish doesn't like those currents either,* I thought aloud.

Bedre! grunted Johannes happily. *Bedre!*

The fight had changed now. The salmon came grudgingly into the deeper water and we forced it slowly toward the shallows. Bruno had heard my shout and arrived as the salmon made a half-hearted run of fifty yards, failing to reach the heavy currents across the pool.

Look at your gallery! laughed Bruno.

The hillside above the pool was filled with a sizeable audience of women and children and workers that had come down from the hayfields. Bruno pointed across the river to the hand-car crew watching the fight. *They travel ahead of the trains to check landslides,* he explained. *They're our Norwegian jungle-telegraph, and everyone at Bulken will know about your salmon before we're back!*

He's not mine yet! I grinned.

The fish wallowed in the shallows and Johannes gaffed it cleanly and carried it ashore. Our gallery applauded and came down to inspect the fish. Bruno disappeared into the farmhouse and returned with a bottle of *akevit* and we passed it among the men, toasting my first Vossa salmon.

Thirty pounds! Bruno studied the scale.

Sigurd had gone fishless when we met in the farmhouse for a lunch of smoked salmon and hard-boiled eggs and cheese and beer chilled in the Kjeilo rapids. Our fishing began again in the late afternoon, with the shadows lengthening across the river, and I killed a second thirty-pounder in the Mehrhølen. The others went fishless again, but we travelled happily up the lake in the darkness.

The river was generous today, said Sigurd.

Vossa is an old friend, Bruno added. *We've fished it all our lives, and we don't expect a salmon every time—but we keep fishing it for days like yours.*

The mountains loomed above the dark mirror of the lake, and the lights of villages and farms danced in the water. Moonlight was pale on my brace of thirty-pounders wedged across the bottom of the boat. *Great day!* I said.

They happen sometimes, said Bruno.

The history of the river tells us that moodiness has always been the hallmark of the Vossa and its salmon. Many anglers have gone fishless in the past two centuries, but its generous moods have earned it a place among the great salmon rivers of the world.

Its reputation for trophy-size salmon was already well established in 1900, when a famous London club—with membership requirements that included a royal Scottish stag, a successful tiger *shikar* in Bengal, a forty-pound Atlantic salmon and enough money to travel the world fulfilling such requirements—regularly advised its probationary members to lease expensive fishing-rights on the Vossa for the big salmon they needed.

The river had surrendered so many fish over forty-pounds in the decade that followed that a syndicate of British anglers leased several miles and built the Skorvelienhus fishing-house high above the Evanger beats. Its slate-roof porches and clapboard walls sheltered a parade of anglers—wealthy manufacturers and fishing writers and bankers and members of the British peerage—in the Olympian half-century of fishing that followed.

Their sport was interrupted during the German Occupation, and those years produced a wry incident on the Vossa that has become part of modern Norwegian folklore. The incident involved a Wehrmacht colonel who arrived in Evanger, complete with his Mercedes staff-car and an escort of motor-cycle troops, and demanded two weeks of fishing.

We will move into Skorvelienhus, the colonel announced, *and begin fishing tomorrow.*

The assembled gillies muttered and the old riverkeeper from Skorvelienhus shook his head. *You cannot fish,* he said. *The fishing-rights belong to Englishmen.*

Ridiculous! snapped the German colonel. *Englishmen no longer control anything in Norway!*

They'll be back, said the old man softly.

Skorvelienhus records show that British anglers killed thirty-three salmon better than fifty pounds during their tenure on the Vossa, including six brutes over sixty. That roster includes such names as Lord and Lady Haworth, Sir Percy and Lady Barlow, and the Countess of Elgin. There were also fishing writers whose books have become part of the literature of angling—men like Negley Farson and Tate Regan and the celebrated Arthur Hutton, who wrote *Life History of the Salmon,* and holds the Vossa fly-record with a cockfish of fifty-nine pounds killed in 1922.

Such history is also found in the memories and memorabilia of the boatmen and riverkeepers and gillies who lived and fished the river in those storied years.

Mathias Bolstad is the village postmaster in Bolstadøyri

and a riverkeeper whose memories reach seventy-odd years into the past. *Sometimes it all comes sharp in the mind,* he sucked thoughtfully on his pipe and squinted downriver into the late afternoon sun, *and I can see it all like yesterday—the English sailing their yachts up the fjord and anchoring below our village, staying in the farmhouses, and hiring us for gillies and boatmen—the English fished beautifully, and I remember their tweed coats and plus-fours and hats, and laying out their long faultless casts.*

Johannes Horveid has similar memories. His weathered face and oar-roughened hands are typical of the veteran gillie, and we sprawled in the hayfields along the river when the salmon were not in the mood, talking about the past. *We have three months of salmon-fishing,* his voice has the authority of sixty-odd years of sport on the Vossa, *and the rest of the year we work our farms and cut timber and ship out with trawlers and packet-boats on the fjords—but our hearts are really in the river.*

Horveid remembers the morning Johannes Grimstad killed the record salmon on the Vossa, the giant hook-billed male that weighed seventy pounds. Johann Bolstad was working at Skorvelienhus when H.R.H. White caught six salmon between forty and fifty-seven pounds in a fortnight—a record unequalled anywhere in the salmon angler's world, even on such storied rivers as the Årøy and Alta.

The river still holds trophy-size secrets. During the solar eclipse in 1954, when a strange half-light shrouded its valley through the midday hours, the pools below Bulken produced three salmon better than fifty pounds. George Strøme was fishing that incredible morning and killed two fantastic salmon —cockfish of fifty-four and sixty-three pounds—on successive casts in perhaps the most fantastic feat of Atlantic salmon-fishing on record.

The past three seasons have seen the Vossa surrender twelve salmon over fifty pounds, eight of them on the three-mile beat above Bolstadøyri, including a mammoth sixty-one pounder killed by Odd Haraldsen at the Rongenhølen Pool early in 1966.

The tradition of famous anglers continues in our time. Recent years have seen expert Norwegian fishermen like Odd Haraldsen, Fritz Rieber, Sigurd Liland and Thomas Falck on the river. Americans like Richard Sweet, William Newbold, Sampson Field and the Honorable Graham Parsons, who served as the Ambassador to Sweden, have fished at Bolstadøyri. The present American ambassador in Oslo, the Honorable Philip Crowe, has fished there in past months. British tradition is maintained through the fishing holidays of rods like Arthur Oglesby, Eric Horsfall Turner, and Sir Thomas and Lady Sopwith.

The watershed of the Vossa is travelled by most of the tours and cruise-ships that visit the Sognefjord region each summer. Its countryside is famous for its peaceful scenery and picturesque stave churches and mountain farms, along with first-rate hotels like Ulvik and Kvikne.

The fishing is varied. Salmon travel the thirty miles of river between the fjord and the Storfossen waterfalls. There is considerable market netting in the three lakes below Voss, and fishing above the town is relatively poor as a result. The country town of Voss is well-known for its charming streets and its twelfth-century church and the summer visits of the late composer Edvard Grieg.

There is only commercial fishing in the six-mile lake below the town. Bulken lies above its outlet, and its Hotel Lilands can sometimes arrange fishing between Bulken and the Seimsvatn farmstead downstream, as well as occasional access to the beats at Evanger.

The famous pools upstream from Evanger, with their rambling clapboard fishing-house at Skorvelienhus, are still held and fished by British families. The worst commercial fishing is found in the fjord-like Evangervatn, and below its obstacle course of nets and fish-traps are great pools like Langhølen and Bridge Pool and Kjeilo.

Salmon-lies on the Vossa are strong and deep, and its brawling big-water character dictates its tackle requirements. Sinking lines and relatively large flies are needed to reach salmon in such currents, and this often makes the light tackle fashionable on American and Canadian rivers impractical. Most fishermen on the Vossa use two-handed fly rods between ten and thirteen feet, although I have fished it successfully with a powerful 9½-foot young parabolic under most conditions. Greased-line tactics are suitable in the tail-shallows of several pools after mid-July, and floating lines are sometimes useful. Reels should be durable, have a firm drag-system, and hold at least two hundred yards of thirty-pound dacron backing. Leaders should measure twelve feet, since the water is very clear over its dark bottom, with tippets testing between twelve and thirty pounds depending on fly-sizes. Fliers should vary between 5/o and four, with darker patterns like the Black Dose, Blue Charm, Brown Fairy, Orange Charm, Jock Scott and Black Doctor most useful, although brighter flies should be carried like the Peter Ross and Silver Grey and Dusty Miller—which killed me a record fifty-one pound salmon in the Langhølen Pool.

Such trophies are usually taken when least expected, and mine was no exception. The week's fishing that followed the brace of thirty-pound salmon taken with Bruno Jensen and Sigurd Liland ended without another sign of salmon. Vossa proved its fickle reputation two other years, although my visits were too late in the season, and I had about decided the river was a waste of time—in spite of those big fish from Kjeilo and Mehrhølen that first day.

Odd Haraldsen changed my mind. We met over dinner in New York just after he took the fishing-rights on the Bolstadøyri pools, and he talked me into fishing it again on my next trip to Oslo. Haraldsen was persuasive.

You should know better, he chided when I expressed mixed feelings about the Vossa and its salmon. *Salmon rivers are like beautiful women—bored when you're interested and eager again when you're losing interest!*

You're probably right! I agreed and laughed.

Six months later the porter loaded my baggage aboard the train in Voss, and the shrill stationmaster's whistle signalled our departure for Bolstadøyri. The train gathered speed and wound down the valley, offering familiar glimpses of its lakes and villages and mountain farms.

Odd Haraldsen was waiting at Bolstadøyri. *Where've you been?* he yelled as the train left for Bergen. *We've been expecting you to arrive all afternoon!*

How's the fishing? I asked.

Great! he answered. *Took two thirty-pounders at Rongenhølen just before lunch!*

Story of my life! I groaned unhappily. *Vossa gets generous when I'm riding around on trains!*

Still two hours of fishing, he laughed.

Nils Bolstad was waiting with his boat on the famous Langhølen Pool. The pool is four-hundred yards from the tumbling rapids at its head to its spreading tail-shallows downstream. Salmon are scattered down its entire length.

Fishing light was already waning as we reached the head of the pool. Nils pointed to the holding-lie between two converging currents, and watched me select an Orange Charm and study it with uncertainty.

God flue! he finally nodded his approval.

His confidence in the fly-pattern helped, and we began casting across the oil-smooth water. Fifty-odd casts were unproductive, and I was mentally punishing myself for coming late and missing a good morning on the Vossa. Downstream we stopped fishing and changed to a larger fly-pattern—a pale Dusty Miller with a silver-tinsel body to catch the light in the gathering darkness.

The line dropped the fly tight against a granite outcropping where the current flowed smooth and deep. The third cast came around deep and finished its current-swing and hung deep below the boat—and as I started a rhythmic retrieve before casting again, the rod snapped down sharply.

Salmon! I turned and Nils grinned.

The fight was powerful. The fish held deep and shook itself sullenly. Salmon-fishermen feel helpless with a stubborn head-shaking fish, because snubbing it firmly will tear out a well-hooked fish and slacking off is more dangerous. This salmon simply bulldogged deep under the boat, telegraphing its angry convulsions back along the rod until the fly worked out and it was gone.

Nils shook his head unhappily and maneuvered the boat opposite a towering ledge where the river eddied deep over unseen boulders. *Beste plass,* he whispered.

How deep are the fish? I asked.

Åtte meter, Nils answered.

Twenty-five feet is deep for fly-fishing. It means breaking the rules of salmon-fishing, with a long quartering cast upstream, letting the line sink back deep until it was opposite the boat. Lowering the rod downstream, I waited while the line bellied deep across the river and felt the fly begin to swim properly.

Suddenly the fly stopped swimming, the line tightened with weight that spelled salmon, and I struck firmly. Nothing happened. There was only a ponderous sense of power while the fish ignored the pressure of the tackle. Nils maneuvered the boat below the salmon and I stripped off line, forcing the fish off balance with downstream pressure.

That worked and the fish moved, but slowly upstream with a strength unlike any salmon in my experience. *Well,* I laughed nervously, *we're not snagged on the bottom!*

It's not Mother Norway! Nils agreed.

Suddenly the salmon bolted fifty yards upstream. *Hardly!* I shouted unhappily, and it stripped another fifty yards off the reel in great rasping jerks of line.

Twenty minutes passed and we played the fish cautiously, losing and gaining and losing line again. Nils was worried about gaffing it from the usual beach near the bottom of the pool, since even a spent salmon can force a fight into the rapids when its bulk is caught in the current. The boulder-paved beach fifty yards above the boat looked better, but it meant working the fish from the main current and forcing it upstream. Salmon can sometimes be led with steady pressure, but I had never tried it on one over twenty pounds.

Thirty-five minutes. Salmon experts figure par in playing the fish at a pound per minute, and such a long fight without tiring this salmon spelled considerable size.

Nils nodded toward the upper beach and I forced the fish carefully into the quieter water below the boat. We rowed slowly and smoothly upstream while I braked the reel and held a constant rod-pressure. The oars thudded once and broke rhythm, and my heart stopped as the fish bolted forty yards. We regained the line and led it upriver until my fingers slipped on the reel, and its ratchety clatter triggered an erratic head-jerking run that stripped off thirty yards.

The boat grated on the rocks and I waded ashore. *I'm tired,* I thought suddenly, surprised at the aching in my shoulders and wrists and arms. *I'm really tired!*

The fish seemed spent, but it still wallowed powerfully in the huge counter-clockwise currents off the beach. Several times we tried to work the salmon within gaffing range, and each time it bulled off into its nightmare merry-go-round currents. Nils said nothing and waited with the gaff.

He's coming! the thought was almost prayerful.

The salmon rolled weakly under the surface and the current carried it toward the beach. Nils stared hard into the black water as I worked the fish close, reached out cautiously with the gaff and struck hard.

There was an enormous splash that showered us both. Nils shouted and almost went down in the river, wrestling the huge salmon ashore. Its size seemed awesome in the gathering darkness as Nils delivered the coup-de-grâce. *Twenty-two kilos,* he guessed, and the fifty-pound scale hit bottom.

Fifty-one pounds! I thought wildly.

Salmon fishermen spend their lives dreaming about such trophies. Friends looked at the photographs and tracings of the fish and shook their heads. *Those outlines are obvious forgeries,* said one waggishly, *and those pictures look like a thirty-pounder with two midgets!*

Others were like the scholarly friend who has fished Atlantic salmon for more than sixty years without bettering thirty pounds.

Killing a salmon like that at your age is tragic, he smiled philosophically. *It's like stumbling over the Grail on your first mission from Camelot.*

There are long odds against a larger salmon in my lifetime, but salmon fishermen are dreamers. Cyril Mowbray Wells was headmaster of Eton College, and he fished the Vossa faithfully each summer for twenty-odd years. Wells caught almost fifteen hundred salmon during his tenure on the river, and his catch totalled over fifty thousand pounds. His record fish was a salmon of fifty-three pounds, but he fished diligently each summer, hoping for a bigger salmon all through the twilight of his life. Wells insisted that his luck resulted from the skills of Mathias Bolstad, the postmaster who was his riverkeeper during his years on the Vossa.

Cyril Mowbray Wells had strong emotional ties for the river and its gillies, and his feelings are not uncommon in salmon-fishing circles. His will stipulated that his ashes would be scattered into the river. The villagers gathered on the bridge at Bolstadøyri with the boatmen and gillies not long after his death. It was a bright morning when the first spring salmon had been seen in the estuary. Mathias Bolstad gravely scattered the ashes of his British friend into the river, and the men stood bareheaded in the wind as the current carried them swiftly toward the sea.

The Canary
in the Mine

IT was hot that afternoon below Roscoe, and
the river simmered like a series of millponds in the sun.
Locusts murmured in the trees until the shadows of the mountain reached the current. Our supper cookfire threaded its blue
hackle-colored smoke across the pool.

Our camp was filled with the smells of biscuits and trout
chowder and coffee. It was getting cooler with the sunlight off
the river, and the first trout of the evening porpoised tight
against the rocks. It was the middle of July, and there had
been fine *Potomanthus* hatches at twilight for two weeks. Big
trout sometimes took the big cream-colored mayflies then, just
at dark when the river flowed cool again.

There was plenty of time before the hatch, and the still
Beaverkill flats were so low and clear that wading too soon
would frighten the fish. It was getting dark when the first pale-

winged drakes fluttered down the pool and two fish started working in the main current.

It's about time, said my father.

He waded out stealthily into the pool. My father took the smooth run above its tail and I worked carefully into the rib-deep current along the railroad. *Good luck!* he said.

There was a heavy fish swirling rhythmically, tight against the rip-rapping. It would roll to take a fluttering drake with a heavy splash, and the silken current became still again, before it sipped the next dun coming down. The big mayflies were coming often now, and the fish worked greedily on the hatch. It looked easy enough, but it soon proved difficult. It was a long cast with a big straw-colored variant, trying to punch it out on a fine tippet into a slight wind. It kept falling back on the delicate tippet in a dragging tangle of moss-green nylon that spooked the fish.

Time after time it floated down, almost reaching the fish before it dragged and was refused again. *It's got to be a big brown,* I thought. *He's pretty smart!*

Finally I waded deeper to shorten the cast, soaking the fly-boxes in my fishing vest. The cast worked out softly and settled the variant two feet above the fish. The leader fell in a nice loop and the fish took the fly without hesitation.

The reel growled angrily as the fish bored upstream. The line sliced through the still current.

Big fish? yelled my father.

Feels pretty strong! I answered.

The fish sulked deep among the rocks, and it was almost dark when I heard my father wading out of the river to help. The fight went bulldogging along the bottom, punctuated with sullen headshaking pulls. It was a stubborn fish and a strong fight. Several times it worked well into the backing, threshing and rolling down the current until its splashing covered the full length of the pool.

Is he getting tired? yelled my father.

Not yet, I answered.

The fish worked down along the railroad, its cartwheeling jumps echoing from the rocks. Finally I worked it back into the pool and waded toward our camp. My father had his electric torch.

You want the light? he yelled.

Wait until he's tired, I answered. *The torch could spook him if you turn it on too soon.*

Okay, he waited on the bank.

We worked the fish into the shallows. *Seems like a big brown,* I grinned happily in the darkness. *It's the biggest fish in the Beaverkill—feels strong as a salmon!*

Good work! said my father.

The fish made a few half-hearted circles, stubbornly taking line off the reel, until I forced it back into the quiet water along the trees. Whippoorwills called softly across the river and the moon rose slowly above the mountain. The fish rolled weakly in the shallows and my father switched on the torch. *It's a bass!* he choked.

Damn! I groaned. *I thought it was a trout!*

He netted the husky smallmouth and carried it ashore, threshing muscularly in the meshes. *Don't be disappointed,* he laughed. *It's at least four pounds.*

It's big enough, I smiled, *but it's not a trout.*

There is nothing wrong with a four-pound smallmouth, except that fishing luck is really fickle when you catch a trophy fish of the wrong species on the wrong river. Smallmouth bass are first-rate sport on their own streams, like the Cacapon or the Shenandoah or the Current, but a big smallmouth on a trout stream is a serious symptom.

It means the Beaverkill might be getting too warm, said my father, *and the trout are like the canary in the mine—when they begin to go the river is dying.*

Tigerfish of
the Himalayas

Nepal? said a British shooting friend over lunch in Manhattan. *It's an incredible place, and you should try fishing mahseer with flies!*

Mahseer? I asked. *What are they?*

They run like salmon into the cold rivers that drain the Himalayas, he explained. *They come upstream from the Ganges in March and April.*

Will they really take flies?

Can't tell you, he ordered coffee and chocolate mousse. *They catch them on small plugs and spinners and spoons in Burma and Kashmir—they'll probably take a saltwater bucktail fished fast.*

How big are these mahseer? I asked.

They're extremely strong fish, he filled his pipe. *The small ones run about fifteen pounds.*

The small ones! I said.

The Ganges record bettered a hundred and twenty, his chocolate mousse arrived. *You'd better use gear strong enough for a tarpon!*

They must fight like tigers! I laughed.

Mahseer means tigerfish, he said.

Kathmandu alone is worth the twenty-odd hours of airport hopscotch around the world past Karachi and Calcutta. Its name still has the cadences of Kipling. It has a dreamlike half-reality until you reach the steaming darkness of Karachi, smelling jet fuel mixed with the silt-laden Indus after its thousand mile journey from Karakorum and the Khyber Pass. Calcutta was a simmering landscape of mud-colored houses under a white-hot noon. Its rivers were like a tangle of giant ropes coiled in the dust of centuries. The apron crews wrestled baggage from the plane, wearing red loincloths and turbans, and I waited until all my gear was safely unloaded. There was a young girl poised like a heron in the shade of the plane, standing strangely on one leg with both hands on her head. Beggars dozed in the shadows of the terminal, and when I found my gear in the open customs hall there was a raven sitting on my pile of duffle.

The flight to Kathmandu reached a climax in the wildest airport approach in the world. Our pilot held at thirty-five thousand feet with the Himalayas lurking behind the clouds. When he finally saw the field, the Caravelle dropped straight down in a series of tight ear-popping spirals. The plane roared in past the terraced rice fields, until it touched down and its landing roll shuddered and braked abruptly.

Drag chute! I muttered in disbelief.

You're right! said the young Norwegian engineer beside me. *Gauchar's too short for the Caravelle!*

Nepal has been fully open to visitors less than twenty years, and for over a century British advisers were the only foreign travellers permitted into Kathmandu. Its mountain kingdom is a narrow enclave tucked between India and Tibet, rising from the hot floodplain to the polar altitudes of the Himalayas in a hundred miles. Most of its valleys have never been seen by outsiders, and Kathmandu is still a medieval city with roots twenty centuries in the past—ancient as Rome and much less touched by the cacophony of the modern world.

Most Americans know Nepal through the exploits of the Alpine expeditions of Herzog and Dhyrenfurth and Hillary. Their heroism on peaks like Annapurna and Dhaulagiri and Everest are common knowledge.

Others have read about the Gurkha regiments that helped Britain end the Sepoy Rebellion in 1857, terrified Italian infantry in Egypt and Libya, fought the Japanese in the liberation of Burma, and mercilessly tracked communist guerrillas with their *kukris* in the jungles of Malaya after the war. Still others know that Buddha was born six centuries before Christ at Lumbini, ninety miles southwest of Kathmandu.

The capital lies in a high amphitheatre of terraced mountains. Its streets are crowded with ancient temples and stupas and monasteries. The sacred Bagmati flows through a richly-tangled tapestry of streets, its currents silt-red among the temples and earth-colored houses. It passes the steps where the dead are cremated and the pious bathe to purify themselves, and flows underneath the intricate platforms and terraces below the huge Pashupatinath temples of Shiva.

The tiny courtyards and streets teem with life, and the sweet odors of *gaja* and *hash-hish* are mixed with the curried cooking smells. Barefoot women pass over the cobbles, their red-hemmed skirts moving against tattooed calves. Gurung tribesmen wander the crowded squares, carrying their possessions on their heads, and schoolgirls in bright saris mingle with crowds of saffron-robed monks.

Tibetan refugees fill the markets of Patan. Sherpa porters down from the fifteen-thousand-foot villages below Thyangboche and Ama Dablam stare like tourists at the street-life of the capital. Women squat in carpets of bright peppers and spread *cannabis* to dry on the cobblestones, and bearded holy men sit crosslegged in their breechcloths, staring at their bowls and prayer wheels.

The market streets are walled with tiny shops like carved mahogany armoires. Their miniature arcades are stacked with Indian silks, cloth goods from Bhutan, herbs and curry and spices in huge jars, roots for the beer-like *chang* from the foothills, aluminum saucepans and egg beaters, hand-beaten brass water-jars from Bharatpur, and twisted pine-smelling incense hangs beside piles of American bubble gum.

There are treasures everywhere in Patan. Tiny stalls in the alleys near the Golden Temple of Mahavihar are filled with silver rings from Sikkim, tarnished sixteenth-century Buddhas, erotic *shakti* figurines smuggled through the high mountain passes from Tibet, and silver prayer wheels from the monastery at Pokhara—stuffed with rice-paper prayers and covered with rubies and lapis lazuli and jade.

Patan courtyards are the workshops of artisans who practice ancient skills, just as their ancestors have worked metals and mahogany and jewels since the reign of Kublai Khan. Children sort the tiny stones and shape filigree wire in darkened lofts. Young girls encrust the heads of tiny dragons with rubies and gold wire, while their fathers still cast idols, using wax effigies and crude courtyard smelters, and filing the castings held between their calloused feet.

Our tiger-striped taxi pushed through these crowded streets from the airport, stopping while sacred cattle crossed lazily or sprawled on the cobblestones. Several *saddhus* perched like fish eagles on the compound of the Hotel Royal, and inside its walls we wound through the araucarias and bottle-brush trees to the entrance.

The Royal is a former Rana palace, confiscated from the family that ruled Nepal for centuries until it was unseated in a *coup d'etat* in 1951. Its corridors and galleries are filled with fading Rana portraits in spectacular uniforms and scarlet tunics. The hotel is old, and there are tiny lizards in its crumbling stucco, but its cuisine is superb. There are usually one or two mountain climbing parties shaking out equipment for assaults on Annapurna and Dhaulagiri and Everest.

Its proprietor is a living legend. Boris Lissanivitch is the last of a distinguished Russian family that raised thoroughbred horses in Odessa. His career has included several years with Diaghilev and the *Ballet Russe* in Paris. Later he worked nightclubs in Calcutta and Singapore and Shanghai with a dancing act.

Those years in the seaports of Asia were something less than working with Massine, Balanchine and Pavlova, and the Bohemian life with Matisse, Cocteau and Stravinsky in Montmartre. His cabaret career ultimately led to ownership of the posh Club 300 in Calcutta. Camaraderie with a continent of kings and maharajahs and princes soon followed. King Tribhuvan of Nepal was a frequent customer, before the revolution that restored his power twenty years ago, and Boris returned with him in the royal plane to Kathmandu.

Boris was waiting at the portico. *Welcome to the Royal!* We shook hands. *You look tired—how about a drink?*

The hotel bar lies down a cloistered gallery. Its hammered copper fireplace and inglenooks are famous from a half-dozen books on climbing the Himalayas. There were four climbers lounging around the fire, their cleated boots resting on the hearth.

Dhaulagiri changes everything, one said.

Boris nodded toward the climbers. *They were getting ready to climb in India when they got permission to climb Dhaulagiri,* he explained. *Its bad to change mountains in midexpedition.*

There's no time to acclimate, said another climber.

Tough! said a third.

Raindrops rattled on the windows and Boris frowned into his Yaktail. *Something wrong?* I said. *Rain?*

It's too early in April for rain, and it's a bad sign for these climbers. It began raining steadily before dinner. We climbed the flower-patterned spiral staircase to Boris' atelier and met his other guests. Prince Basundahara was talking with an Austrian manufacturer and a young Australian journalist from Hong Kong. Boris and his wife were showing her paintings to several of the climbers, and his mother-in-law showed me her collection of miniature silver Buddhas.

Mahseer? asked Boris.

Yes, I said. *I'd like to try fishing them.*

They are very strong fighters, Boris nodded. *They fight like tigers in the Karnali—and its current is very swift!*

Can someone arrange a trip? I asked.

It's easy to arrange, he waved the Colonel across the room. *Colonel Rana can help you mount a party.*

The Colonel agreed to meet for lunch. *We have a tiger camp on the Karnali,* he explained, *and there is good fishing in the gorge upstream when the mahseer are migrating to spawn.*

Are they coming now? I asked.

They started last month, he nodded.

It sounds good, I said.

Dinner was announced with a silver gong. The rain had stopped and we walked back along the roof parapets toward the stairs. The mountains were strangely bright in the moonlight. We crossed the sitting room downstairs and Boris led me across to his collection of stones. Several of the Dhaulagiri climbers joined us.

These are my bits of rock, Boris smiled.

Bits of rock? asked one climber.

The stones have been carried back to Boris from the summits of Annapurna, Dhaulagiri, Makalu, Nilgiri, Jannu, Choyo, Himalchuli, and Everest. *Aren't they fine?* Boris concluded his roster of successful alpine assaults, holding the tiny, sepulchral piece of granite from the highest mountain on earth. *Everest,* he said softly.

The climbers' eyes were very bright.

Our venerable DC-3 waited on the apron an hour after daybreak. Flights to Mount Everest leave early, since haze builds each morning and there are violent thermals that can drop a plane thousands of feet, or force it into a wild roller-coaster climb to oxygen altitudes in seconds. The cool wind eddied across the airfield. The dogs sleeping under the wings were startled when the engines whined, coughed and stuttered and choked, and finally caught and roared. *Good!* I thought. *Never trust an engine that starts too quickly!* We climbed in a lazy circle above the earth-colored houses and pagodas of the capital. The mountains looked lifeless until the sun reached them, first touching Himalchuli and Annapurna and Machupuchare. It exploded into the glittering ice-fields of Ganesh Himal as we climbed east along the mountains. The engineer came back wearing a Sikh turban above his white beard.

Everest! he shouted. *Everest coming!*

The plane shuddered and droned past the Himalayas and we stared like children at peaks that towered above the cockpit. Guari Shankar reflected its snowfields in the rivet-patterns of the wing, and Cho Oyo towered above the pass at Changri-La.

Everest was ahead. *Which one?*

Clouds drifted across the terraced foothills. Fresh snow covered mountain ridges that layered steeply into ice-fields below the summits. Peak after peak towered into the sun, until in the distance beyond Kachenjunga they disappeared into the mists of China.

Sahib! the old engineer pointed. *Everest!*

Ama Dablam seems higher. Its escarpments rise almost vertically above the villages and monasteries above Thyangboche, but its twenty-three-thousand-foot summit is only a minor prelude. Lhotse is higher still, with serrated ramparts showing through its pale snowfields, but Everest lies behind its lesser twenty-seven-thousand-foot sister. Its glowering face looms above a jumble of ice-fields and glaciers, dark and brooding in the sun. Sherpa tribesmen who live at its feet watch the snow plumes trailing in its unseen winds, knowing its moods and calling it their Sagarmatha—the Mother of the Mountains.

Colonel Rana called after lunch. *We can fly down to Nepalganj tomorrow,* he said. *The jeeps will meet us at the airstrip. We'll meet you at Gauchar,* I said.

The airport swarmed with women in bright silks and a hundred children clamoring to carry our rifles. Two old men were holding chickens, legs tied together and wings flapping. Gurkha troops settled their gear in a huge pile. The pilots were young and had taken their training with the Royal Air Force in England. The flight engineer was another bearded Sikh, and the stewardess was a tall Gurung, wrapped in a sari of dark silk that bared her slender waist.

The rainforest of the Terai is another world three hours west of Kathmandu. The chickens squawked and cackled, and feathers drifted back in the cabin. The hot plain was a lacework of dry paddies waiting for the monsoon, like a vast earth-colored jigsaw puzzle. Nepalganj was a dirt strip shimmering in the heat. The pilot made a low downwind pass, growling his engines to clear the sacred cattle, and we turned back to land. The engineer wrestled with a cargo hatch and we climbed down and stared into the blinding heat.

Look at the faces! I thought.

There were tall Raji tribesmen, slender and almost naked in breechcloths and turbans. The terminal was a huge mango with several graceful Tharu women in its shade. They wore jewels in their noses and stood apart from the men, regal and strangely aloof. Two sacred cows ambled back and flopped in the shade of the DC-3.

Six hours later the trail left the last village and wound into the jungle. It was getting cooler and our clothes were covered with dust. Wild pigs scuttled past the jeeps, and at twilight we watched a huge python slide endlessly across the bullock track.

It looks like a wandering fire-hose, somebody laughed.

Wearing a camouflage suit, I added.

It was dark when the jungle ended and our jeeps worked down through the rocks. We could hear a river roaring ahead in the darkness when we stopped. *It's the Karnali,* said the Colonel. *We'll go upstream tomorrow.*

It was cool under the breakfast-fly and the huge river glittered in the sun. We finished breakfast and collected our rifles and other gear for the trip upriver into the gorge. Three dugouts of Raji boatmen waited on the beach below Chisapani. We loaded the mahogany canoes and the Rajis poled expertly upstream along the banks. Fish eagles circled lazily along the cliffs. Otters splashed and played in the gathering currents that eddied along the rocks. Crocodiles slipped into the river.

They come upstream to spawn too, said the Colonel, *exactly like the mahseer.* His lieutenant pointed to a steep sandbar that rose between the boulders and cliffs. There were scuffling tracks and a huge serpentine scar in the smooth river-sculptured sand.

That was a crocodile? I asked.

The Lieutenant nodded. *It probably laid its eggs there this morning.* River bitterns fished among the rocks. Parakeets and flocks of myna birds chattered in the trees, and hundreds of quarreling monkeys busied themselves in the vines of a sunny ravine.

What are mahseer like?

Colonel Rana smiled. *There are several kinds,* he said. *These Karnali fish are mostly goldens, but we catch the odd black mahseer—and they're the real tigerfish!*

The river warden nodded. *But they're all strong in the Karnali,* he added, *with these currents.*

How do you fish them? I asked.

Mahseer will eat almost anything, said the river warden. *Baitfish, insects, mussels, seeds, berries, birds, worms, bread—they'll take anything that moves!*

Minnows and shellfish mostly, added the Colonel.

They crush the shellfish in their throats, explained the Lieutenant. *When they're hooked deep their shell-crackers can smash a spoon or treble hook like a vise!*

Smash a treble hook! I gasped.

It's true! they insisted.

The warden passed me his tackle box. *These are the plugs and lures I use,* he said, *but these big spinners are the best.*

He handed me a huge handmade lure: its two-inch blade was hammered from raw copper and polished on rock, its clevices were twisted from heavy brass wire, its shaft was strung with coarse ruby-colored stones, and it hung with a saltwater treble.

They can crush those hooks?

The warden nodded. *They're made for me by an old man in Kathmandu,* he explained. *We get hooks from England.*

Are mahseer only found in the Ganges watershed? I examined the lure.

No, answered the Colonel, *they're in Pakistan and Burma as well as Nepal, but the best fishing is probably in Kashmir, and here in this Karnali gorge to its junction with the Bheri!*

The spawning runs come upstream like salmon, said the warden, *about five to seven days apart.*

They are a little like salmon, agreed the Colonel. *They like the cold water that comes down from the Himalayas—and a spate of discolored water means poor sport.*

The current was swifter now, murmuring and sucking at the rocky walls of the gorge, and we reached the bottom of the rapids just before noon. The Raji boatmen beached our dugouts where springs trickled into the river through beds of moss and ferns, and quickly built reed shelters to protect us from the sun.

It's getting hot! I said.

Colonel Rana smiled. *We're used to the heat,* he said. *It warms the river and starts the fishing.*

Yes, said the river warden, *the mahseer should start chasing baitfish in a few minutes.*

Look! pointed the Lieutenant.

There was a huge splash and tiny silver minnows skittered in terror. The swift current tumbled a mile down the rapids and turned into the gorge. It churned and eddied and hissed against the cliffs, slowing in a long chest-deep run along the rocky bar below the huts. Huge half-drowned trees were piled across river. The mahseer were slashing everywhere in the shallows, scattering baitfish ahead of their jaws.

Their table manners are awful! I laughed.

We hastily assembled our tackle. The district warden mounted a huge saltwater spinning reel on his rod, his son put up a stiff bait-rod, and I strung a salmon fly-rod with three hundred yards of thirty-pound backing on the reel. The Rajis squatted in the river among the rocks to keep cool, watching and seining tiny minnows with fine-mesh nets that looked perfect for butterflies.

Good luck! said the warden.

His big spinner looped out across the currents, its polished blade glittering in the sun. It splashed heavily and started a pumping swing across the current, and suddenly the rod dipped wildly.

Mahseer! he yelled. *Mahseer!*

The Raji boatmen watched impassively, except for a small grinning boy in a red turban. Line burned off against the clutch and the warden pumped powerfully against the threshing fish. Six times the mahseer jumped like a small tarpon, somersaulting clumsily until it landed in a massive splash. It was a long fight, but finally the fish threshed weakly on the surface and was wrestled ashore. Its sleek length was sheathed in silvery scales, half bonefish and half tarpon. Its muscled back was golden brown, faintly striped like a striped bass with pale yellow fins. The huge spinner was crushed in its throat, almost as if it had been flattened on an anvil. The fish scaled about twenty-five pounds.

Tigerfish is right! I said.

It's about average, smiled the Colonel, *wait till we hook a really big mahseer in that current.*

Let's try a bucktail that looks like those minnows!

Mahseer were still rolling and splashing at baitfish in the shallows. The minnows seined by the boatmen were silvery little sardines with pale amber backs, and I picked a big mylar marabou that matched them with a mixture of white and pale brown feathers. It was tied with silver mylar flanks along its wings. It was clinched tightly into a tarpon knot on the heavy nylon leader, and I worked out line into the sun as two big fish rolled within range.

Anything you catch will be the fly-record in Nepal! smiled the Colonel. *Make it good!*

There was a quick tug and a small fish skipped in across the current, impaled on my huge marabou. *Six inches!* laughed the warden. *It's a Karnali fly-fishing record!*

Sardine! I said ruefully.

We released the little mahseer and I teased the fly back through its full-grown relatives, boiling and chasing minnows in the current. There was a pesky six-pounder that danced across the rapids for twenty minutes before it surrendered, and finally there was a giant swirl behind the fly and a huge maw worked shut across its feathers. The rod doubled into a tight, throbbing circle and the reel protested as it shriekingly surrendered line.

The fight lasted less than sixty seconds. The heavy mahseer catapulted high into the sun and the reel rasped and clattered and its gear-system fell apart. The rod worked wildly until I wrapped my arm in the line, pointed the tip at the fish, and waited until the heavy leader snapped.

That was over quick, I sighed.

The walls of the gorge held the heat and reflected it like an oven. We ate briefly and drank some beer chilled in the river and huddled in the huts or the shade of the rocks until the sun passed. The fish stopped feeding as quickly as they had started.

We crossed the river later and rested while the boatmen carried our gear high above the current. Our camp was on the shoulder of the gorge, a hundred feet above the Karnali rapids. The water rises as much as fifty feet in monsoon season, its pale scour-line obvious on the sandstone cliffs below our encampment.

Jhumli tribesmen passed along the trail above our campsite, trekking back into the foothills from Sitapur with trade goods and salt. Their women carried huge bundles on their heads, and the porters balanced as much as two hundred pounds on poles across their shoulders. They climbed slowly without stopping to rest, using the cadence of a sing-song melody that drifted down through the bamboo.

The three Sherpa cooks with our party had originally been recruited to join the American climbing team in its assault on Dhaulagiri. They quickly organized our camp while we settled into our tents, and huge flocks of chattering myna birds settled in the poplars. It was still hot in the meadow above the river.

Swim? suggested the Lieutenant.

We selected a short-barreled Mannlicher rifle and climbed into a deep ravine below our camp. The trail crossed the ravine on a slender three-log bridge. Eighty feet below in its shadows, a stream flowed still and swimming-pool green. Its bottom was bedrock and pebbles. The Lieutenant jacked a cartridge into the rifle and checked the pool for cobras. There were only a few big lizards clinging to its mossy walls.

Tiny baitfish nibbled at our toes. *Mahseer,* said the Lieutenant. *Those are baby mahseer!*

They really are tigerfish! I laughed.

The stream was surprisingly cold. It was more than a hundred degrees in our camp and in the river gorge below, but the dark ravine cooled and refreshed us. The narrow pool was about ten feet in the deepest place, and ten to twenty feet wide. It was long enough for several lazy strokes, and we played like dolphins until we heard voices. Several Jhumli porters and their women had stopped high on the three-log bridge. They were chattering like parrots and pointing down into the ravine.

What's the matter? I asked.

The Lieutenant treaded water and grinned. *You're the matter,* he said. *They're talking about you!*

Why me? I said.

He backstroked into the shallows. *They heard you were an American,* he smiled. *You're the first American these tribesmen have ever seen.*

That evening I hooked and lost another wild twenty-pounder in the gorge when it sliced my nylon on a huge rock and took my marabou. Just as the fish passed behind the rock, the district warden hooked another. His thick fifty-millimeter line melted off the spinning reel and he frantically screwed down the drag; it did not seem to slow the huge mahseer. It jumped twice far down the gorge, and wallowed across the rapids while the heavy rod worked and throbbed.

The warden was helpless. The powerful fish forced him downstream from rock to rock. He followed through the chest deep shallows to the last gravel bar before the walls of the gorge dropped straight into the heavy current. The big mahseer jumped and jumped again in the rapids, threatening to snap the rod into matchwood. The warden retreated to the final gravel shoal below the cliffs and waded out shoulder deep into the current, raising the lashing rod high above his head. The angry mahseer raked the heavy nylon against an underwater ledge and the straining rod snapped back. The warden waded unhappily ashore.

It looked huge! I said.

About sixty pounds, said the warden unhappily. *We stopped a forty-pounder here last week.*

It was cool coming back up the trail from the gorge, but the furnace-like temperatures lingered in the wild thirst that reached into my boots. We wound high into the mahogany trees and rhododendron thickets, and passed several bearers carrying a wild goat and a huge burden wrapped in jute. The jute was dripping and encrusted with sawdust.

Ice, explained the Colonel. *The tiger camp got a bullock cart of fruit from Lucknow today, and the shikaris have sent us some of the ice for our drinks.*

Thank God, I sighed. *Camp meat?*

It's a young goral from the gorge, he answered. *You'll like the way the Sherpas cook it.*

Is there any beer left? I licked my parched lips.

There was still one can of Tuborg. We chipped the Lucknow ice into a huge brass water-jar, layering it carefully around the precious single can of beer.

The bearers and boatmen gathered around the cook tents to collect their wages in camp meat and flour. They squatted almost naked in the darkness, smoking *gaja* in straight clay pipes they cupped in their hands. They inhaled between their thumbs, like boys making leaf whistles, and held the smoke lazily in their lungs. They passed the pipes among them, and the sweet marijuana-like odor drifted through our camp, mixed with the smells of cooking meat and fresh biscuits. The can of Tuborg was perfectly chilled and I punctured it with shivers of anticipation. There are times in the jungle dry season when the canteen water gets almost warm enough for shaving, and the perspiration evaporates so quickly it never collects on your skin.

I rolled the cold beer across my tongue like a fine Chablis. *It's perfect,* I sighed. *It's the first time I haven't been thirsty since Kathmandu!*

Supper was superb. The Colonel worked with his Sherpa cooks, rolling dough with a length of bamboo on a rolling-board surface hacked from a mahogany log. The Sherpas sliced the goat tenderloins partially through like salami, and sprinkled pepper and crushed bay leaves and curry into the diced meat. The Colonel chopped and rolled the richly-spiced goat inside tiny meat pies. The goat pies were baked in the reflected heat of a huge boulder, and the Sherpas carried them bubbling hot to our open dining fly. Roast wild chicken and peacock followed as the Sherpas served us a royal meal with the music of the Karnali rapids below our camp.

The storm hit our camp while I was still half awake in my sleeping bag. It sounded like a freight train coming down the gorge. *It's a train!* I thought and suddenly I was awake. *They don't have trains here!*

The first gust of wind sliced open my tent like an envelope and then it got terribly still in the valley. The sound of the river filled the camp and lightning flashed, and then the freight-train roaring came growing again in the dark. It grew and grew until we were engulfed in a fierce maelstrom of ochre dust and wind.

Dry storm! yelled the Colonel.

We worked out through the tattered canvas and scattered clothing and ran into the open meadow above the tents. Lightning flashed yellow and orange psychedelic explosions through the blinding dust. Debris and leaves were whipped through our camp. Our throats and nostrils were filled with dust. We recovered our cameras and rifles and my expensive Leonard split-cane rod, and huddled half-naked in the darkness. The wind lashed through the jungle above our camp, and huge trees came crashing down.

Watch the trees! yelled the Colonel.

Suddenly the wind dropped again. It was almost silent except for the sound of the river, and the darkness was thick with dust. Debris settled through the trees like confetti and lightning flickered.

It may not be finished, warned the Colonel.

The wind struck again, like a hurricane once the eye has passed, and the hot wind hit the poplars around our camp with a terrible force. Lightning flashed orange through the dust and pebbles rattled across the tents. We crouched and leaned into the gusts, shielding our eyes and nostrils, while the trees whiplashed wildly. Somehow they survived the impacts, while the pieces of our tent flapped like a spectre in the lightning. It tore suddenly and went tumbling off into the darkness, like the special effects in a technicolor Dracula film.

Our Sherpas were struggling to secure their huge army

tent, cutting additional bamboo poles and driving extra stakes. They worked furiously all through the storm, running back and forth through the whipping trees, and their military cook-tent held. The Colonel supervised the staking of huge canvas flies over our fallen tents, while we stood shivering in the wind. Big clumsy drops of rain fell through the trees.

Don't worry, the Colonel yelled through the dust, *I've never seen a storm like this—but don't worry!*

Trees were still falling high on the jungle ridge above our camp, and lightning struck the precipice across the gorge, tumbling a huge mahogany a hundred feet into the river. It finally began to rain, after the wind had passed.

It's the beginning of the monsoon! said the Colonel. *We'll have to leave in the morning while we can still travel the river and ferry the jeeps across at Chisapani!*

We moved downstream on the swelling flood current just at daylight, our dugouts sliding swiftly along the cliffs, riding the sucking chocolate-colored river. The Rajis paddled silently and raised their ragged sails as the sun touched the high shoulder of the gorge, and triggered the chattering of a thousand monkeys and birds. The Colonel passed me boiled eggs and orange juice and canned caviar for breakfast.

First-class passage, he smiled.

We reached Chisapani that afternoon. The boatmen lashed their dugouts together into rafts and ferried the jeeps across. The river was rising quickly as we got the last vehicle over and we made our final camp in the trees below the gorge. There was a farewell supper of cold peacock and *chital* and wild boar, with each cook competing to prepare his tribal dishes for us, and it was dark when we finally slept. It was still dark when the Colonel moved swiftly through the tents, waking the porters and drivers. *It's another storm coming!* he yelled. *It's going to break in about another hour and it could make the trails impassable.*

Could we get out then? I asked.

Downriver with the Raji boatmen into India, he said, *but that way it could take weeks.*

The storm gathered over the foothills, blackening the first morning sky while we loaded the jeeps and started into the jungle. Rain broke across Chisapani, dropping huge trees and erasing the foothills behind us. We raced ahead of the storm, fording the shallow streams with protesting engines and spinning wheels. Our jeeps whined past the steep banks of the half-dry Gogra before the rains filled its channels, and we finally stopped in the marketplace at Minapur while the storm passed behind, its clouds churning and ink-colored over the jungle.

We just missed a boat trip to India, I said.

Our party stopped for lunch under a huge mango two miles below the Nepalganj airstrip. The Colonel drove ahead to check the plane from Kathmandu, and came back shaking his head unhappily.

What's the matter? someone asked.

It just came over the radio, he said. *It's the party on Dhaulagiri—seven were killed this morning!*

What happened? I gasped.

Avalanche! he answered. *These early spring storms triggered an avalanche!*

That night we walked the empty streets of Kathmandu, talking about the jungle storms and the tragedy in the snow-fields of Dhaulagiri. We crossed the darkened squares and passed among the ancient pagodas, where a band of street musicians were leaving a wedding party. We stopped and watched them pass through the domed stupas and terraced shrines and courtyards of silent granite bells. The high *ching-ching* of their cymbals rose above the shrill counterpoint of their flutes, and when they were gone, their music lingered hauntingly in the darkness. The temple dogs put their heads back down and dozed, and it seemed that we had only imagined the musicians and their music.

La Fiebre de las Bocas

THE storm gathered on the broken escarpment
at Chapelco, and sheets of rain láshed across the truck. There
were two riders above the Quilquihue crossing. They hunched
low on their ponies, their flat brimmed hats and heavy
ponchos turned against the wind.

It was still raining and the wind was cold when we
reached Junin de los Andes. The village was dark and silent.
Its adobe houses were shuttered and huddled against the wind
like the gauchos we had passed in the road. There were lights
in the Hosteria Chimehuin, flickering through the tall poplars
that sheltered it from the wind. Below the inn, the river
wound across the open valley past the cattle pens and the
poplar-lined Senoritas, the famous pool named for the camp
followers who live there and offer comfort to the cavalry post
above the town. Its channels split and merge again, flowing

toward the smooth foothills that force the Chimehuin south into the barren pampas.

The lights were warm inside the Hosteria, and the windows were smoky with cold. The storm lashed across the valley for hours, cutting the power lines from the north, and candles guttered and glowed on the tables. Fishermen were eating beef and thick vegetable soup and drinking red wine, and the light flickered in their faces like a painting strangely transplanted from the stories of Dickens.

José Julian is the proprietor of the simple Hosteria Chimehuin, and his little inn at Junin de los Andes has sheltered an impressive log of famous anglers. Their mecca is the storied Chimehuin, which flows fifty miles between its alpine birthplace in Lago Huechulaufquen to its junction with the Collon Cura in the treeless pampas. The entire river is good, and a twelve-pound trout is possible anywhere in its mileage, but the famous fly-casters who journey each winter from both Europe and America are drawn to the tumbling Boca Chimehuin, where the river flows full-blown from its wild wind-tossed lake.

There were two good friends in the dining room, and I smiled when I saw their faces through the windows. They are there each summer, fishing the three-mile reach of water below the Boca Chimehuin the entire month of March. Both are great fly-fishermen who know that reach of river in all its varied moods.

Prince Charles Radziwill is a Polish exile who lives in Buenos Aires, and has discovered a substitute for the shooting and fishing on his family estates in the partridge fields below Buenos Aires and the countless rivers of Patagonia. His best fish from the Boca Chimehuin is a fifteen-pound brown, taken on a big saltwater bucktail in the churning outlet.

Bébé Anchorena is a member of a famous Argentine family, with a sprawling estancia in the foothills at Tandil. Most of the year his skills are focused on the sheep and thoroughbreds in his township-sized pastures, but after Christmas his thoughts turn to Patagonia and Junin de los Andes. Anchorena held the world fly-record with a twenty-four-pound brown from Boca Chimehuin for several years, until it was displaced with an even bigger fish caught at Boca Correntoso.

Both men are addicts and spend their holidays fishing the Chimehuin outlet each summer. *It's never boring,* they explain. *The fish are migratory and they are always dropping down from the lake—we see new ones every morning.*

You'll see tomorrow, they added.

It was clear in the morning. The storm had passed and the sun was bright in the garden. We drove west along the river after breakfast, passing the cavalry post that guards the valley and the mountain pass from Chile. Beyond the rolling foothills, there was a volcano rising Fujiyama-perfect in the distance, its snowfields glittering in the sun.

Lanin! said Bébé. *Lanin guards the Boca!*

Radziwill nodded. *It's clear today,* he added, *but when the mountain wears a sombrero of clouds, fishing is good.*

No sombrero today, I said.

It's still good! laughed Anchorena.

Both men fell silent. The truck whined up the low hills at the head of the valley, where a grove of monkeypuzzle trees was dark against the ridge; and as we reached the summit and started down toward the river, the fifty-mile length of Largo Huechulaufquen was ahead. The volcano towered above the narrow fjord-like lake. The wind moved down the lake and its dark surface churned and rolled with whitecaps. Chile lies in the distance, lost in the squalls that often shroud the border.

Boca Chimehuin lies twelve thousand feet below the summit. Centuries ago some primordial earthquake opened a crevasse in the hills that enclosed the lake, and the river spilled gratefully into the gorge that the Patagonian settlers called the Garganta del Diablo. The river still flows through this outlet toward the sea, spilling through the lava ledges that block its currents. The winds blow down the fifty-mile length of lake, churning its surface into wild breakers that crash and roll into the mouth of the river. There are two black channels in the lava, churning with heavy surf and currents, before the river spreads into a deep riffle that reaches a hundred yards below the lake. The river turns in a deep smooth-flowing pool at the base of the hills and glides down a shallow, weedy reach of water toward the timber bridge.

Bébé stopped the truck. *Come on!* he said.

We walked along the bluffs above the river, carrying a pair of binoculars. The sun was high and we could see deep into the currents of the first pool below the lake.

Look! said Radziwill. *Look there!*

There are several huge boulders and ledges deep in the eddying currents, and a giant log is wedged among the rocks. Radziwill pointed and suddenly I saw them: six huge trout lying ahead of the ledges.

Bébé pointed downstream to a pocket above the weeds. *He's still there!* he whispered.

Radziwill nodded. *The rainbows are new!*

It was difficult to tell how large they were. The fish were lying too deep. *How big are they?* I asked.

The rainbows are three or four kilos, guessed Bébé.

Radziwill agreed. *The one beside the ledge is much bigger,* he added. *Maybe six or seven.*

Fifteen pounds? I exhaled in disbelief.

They both laughed at my excitement. *The brown lying above the weeds is even bigger still,* grinned Bébé.

Let's fish! I said weakly.

We crossed the trestle bridge, where the current gathered and dropped toward the rapids of the Garganta del Diablo, and drove down the beach to the sheltered meadow beside the river. The low hills sheltered our campfire site and its abandoned apple trees.

We rigged our tackle carefully. Charles and Bébé had talked so much about the huge fish in the Boca Chimehuin that I carefully checked my gear. The rod was a powerful 9½-

foot young parabolic, and I seated the big Hardy reel carefully. Running the fly-line between two cypresses, I stripped the dacron backing into the grass.

You like it better than nylon? asked Bébé.

Yes, I answered and reeled it back evenly on the spool. *There's so much stretch in nylon lines that it can bind and damage the light alloy in a fine reel spool.*

The leader knot was seated firmly into the finish of the line and I tested it with several hard pulls. The nylon leader tapered to twelve-pound test, and I ran it painstakingly through the guides, pulling the nail-knot through carefully. The leader survived several nasty jerks and pulls, and when it seemed sound I knotted a big nymph to the tippet.

It was like surf-casting in the outlet. The wind howled down the lake and pounded the surf across the lava outcroppings that block the river. The current churned wildly through its deep chute in the lava, eddied in its fierce whirlpool below the rocks, and plunged over a huge slab of lava that lies in the main current tongue. The wind gusted and carried the spray fifty yards below the lake, and near the outlet, waves rolled and broke around my waist.

It seemed like it was raining horizontally under a cloudless sky, and we wore light nylon raingear as protection from the spray. The wind was so fierce we all wore the Basque berets of the sheepherders, since our hats refused to stay in place. Double-hauling to shoot line into the wind, we cast directly across the current to drop our flies quartering downstream. The lines whistled past our heads in the wind, and I was glad for the tempered sun-glasses to protect my eyes.

Charles and Bébé gave me the best place. It is the first churning hole below the ledges, and I waded deep into the river. The fish were holding below the lake.

They're a little like salmon, explained Bébé. *They stop just below the lake, like a salmon stops above the rapids to rest.*

How deep is that chute? I asked.

Maybe three meters, said Bébé.

It seemed best to work our flies deep into the run below the lake, but the current was so fast that casting upstream was necessary. It was difficult to shoot line quartering upstream into the gusting wind, and it gave me trouble.

I'm not getting deep enough! I yelled.

Radziwill hooked a big fish in the tumbling riffle below the ledges, and we stopped fishing to watch. His reel protested with a shrill soprano when the trout bored deep into the main current. Twice the fish cartwheeled high into the sun, tumbling back clumsily into the river.

It's silver! I shouted above the wind.

But it's still a brown! answered Bébé.

The fish was finally beached in the shallows. It was colored like a salmon, except that its configuration spelled trout and there were dark cross-like markings on its sides.

It doesn't look like a brown! I studied the fish carefully. *It looks like a salmon!*

It's like a sea-run brown, laughed Bébé.

From the lake? I asked.

These lakes are volcanic and there are hot springs everywhere, explained Radziwill. *They're rich in crustaceans.*

Shrimps? I said.

Crabs, they answered. *They look like saltwater crabs, but they're about as big as a silver dollar.*

Cangrejos, added Radziwill. *They're out there by the thousands and they grow fish like crazy!*

Bébé lifted and weighed the trout.

Six pounds! we read on the scales. *Cangrejos or crabs or whatever—that's proof enough for me!*

Buena suerte! laughed Radziwill.

I waded back into the surf-like currents at the outlet where the river tumbled over the ledges into the churning rip below the lake. Finally I succeeded in shooting a long cast low into the wind, and the big nymph dropped across the run.

The fly sunk deep with the heavy current, until I tightened and worked it back slowly along the bottom. The line gathered with a patient hand-twist retrieve as it bellied past me, and suddenly the fly stopped deep in the current. It was a steady pull, strong and holding solid under the pressure of the rod, and for several minutes I thought the fly might be fouled on a ledge. Then the fish moved upstream through the heaviest currents, and its angry headshaking and rolling throbbed back into the rod.

Suddenly it jumped. *It's huge!* I yelled.

It looked like ten or twelve pounds. It jumped again and turned back into the swift-running currents downstream, gathering speed rapidly until the line sliced audibly through the water and the reel wailed in the wind. The fish jumped again and again, and the sun flashed on its wild acrobatics.

Brown? I yelled.

It's a rainbow! they laughed.

Finally it surrendered and I forced it from the strongest currents. Its bright sides and gun-colored back were clearly visible in the shallows. There were no spots and no trace of the red-striped flanks and gill covers typical of river rainbows.

Looks like a steelhead! I yelled.

It's been eating cangrejos! answered Radziwill.

The fish jumped wildly again. It showered me with water and my glasses were covered and it jumped twice more. My arms were getting tired. My heart was pounding and the fish was close, and suddenly it rolled clumsily and the fly came sickeningly free.

My God! I yelled.

I plunged into the river. The fish drifted weakly into deeper water and was gone, and I waded unhappily ashore. My hands were shaking and I groaned.

He's got the disease! laughed Radziwill.

Disease? I grinned.

La fiebre de las Bocas, grinned Bébé. *We caught it years ago and it's incurable.*

Boca fever, Radziwill explained.

I've got it! I agreed.

The hook was slightly bent. My hands were still shaking so badly that I was unable to extract another nymph from my fly-box, and my fingers refused to make the knot when I finally worked another fly from its compartment.

Look at him shaking, grinned Radziwill.

Bébé shook his head mockingly. *Boca fever,* he laughed. *Worst case I've ever seen!*

It's a sickness! I smiled.

We took several big trout the next few days, but nothing like that big rainbow. Bébé and Charles both had several five and six pounders, and I took a brace of four-pound rainbows in the outlet. Charles lost a giant fish below the bridge, and in the smooth Rincon Pool below the bluffs, I watched a monster rise and follow my swinging fly and take it hard. The rod wrenched down and straightened, but the fish turned and was gone. The hook had been broken on the rocks, and when I recovered I replaced it angrily.

That fish was over fifteen! said Bébé.

My fault! I growled.

My first pilgrimage to the Boca Chimehuin was almost over, and I had failed to solve its secrets. Bébé and Charles were staying two more weeks; they have fished the river for years and they were sure their big-fish day would come.

It takes patience, said Bébé.

Radziwill poured another round of wine and the inn-keeper served dinner. *Some morning we'll find the volcano wearing its sombrero of ice-clouds,* said Charles, *and the fish will be taking.*

It'll come, said Bébé. *It'll come!*

It was still and cold outside when we finished our coffee. The stars glittered in the darkness. Their unfamiliar constellations were bright, and the Southern Cross hung high above the town. The valley was silent, and we could hear the river in the distance.

It's just not your trip, I thought when I settled deep in my blankets. *You've only got one more day.*

Two hours before daylight, the wind gathered again and stirred across the dark surface of the lake. It riffled the quiet shallows of the Boca Paimun, moving in the rain forests on the high threshold of Chile. The wind rose and touched the snow-fields and forest shoulders of the volcano. It gathered and forced the fjord-like surface of Huechlaufquen into rolling whitecaps that crashed across the lava outcroppings where the river leaves the lake.

Gusts lashed down the gathering currents, rattling stones across the beach and the timber bridge, and rose again in the steep road above the river crossing. There were silver pesos glittering beside the candles in the shrine at the river, and their light guttered out in the eddying wind. The coins had been left by a traveller walking to a lumber camp in Chile, and two young soldiers had left the candles.

Beyond the simple roadside shrine, where the road topped the rise and wound down past the monkeypuzzle trees, the wind scattered volcanic ash along the valley floor until it stirred in the poplar windbreaks above the town. It moved through the cavalry post and the sentries shivered in the darkness. The wind rose all through the night, moaning across the shuttered town and through the trees around the Hosteria Chimehuin. Dust eddied in the marketplace and the hides drying at the *carneceria* pens, and the wind crossed the river into the treeless hills beyond.

We reached the river early. The sheltered meadows were still in shadow, and the sun had still not reached the tumbling outlet below the monkeypuzzle trees.

It looks good, said Bébé.

Carola Anchorena had come with us that last morning and cooked breakfast beside the river. There were eggs and fried potatoes and small rare steaks and coffee, and we sprawled in the grass and ate and talked about fishing.

There were no ice-clouds on the volcano and the morning sun was bright on the Boca. We caught nothing that morning, although we studied the pools from the bluffs of monkey-puzzle trees, and they were filled with big trout that had dropped back from the lake in the night. We ate lunch in the meadows, savoring the lamb *asado* and wine chilled in the riffles, and afterwards we napped in the warm grass.

The shadows were getting long across the river when we wakened, and it was already twilight in the Garganta del Diablo. We had sandwiches and *maté* and walked down along the river into the canyon. Bébé led me along the trail to the huge pool at the mouth of the Garganta, where he took his record trout six years ago.

It was quite a night, he smiled.

Bébé pointed across the river, describing how he took the giant brown that held the world fly-record for several years. His long casts had worked down the pool, dropping the big saltwater bucktail clear across the river. Reaching the deep holding-water near the bottom of the pool, he worked the fly back into the main current. Suddenly there was a sailfish-size boil that showered water high on the downstream wind. The rise was a strong porpoise-roll, and the huge fish settled back and sulked. The rod held in a stubborn circle and Bébé waited.

He's big, he thought.

Bébé had no idea how big the trout really was. It turned and lunged downstream, wrenching the rod down toward the surface. The reel spun wildly and fouled the line, and Bébé stumbled downstream over the rocks. He tried to untangle the line as he scrambled after the fish. Once he fell hard, bruising his ribs and gouging both knees badly. Finally the line came free, and he quickly reeled it smoothly into place. The fish hung stubbornly at midstream.

It was like I was fouled on the rocks, he said.

His spirits sank and his bruises ached. Bébé walked

downstream and pumped hard. Nothing happened and he tried alternating pressure and slack for ten minutes. *Just when I was sure he was gone,* Bébé continued, *the fish moved and stopped again.*

It was not much, but it was the beginning of the end, and Bébé forced the fish slowly back from the main current. When the fish reached the surface, it rolled and bolted downstream again. The reel rattled and whimpered in protest. The huge trout stopped above a monstrous deadfall tangle of logs, fallen from the shoulder of the volcano and wedged into the rocks in high water.

It was already dark, said Bébé.

He kept working, forcing the trout off balance and chipping away at his strength. The moon was high enough in the last hour that its light illuminated the canyon. Finally the fish floundered on the surface, and the moonlight flashed on its belly. Bébé knew he could win when he saw the pale belly and felt the great fish shudder.

It surrendered slowly, giving ground inch by inch. Bébé forced it into the rocky shallows until its dark length lay at his feet. He reached anxiously with the gaff. The trout rolled and tried to reach the current, but Bébé forced it back patiently.

My arms were shaking, he laughed.

He reached out with the gaff and the huge tail fanned weakly. The gaff stuck and held. The fish threshed wildly, showering him with water. It wrenched violently and twisted free. Bébé floundered and almost went down in the river, but the fish was exhausted too. It rolled weakly in the shallows.

And I gaffed it again! grinned Bébé.

His daughters Carolina and Paola had come downstream in the darkness to find him. They saw the fish carried ashore and shouted questions across about its weight.

Fifteen or twenty pounds! he shouted back.

The girls laughed derisively at that estimate. *They thought I was joking,* said Bébé.

His scale stopped at twenty pounds. He hooked it into the gill covers and struggled to raise it in the darkness. The scale hit bottom. *It's over twenty!* he yelled. The girls stopped laughing and ran upstream to meet their father at the bridge. *It went twenty-four at Junin!* he finished.

Radziwill was fishing the huge pool from the other bank and we watched his flawless casting for several minutes. The pool had produced the world fly-record and it seemed a little like a shrine. Finally we walked down into the high-walled canyon of the Garganta del Diablo.

Bébé stopped to fish the first deep pool. I walked farther down the canyon, clambering along the steep trail above the river past the cypresses and monkeypuzzle trees. The river churned far below until the trail dropped back sharply toward the water.

Looks good, I thought.

It was a big pool below a heavy chute of rapids. The Chimehuin danced down a tumbling riffle, turned against a huge outcropping of basalt, and churned like a spillway at flood water through its last hundred yards into the pool. The pool itself stilled the rapids in its depths, swelling smooth and deep for fifty yards, until its currents gathered again above the lava ledges and it tumbled back into another mile of rapids. It was really big-trout water.

The sky was darker now and I had taken a single fish of eighteen inches. It was an average river brown, bright ochre and orange on its flanks and belly, and covered with poppy-colored spots. It held softly in my hands while it recovered, and finally it bolted off into the darkness. It was almost time to climb out of the canyon. Later it would be too dark to see the trail up the rocks.

It's over, I muttered.

There had been no trophies for me at Boca Chimehuin. The week of fishing had passed, and my best fish was still a four-pound rainbow. *But four pounds isn't bad,* I thought wryly, thinking I had become pretty spoiled.

Suddenly there was a great salmon-sized boil behind the swinging bucktail. It engulfed the fly in a wild lunge, and the reel screeched out huge stacatto lengths of line. The fish bored deep into the heavy current at the head of the pool. It was a mistake. I tightened and held a firm circle in the rod, without enough pressure to frighten the fish. It was fighting the currents below the chute, and my pressure was just enough to force it off balance. It struggled to hold its position, and I nagged at its strength with the rod.

The tactics worked and the fish lost the edge of its power in those first fifteen minutes, and when it broached in the smooth twilight of the pool, it was already beaten.

Careful! I thought wildly. *Careful!*

There was a dangerous moment when it drifted back on the currents, threatening to slide into the rapids. It seemed impossible to hold even its weight in the quickening current, unless I tricked the fish into helping. Sometimes a fish will move away from the pressure of your tackle, so I stripped six yards of line off the reel without releasing the line under my fingers. Lowering the rod downstream, I let it all slip suddenly into the current until the line bellied down below the trout. It throbbed in the swift shallows at the lip of the pool and its pressure from below alarmed the fish. It moved quickly upstream and sulked into deeper water.

The shallows were still and the bottom was good. The fish rolled weakly now, and I forced it close until it sensed me in the darkness, and bolted across the pool when I tried to pick it up across the shoulders. The run was half-hearted and I snubbed it short. It came back stubbornly and floundered until I seated my fingers around its head, pressing the gill covers, and carried it ashore. It was a powerful rainbow of fourteen pounds, and in the darkness it seemed huge.

It was difficult climbing out of the canyon, wrestling the

big fish up the steep, rocky path in the dark. Finally I reached the top and crossed the brushy plateau until I touched the road. The constellations were very bright, and I stood a moment in the road looking at the Southern Cross.

The mountains were purple against a cloudless twilight and the vast surface of the lake was still. It was quiet and I could hear the river tumbling below in the Garganta del Diablo. Bébé and Carola and Charles had already reached the trucks, and I could see their cookfire in the meadow below the Boca. My body ached and the tail of the great fish was dragging in the dust.

The wind stirred and moved in the monkeypuzzle trees, riffling the still surface of the lake. There was an Araucan woman resting with her children beside the shrine, and their candles flickered in the darkness.

Homage to Henryville

THE muses of remembrance and history are
fickle at best, and the muse of angling tradition is no exception. American fishing tradition has made the Beaverkill and
her Catskill sisters the cradle of fly-fishing innovation and the
fountainhead of American fly-fishing literature. But in recent
years, considerable evidence has emerged that the lesser-
known Brodheads in the Poconos of Pennsylvania is probably
the true wellspring of American trout-fishing tradition.

There is also considerable evidence that Henryville House
on its laurel-sheltered upper reaches is the oldest trout-fishing
hotel in America, and its rambling clapboard structure sheltered every major American angler from its establishment in
1835 until the Great Depression of the nineteen thirties.

The Brodheads tradition is old and rich. Its watershed

229

was already famous for trout when Indians camped on its banks to fish and hunt through the pleasant Pocono summers. The Indians never killed more fish than they could eat or cure for the winter or plant with their corn, and trout were still plentiful in the Colonial period. Apprentice indentures throughout the Poconos stipulated the maximum number of brook-trout dinners that frontier laborers would eat, and both Indians and trout were still numerous when the Brodheads was called the Analomink. That poetic Indian name was soon forgotten after the Indian lands were settled.

Captain Daniel Brodhead negotiated for Pennsylvania lands in 1734, dealing with the sons of William Penn. Brodhead emigrated to the Analomink country in 1737, soon after the infamous Walking Purchase had secured the watershed from the Indians. His wagons passed through the primeval forests that cloaked New Jersey and the Delaware Water Gap. Brodhead carved fifteen hundred acres from the wilderness and sowed his crops and prospered. His original log cabins were replaced with a beautiful fieldstone manor house. The Analomink flowed through Brodhead Manor and emptied into the Delaware, and it was not long before its older Indian name had passed from the speech of its settlers. The little river that empties into the Delaware above the Water Gap had become known as Brodhead's Creek.

The Indians were hostile in those years. Old hatreds still smouldered after the Walking Purchase, which defrauded the Delaware and Minisink tribes of some twelve hundred square miles that included the Analomink and Brodhead Manor. That festering hatred travelled west with the displaced Indians, and erupted later in the Indian wars of 1755.

Painted war-parties ravaged isolated farmsteads and settlements above the Kittatinny mountains, and settled the Walking Purchase score in a series of massacres that drove the settlers south in terror. Brodhead and his five sons refused to join these refugees, barricading themselves into the fort-like manor house, and successfully defended their families and neighbors. Soldiering was an old tradition with them, and went back to an earlier Brodhead who served as an officer with the British grenadiers that took New Amsterdam from the Dutch in 1664. The five Brodhead sons, tempered in these frontier Indian wars and skirmishes, later served as officers under Washington.

There was little fly-fishing in this period, and the Pocono angler commonly included his Lancaster long-rifle in his fishing tackle. Although there were fly-fishermen in the colonies in these early years—mostly British officers and officials—trout fishing was a matter of food rather than sport. The little Brodheads and its sister rivers did not really become angling meccas until a century after the Walking Purchase.

The genesis of angling tradition on the Brodheads is found in the little Halfway House, which Arthur Henry built on the freight trace between Easton and Scranton in 1836. His primitive log-framed inn prospered with a clientele of mule-skinners and occasional sportsmen, and was expanded twelve years later into Henryville House. George Washington Bethune served as editor for the first American edition of *The Compleat Angler* in 1847, and his appendix included fly-pattern and tackle recommendations for the Brodheads and its sister rivers. Bethune undoubtedly visited the Halfway House in his pilgrimages, and was probably the first angling writer who paid his homage to Henryville.

The first fly-fishing notable to appear was Joseph Jefferson, celebrated both as an actor and a later angling companion of Grover Cleveland on many trout streams and salmon rivers. Jefferson boarded with his family at Henryville House through the summer of 1848, and tells us in his later autobiography about fishing on the Brodheads, and how the little river tumbled through mountain meadows and a forest cathedral-dark with towering pines and hemlocks.

Frank Forester omitted specific mention of the river in his *Fish and Fishing* of 1849, the first American angling book, but like Bethune he recommends the wonderful brook-trout fishing in the Brodheads region, and was probably the second angling writer to explore the river and its tributaries. The third was Robert Barnwell Roosevelt, and the Brodheads was already well-known in American angling circles when his famous *Game Fish of the North* called it a great trout stream in 1862. The freight wagons and canalboats were waning, and as the railroad pushed through the Brodheads valley toward the developing coal fields, the Poconos experienced the beginnings of a fly-fishing invasion.

Thaddeus Norris is perhaps the most famous of these early Brodheads regulars. His signature is found in the old registers of Henryville House as early as 1851, and he wrote of the Brodheads in considerable detail in his *American Angler's Book*, which appeared in 1864 and firmly established him as the father of American fly-fishing literature. James Henry was then the proprietor of Henryville House, and his son Luther often accompanied Norris on the river. The prose of the legendary Norris has a curious cadence in our ears, patterned on the fishing dialogues fashionable after Walton, and in one passage he exclaims to his young disciple Luther Henry:

> What pretty bright trout there are in this bold rock creek! It would be called a river in England, and so it is!

The hallowed dry-fly method first emerged in England in 1851 with the *Vade-Mecum of Fly-Fishing for Trout*, which codified tactics worked out by G.P.R. Pulman on the Barle and the Axe in Devonshire. Norris also experimented with a dry-fly method in those same years, and his exploratory tactics— described in detail in his *American Angler's Book* fourteen years later—used two flies that settled softly on the current and floated and were taken by the trout before they sank. It seems unlikely that his dry flies were more than well-dubbed heavily-hackled wet flies, but however crude, such primitive dry-fly methods were practiced on the Brodheads almost twenty-five years before the innovations of Theodore Gordon and the Golden Age of the Catskills.

Norris also played a principal role in the evolution of the modern split-cane rod. His companion astream on the Brodheads was often Samuel Phillippe, the gunsmith and violinmaker from Easton who invented modern bamboo rod construction. Although British rodmakers had long experimented with various bamboo systems in their rod-tips, as Edward Fitzgibbon wrote in the *Handbook of Angling* compiled in 1847, their most successful systems employed three-strip construction with the power fibers of the cane inside the finished sections. Phillippe worked with power fibers outside his finished sections in the present manner, having independently hit upon this revolutionary theory with a rod builder at work in England. However, the skilled hands and inventive mind of Phillippe must be credited with devising the modern four- and six-strip cane construction. Phillippe passed his techniques on to Norris, who became one of the great rod builders of the nineteenth century, and their buckboard expeditions along the Brodheads played a considerable role in the refinement of their revolutionary fly-rod designs.

Norris and Phillippe were joined in those halcyon days by other American anglers of considerable fame. Perhaps the best-known was Chancellor Levison, whose first visit to Henryville is recorded in the register more than ten years before the Civil War. Levison was later a founding member of two organizations that have Olympian stature in American trout-fishing history: the Brooklyn Flyfishers' Club and the Anglers' Club of New York.

The Civil War limited his fishing trips to Long Island waters, but Appomattox saw his return with two equally famous cronies—Charles Bryan and Henry Wells. Levison later became a well-known tournament caster who drew sizeable crowds demonstrating his prowess at Prospect Park in Brooklyn and Haarlem Mere in Central Park. He also served as the impeccable bowler-hatted fisherman for the casting plates in *Fly Rods and Fly Tackle,* written by Henry Wells several years later in 1885.

Bryan was another familiar Brodheads pilgrim in later years, with an attendance record of weeks and weekends through the eighteen seventies that remains enviable in terms of modern transportation. These three anglers are remembered on the Brodheads for their impressive catches of brook trout after the Civil War.

Levison and Bryan first joined two other historic founders of the Anglers' Club of New York on the opening weekend of 1885, and their names can still be found in the faded pages of the Henryville register: Edward Baldwin, Chancellor Levison, Edward Rice and Charles Bryan. The following year they were joined on that April weekend by two British guests, and in 1887 their arrival was cheered with six inches of fresh snow. Bryan and Rice stayed while their less hardy companions returned to New York. Their comments in the register record a river discolored with snow-melt, and include a candid confession that their catch of forty trout was taken on worms.

These men were soon joined by another early member of the Anglers' Club, the late Henry Ingraham, who first visited the Henryville water in 1887. Ingraham later wrote his classic *American Trout Streams,* a collector's item that now brings a hundred dollars in the sporting-book market. His angling poem *On the Heller Branch* was written during a December grouse-hunt in 1888, and its happy verses appear in his elegant nineteenth-century hand across two full pages of the Henryville register. Its mood captures an idyllic morning astream with the full-blown romanticism of the nineteenth century, and concludes with these lines about another kind of romance:

> *Then when grows the sun more fervent,*
> *And the wary trout, observant,*
> *Says at last, "Your humble servant,*
> *Now we see your treacherous hook!"*

Maud, as if by hazard wholly,
Saunters down the pathway slowly,
There to dangle
While I angle
With her book.
Then, somehow, the rod reposes,
And the book no page discloses,
But I read the growing roses
That unfold upon her cheek;
And her small hand, soft and tender,
Rests in mine. Ah! What can send her
Thus to dangle
While I angle?
Cupid, speak!

The setting for his idyllic verses was the Heller Branch, the small brook-trout feeder also mentioned in the Henryville register as the source of a twenty-fish basket of trout taken by the redoubtable Chancellor Levison in those years.

Another regular on the Brodheads before 1890 was the venerable John Wise, long considered the Dean of Pennsylvania trout fishermen. His three-fold renown lies in the disparate worlds of Pennsylvania commerce, politics and trout-fishing. Wise is an engineer whose canny executive skills forged the extensive holdings of the Pennsylvania Power and Light Company. His political conservatism worked in chess-like opposition against another Pennsylvania figure of myth-hero stature, the courtly and courageous Gifford Pinchot, the progressive governor of Pennsylvania who served as a trusted advisor to Theodore Roosevelt. Wise learned fly-fishing from his father and his two fishing cronies—George Reeder and Morris Carpenter—who are still considered the first fly-fishermen to explore the Brodheads.

Wise caught his first trout on the Henryville water in 1887, using flies tied by his mentors and leaders made of hairs lovingly gathered from the horse that carried them on the final leg of their eighteen-hour trek from Philadelphia. Wise acquired his extensive trout stream holdings in the Poconos during the First World War, including much of the Tunkhanna and Tobyhanna, and his twenty-odd miles of water have spawned a half-grudging half-admiring limerick among old-time Pocono fishermen:

> *Of all the guys*
> *That fish with flies,*
> *Old Johnnie Wise take the prize;*
> *And we'll post our bets at ten to seven:*
> *He'll buy a trout stream*
> *Up in heaven.*

Wise still fishes after more than seventy-five years on the Brodheads and its sister rivers, and is usually found studying the current for rising fish each opening day morning from the simple bench above his Sawmill Pool on the Tunkhanna.

William Cowper Prime was another multi-talented figure who fished the Brodheads in those same years. His worlds included an extensive legal practice in Manhattan, another career teaching art history at Princeton, and a third career as the author of popular angling books like *I Go A-Fishing*, which first appeared in 1873. Prime was the bellwether for a considerable parade of well-known Princeton fly-fishermen whose ranks include men like Henry Van Dyke, Edward Ringwood Hewitt, Otto von Kienbush, Eugene Connett, Russell MacGregor, Philip Nash and Dana Lamb. Books like his *I Go A-Fishing* were perhaps the best-known American angling works of the period, and provided fireside reading for an entire generation of gentleman anglers.

Other inns and boarding houses appeared and also prospered in the closing years of the nineteenth century. Other anglers made regular pilgrimages to the Brodheads from Philadelphia and New York during an epoch of trout-water greatness. The emerging shrines of those storied years—the ledge pools on the water of the Haase farm, the productive dry-fly flats on the LaBar stretch, the austere little hotel operated by

Analomink Charlie Rethoret on the lower river, the little Spruce Cabin Inn, and the Lighthouse Tavern—have all passed into literature and legend. These places from the old days on the river have fallen victim to fires and floods, or have evolved into private fishing clubs. Henryville House alone has survived as a living symbol of those earlier years, a fishing inn as old as American fly-fishing, although its historic river mileage has finally become club water too.

James Henry died after the close of the trout season in 1888, and the great brook-trout years on the Brodheads died with him. The Henryville register is filled with yellowed records of phenomenal catches in the twenty years after the Civil War, but then the little river declined. The impressive forty-fish baskets of trout, and the almost carnal lumbering that ravaged the conifers for railroad structures and mine timbers—and left great hemlocks rotting in the woods, their acid-rich bark stripped off for the tanneries—has taken their toll. Lumbering and clearing farms had changed the watershed. Its currents had become too warm for its native trout, and the last big stream-spawned brookie recorded in the fishing log at Henryville was a two-pounder taken early in the spring of 1893.

Fly-fishing celebrities began arriving to sample the fishing with these well-known anglers. Henryville House was visited by John L. Sullivan and the storied Lily Langtry and Jake Kilrain, adding the brash glamour of the prizefight world and the music hall. Grover Cleveland and Benjamin Harrison were registered simultaneously for an enigmatic week of fishing before their election campaign in 1880. Fishing and fishing writers were still the nucleus of Brodheads life in spite of such glamorous outsiders, and the Henryville register of that period also includes these light-hearted lines from Henry Van Dyke:

> Over the hill to Henryville
> 'Tis oft' the fisherman's cry,
> For I'll catch a fourteen-incher
> With an artificial fly!

The celebrated Henry Van Dyke achieved equal fame as a professor of literature and religion at Princeton, and as a trout-fishing writer of eloquence and skill. He became a familiar figure along the Brodheads in the eighteen nineties. His angling classics like *Little Rivers* and *Fisherman's Luck* tell us that he often fished the Swiftwater, tributary to the Brodheads above Henryville. Van Dyke writes of his encounter there with Joseph Jefferson, when the old thespian had made a sentimental fishing pilgrimage back to Henryville, where he had spent the idyllic summer fishing with his family a half century before; but let these lines from *Fisherman's Luck* describe that meeting astream:

> One May evening a couple of years since, I was angling in the Swiftwater, and came upon Joseph Jefferson stretched out on a large rock in mid-stream, and casting his fly down a long pool. He had passed the three-score years and ten. But he was as eager and happy as a boy in his fishing.
>
> "You here," I cried. "What good fortune brought you to these waters?"
>
> "Ah," he answered, "I fished this brook forty-five years ago. It was in the Paradise Valley that I first thought of Rip Van Winkle. I wanted to come back again for the sake of old times."

Paradise Valley is a local name for the Henryville Branch of the Brodheads. Local legend tells us that the name originated with General Sheridan, who spent a quiet recuperative summer fishing at Henryville after his Civil War campaigns. Rip Van Winkle was the role that made Jefferson famous, and led to his fishing comradeship with Grover Cleveland.

The opening weekend in 1895 marked an historic event in the tradition of American trout-fishing. The time-stained pages of the Henryville register reveal in intricate nineteenth-century penmanship that fifteen well-known anglers had formed the Flyfishers' Club of Brooklyn. That circle of fishing greats has been immortalized in *Fishless Days*, an American collector's item from the equally famous Sparse Grey Hackle.

These founders of the Brooklyn Flyfishers' were a wealthy group of brewers and businessmen, and included Ernest Palmer, Abraham Snedecor, R. J. Sayre, James Rice, Lodie Smith, C. B. Boynton, Chancellor Levison, H. B. Marshall, Charles Bryan, R. M. Coleman, J. L. Snedecor, F. S. Howard, Ralph Burnett, J. E. Bullwinkle and C. H. Fitzgerald. Their annual ritual of the membership scroll was repeated each season in the Henryville register until 1897, when James Walker and William Oxford were added. Charles Bryan was abroad in England that April. The Brooklyn Flyfishers' registered him *in absentia* and fondly wished him good hatches on the hallowed Itchen and Test.

The circle of Brooklyn regulars left Henryville House after that season of 1897, and several members observed with sadness in the fishing log that its storied brook-trout fishing seemed finished. Their clan emigrated north to the Hardenburgh farm on the Beaverkill, and established themselves in a log-framed fishing house on a sunny slope above the river. These earlier Brodheads fishermen played a major role in the growing reputation of the Beaverkill and the other Catskill rivers, and their departure from the Brodheads marked the end of another era.

History tells us they left too soon. Records that survive for the Commonwealth of Pennsylvania in those years reveal that the European brown trout was introduced in 1889. Specific records of such stocking on individual rivers have not survived, but the fishing log at Henryville House records the capture of seven strange-looking trout under the cribbing of the Dam Pool the following summer. These unfamiliar trout averaged fifteen inches, much bigger than the native fish, and the faded notation in the fishing log described them as dark and curiously colored.

Brodheads fishermen did not realize that the brown trout planted that prior year had survived and multiplied under the conditions that were slowly eradicating their native species, and this seven-fish basket of trout signalled the Renaissance that would rescue a famous river in decline.

The fishing log that covers those first brown-trout years was started just after the Civil War, and in spite of thoughtless vandals who ripped and sliced several famous signatures from its pages, there remains a wealth of historic names and records. Henryville regulars took ten of the European trout better than twenty inches before 1900. Sixteen bigger browns were registered in the decade that followed, including three brutes better than six pounds. The record Henryville trout on flies is a twenty-seven inch brown caught in 1901. Three twenty-two-inch browns are tied for the dry-fly record, and a thirty-inch ten-pound monster was captured with worms.

Several of these trophies were laid diagonally across the open Henryville register and their outlines were traced for posterity. These tracings are authentic, since the fish-slime that penetrated the pages had discolored over the intervening fifty years, and trout scales have adhered to the silhouettes or scattered through the bindings.

The immigrant European trout proved much harder to catch than the native species they displaced, and their challenge soon evolved anglers of greatness. Those skilled anglers who banded together at Henryville to form the Brooklyn Fly-fishers' later formed the founding nucleus of the Anglers' Club of New York. These patron saints of American angling and fly-fishing literature are registered in the guest books and fishing logs of inns and boarding houses and fishing clubs the full length of the little Brodheads. Their roster includes figures like Albert Rouselle, John La Farge, Henry Ingraham, Alden Weir, Chancellor Levison, Charles Bryan, and the ubiquitous Smith brothers—famous for angling rather than cough-drops —James, Milton and Lodie.

Such pioneers were soon followed by others like John Taintor Foote, Jason Lamison, Edward Ringwood Hewitt, George La Branche, Henry Van Dyke, Edward Rice, Perry Frazer, Edward Cave, Robert Lawrence, Reuben Held, Har-

George La Branche

old de Rasloff, Edward Boies and Charles Stepath. Nine of these regulars were fishing writers of importance, two served as editors on the staff of *Field & Stream*, six were later presidents of the Anglers' Club of New York, and four wrote angling works that have achieved major importance in American fly-fishing literature.

John Taintor Foote authored many books and essays and stories on shooting and trout fishing, and his work is a milestone in the literature of American field sports. Perhaps his masterpiece is *Wedding Gift*, written some years after Foote had passed a similar honeymoon fishing at Henryville House. The later *Pocono Shot* was written there in another summer devoted both to the typewriter and the stream. Foote is well remembered on the Brodheads. The sitting room at Henryville House embraces the original log-cabin inn built in 1836, and was once partitioned off for Foote to serve as his studio.

Foote took his breakfast punctually each morning at six, and then spent the next four hours in the studio, drinking coffee and writing. The children of the Henry family policed the children of the other guests to prevent porch games outside the sitting room when the writer was at his work. Foote finished punctually at ten, just in time for the late-morning rise of fish, and disappeared down the Brodheads with a lunch of cold chicken and thick-sliced bread still warm from the Henryville ovens.

Edward Ringwood Hewitt was a lovable and irascible character who needs no introduction to the fly-fishing fraternity. Hewitt was long considered the Dean Emeritus of American anglers, and well-known Hewitt books like *Telling on the Trout* and the later *Secrets of the Salmon*, recently incorporated into the autobiographical *A Trout and Salmon Fisherman for Seventy-five Years*, are the high points of a fishing career that contributed ten books to the literature of fly-fishing. This master of the American dry-fly technique first used English floating flies at Henryville in 1905, according to his own writings, after his usual methods had failed during a remarkable rise of trout. Hewitt returned the following week, armed with a new Leonard rod and proper flies and the legendary Hewitt determination—and soon captured his first dry-fly trout from the Buttonwood Pool.

Hewitt fished and quarreled and competed with an angling colleague of equal stature in those Olympian summers on the Henryville water. George La Branche was another giant of angling literature whose early reputation had its beginnings along the Brodheads. Thaddeus Norris and the better-known Theodore Gordon—whose fame in angling circles is more closely linked to the Catskill rivers, although he also fished the Brodheads in his native Pennsylvania—are considered the fathers of the American fly-fishing, but it was George La Branche who really taught Americans to fish with dry flies on the swift, boulder-broken current of our rivers.

His little volume titled *The Dry Fly and Fast Water* outlined the emerging American method, and has a deserved reputation for both its technical innovations and the qualities of its writing. That slim little masterpiece was published in 1914, when La Branche was thirty-nine and at the height of his powers, and it remains in print fifty years later. Its passages are rich with references to his experiences along the Brodheads. La Branche worked his dry-fly sorcery from Henryville House and the Spruce Cabin Inn, and once owned a reach of water now controlled by the Parkside Club of Philadelphia. The sparkling riffles and swift runs of these beats played a major role in the evolution of his theories. George La Branche loved the little Brodheads, and its quicksilver rhythms have passed into his prose.

The river became a fishing shrine after 1900, and other Brodheads regulars continued their pilgrimages. Forty years after his Henryville fishing poem, Henry Ingraham wrote *American Trout Streams* and was elevated to the president's chair of the Anglers' Club of New York. Edward Cave and Perry Frazer long served with *Field & Stream*, where the first meetings of the Anglers' Club were held. Frazer was one of the great tournament casters in those years, and contributed books like *Amateur Rodmaking*, which remained a standard work for sixty-odd years. Edward Rice and Reuben Held collaborated on the *Angler's and Sportsman's Guide*, which appeared in 1912. Alden Weir was an almost-forgotten painter who was a companion of Whistler, Ryder, Sargent and Winslow Homer, who was also a diligent and skilled trout fisherman. Weir was the first American painter to embrace Impressionism, and had a principal role both in the Golden Age of American trout fishing and the Gilded Age of American painting.

Still others made pilgrimages to the Brodheads shrine. The last season before his death—after ninety-odd years as a market hunter and poacher of fearsome skills—the legendary Henryville Charlie Ross sprawled with me in the shade below the Upper Twin Pool and talked about the past. His memories of the river were rich and varied. Calvin Coolidge failed with flies he borrowed from an old poacher, but finally caught two Henryville trout on nightcrawlers. Theodore Roosevelt and Gifford Pinchot had also visited Henryville House, and had excellent luck with flies and their elegant split-cane rods.

Roosevelt and Pinchot could fish! Henryville Charlie had austere standards for politicians. *Coolidge couldn't!*

The old riverkeeper also remembered Buffalo Bill and Annie Oakley, who came to Henryville House both to fish and demonstrate their marksmanship on the rolling lawns. Henryville Charlie had helped transfer their baggage from the train depot and guided them on the river. He remembered the mountainous pile of baggage he finally assembled on the Henryville porch. There were leg-of-mutton gun cases and leather rod-luggage and boxes of targets and special ammunition in addition to steamer trunks and suitcases, and a small crowd gathered in awe.

Annie Oakley warn't no beauty, the old poacher winked and his time-faded eyes twinkled with humor, *but she sure had hell's own pile of trunks for a plain woman!*

Theodore Roosevelt
and Gifford Pinchot

Buffalo Bill is still remembered at Henryville for his buckskin suits and elegantly-trimmed mustache and beard. Annie Oakley is remembered for her bright blue eyes and soft chamois-skin skirts and gentle disposition. The gallery of guests and local people was amazed with her shooting, especially the market-hunter friends of Henryville Charlie. Their attitude was one of grudging admiration, with some unchivalrous muttering about the difference between breaking thrown targets over an open meadow and shooting ruffed grouse in a hemlock thicket.

Henryville Charlie finished his long career policing the Henryville water against poachers, an irony that would have been fully understood only by his long-dead cronies, since the owners of Henryville House decided that the most accomplished poacher in the entire valley would be the best protection against midnight raids on their trout. Henryville Charlie was still able to fish the river in his ninetieth year, and could mend a skilled wet-fly swing and work a deceitful poacher's retrieve almost to his death.

Henryville had become justly famous and its heritage of famous guests continued to grow. The patriarchal Chancellor Levison, impeccable in his shooting tweeds and regimental tie, rose in those years at a meeting of the Anglers' Club of New York to move that the membership petition the Delaware, Lackawanna and Western about better rail service to Henryville. Presidents and politicians had mingled with great anglers and prizefighters and theatrical celebrities in the fishing inns along the river, but with the guns of the gentle Annie Oakley—and the ominous cannon that rumbled across Europe in the summer of 1914—an epoch of tranquil order ended for both the Brodheads and the world.

Chancellor Levison was the first regular who returned to the river after the Great War, as he had after the Civil War, and the old master is still remembered from those years—not for the flawless casting and impressive catches of his youthful years, but for the seven blankets and hot-water bottle he required for his room. The old angler was accompanied in those years by his nephew-in-waiting, the infamous fortune-hunting Victor Grimwood, who shares the dry-fly record on the Brodheads with a four-pound brown from the Barn Pool below the Haase farm.

Grimwood was a charming anti-hero. He arranged for the seven blankets, hot-water bottles, thick slices of lightly-browned toast, special British marmalade, and six-egg omelets specified by his venerable uncle. Grimwood fished beautifully with the most expensive tackle, and like his uncle in earlier years, wore his Burberry shooting-coat and regimental mustache with considerable *elan*. His bearing was always ramrod straight, and there are still Henryville ladies who remember his flashing eyes and the dance-floor grace that never faltered, even after long hours astream. These romantic ladies never dreamed that Grimwood would later defraud both friends and relatives of thousands, in a scandal that rocked society in both Philadelphia and New York, and that after an infamous trial his dance-floor manners would be wasted in prison.

There was another society scandal in those years, when Broadway glamour and glittering wealth were meshed in the streamside *liaisons dangereuses* of Louise Groody and Jack Harriman. The famous musical-comedy star dominated shows like *No, No, Nanette!* and *Hit the Deck!* Henryville oldtimers remember both her skilled casting, and her impromptu performances for other guests, especially the lilting *Tea for Two* that she had first performed and taken as her trademark. The oldtimers also remember the sleek cream-lacquered Stutz she gave Harriman after a particularly successful Broadway season, and the Henryville ladies still remember the quarrels that ended the affair. The final argument erupted in the tackle-hung Henryville dining room and ended in the New York gossip columns. The regulars remember the beautiful actress and the flawless working of her amber English line in the sun above the Ledge Pool, and the Henryville ladies smile sadly as their thoughts retrace the fickle past.

Brown-trout fishing on the Brodheads was still good in the twenties and thirties, and there were new fishing writers of considerable reputation as well as angling *innamorata* working its storied pools and flats. Eugene Connett fished the Brodheads regularly in those years, and authored such sporting classics as his *Magic Hours* and *Random Casts* and the lovely *Any Luck?* Connett immortalized the difficult stillwater pools on the Brodheads with his essay *In the Tail of the Flat*— included in several angling anthologies and rumored to describe Mary's Flat, a famous reach of water on the Parkside Club holdings. Connett was the energetic president of the New York Anglers' Club who was instrumental in leasing its first Hanover Street quarters in 1920, near the old Hotel Lucerne. Brodheads acolytes gravitated toward three fishing shrines on the river—the group that fished the lower river from the clapboard Hotel Rapids at Analomink, the group that fished Brodheads Forest and Stream and the Parkside water and the Haase farm, and the Henryville regulars.

The anglers who fished from Analomink before the hotel burned are a famous group that includes names like James Leisenring, John Alden Knight, Ed Zern, Preston Jennings, Vernon Hidy, Chip Stauffer, Dick Clark, Sibley Smith, William Thompson, Charles Wetzel and Don Brooks. Leisenring has achieved legendary stature since the publication of his little *The Art of Tying the Wet Fly* in 1941, and the series of articles about his flies and techniques that appeared a few years after his death in *Sports Illustrated*. Big Jim was the solitary bachelor-master of the Brodheads until his death, and was the acknowledged leader of the Twelve Apostles, a circle of dedicated Brodheads fishermen whose ranks included expert fly-dressers like Dick Clark and Chip Stauffer.

John Alden Knight needs no introduction to American trout fishermen. His distinguished career embraced countless articles and twelve-odd books that range from the *Field Book*

James Leisenring

of Fresh Water Angling through the *Modern Angler* to the recent *Complete Book of Fly Casting*, done in collaboration with his son shortly before his death.

The first major work on American trout-stream entomology was the beautiful *Book of Trout Flies* written by Preston Jennings in 1935. Its pages are filled with references to both the Brodheads and the Hotel Rapids, and its first edition has become a collector's item worth almost a hundred dollars. The peripatetic and puckish Ed Zern, whose humorous works range from *To Hell with Fishing* to the hilarious *How to Tell Fish from Fishermen*, was another Analomink regular in those days before the little hotel was destroyed. Sibley Smith was a painter who followed in the tradition of Alden Weir in making regular pilgrimages to the Brodheads valley. Charles Wetzel is now the venerable Dean of the Weikert water on Penns Creek in central Pennsylvania, but in the past he was regular on the Brodheads. Wetzel is the author of such angling books as *Practical Fly Fishing* and *Trout Flies*, works that continued the entomological beginnings found in the writings of Preston Jennings.

The gentle and venerable Ray Bergman was the best-known fishing writer in America, after a writing career that produced books like *Just Fishing* and the best-selling *Trout*, which counselled an entire generation of fishermen in tackle and tactics. These men and many others came to the Hotel Rapids, and the passages of American angling literature contain many references to Charlie Rethoret and the wonderful French cuisine he prepared at all hours for hungry fishermen, and about a legendary trout named Herman that inhabited the Railroad Pool across from the hotel. Herman was the subject of an epic poem of fishing doggerel called *Herman to His Grandchildren*. Its seemingly endless fifty-four stanzas mention many of the Analomink regulars.

The regulars who fished above Analomink on the club waters at Brodheads Forest and Stream, Parkside and the

Haase farm are equally distinguished, and include fly-fishermen like the late Manning Barr, Walter Steel, Robert Kahn, Scotty Scott, Curtin Windsor, Philip Nash, Page Brown, Allen Du Bois, Guy Jenkins, Dana Lamb, and Sparse Grey Hackle. Their founding members included expert anglers like Henry Jenkins, who fished with Theodore Gordon and all of the other great fly-fishermen of the Catskill School, and the late Richard Hunt, whose writings include the little masterpiece *Salmon in Low Water*. Fire also destroyed the Spruce Cabin Inn, and other than Henryville House, only the Brodheads Forest and Stream and Haase farm survive from the old days on the upper Brodheads. They have evolved into small private fishing clubs with some of the best water in the east.

During the week, when most of their regulars are occupied with their corporations and brokerage houses and law practices in Philadelphia and New York, the old fishing quarters of the farms fall silent. April rain trickles softly on the windows, and the afternoon duns are coming off the riffles— inside there is still an aura of the Brodheads past in the sitting room memorabilia and the photographs of the famous that watch silently from the walls.

The celebrated Richard Hunt was often accompanied on the Haase beats by anglers like Sparse Grey Hackle and General Theodore Roosevelt and the scholarly Dana Lamb, whose writings include the recent collections of essays and stories entitled *On Trout Streams and Salmon Rivers* and *Bright Salmon and Brown Trout*. Roosevelt and Hunt also fished the Henryville water, and with Robert Barnwell Roosevelt and his father, Hunt became the third member of his distinguished family to fish its storied runs and pools. Richard Hunt is perhaps best known for his writings on salmon fishing, but he also wrote the following lines about his beloved Brodheads in 1934:

> The lovely stream flows through its friendly valley, and pleasant days await me there. I can feel at one with those who have fished and loved it. I

can foregather again with those whose companionship means much to me. I can tell tales of the big ones which got away or would not rise in the biggest of little rivers.

Russell Henry succeeded his father Eugene as the manager of Henryville House in the thirties, and became the fifth generation of his family to shelter fly-fishermen on the Brodheads. Their rambling white-clapboard hotel had served four fishing presidents and every major fishing writer in America for almost a century. That parade of famous rods that had begun with Thaddeus Norris before the Civil War, and included both Hewitt and La Branche after 1900, began to decline in the middle thirties. The fishing pressure that came with a reputation for greatness eventually caused some regulars to enlarge the private clubs which controlled the better beats above the Junction Pool. The biggest of little rivers was no longer public water.

Rationed gasoline and tires during the Second World War gave its public reaches some much-needed respite. The brown trout began to thrive again, but the headlong release of peacetime and postwar population explosion soon ended their brief period of euphoria. The once great river declined rapidly until after 1950, it offered little more than the popular hoax of put-and-take stocking, and there was little or no decent sport on the public pools. The regulars were in mourning.

Disaster struck in the August hurricane of 1955, and the Brodheads instantly became a maelstrom that tumbled forty feet of dark water toward the Delaware. Bridges were obliterated. Barns and houses were hammered into water-soaked matchwood. Campers were caught and drowned in their bedrolls. Miles of highways were erased and eroded. The Delaware, Lackawanna and Western found much of its roadbed gone, its tracks and ties and rolling stock scrambled into hopeless spaghetti-tangles. The flood churned toward Stroudsburg and the Water Gap in a straight, inexorable line that escaped and ignored the looping tree-lined course of the river. Its force crushed everything in its path. When the flood waters receded, there was a raw linear wound that reached down the valley for miles. Trout were found rotting in the forests and fields, hundreds of feet from the river and as much as fifty feet above normal water. Fly-hatches were almost completely eradicated, and the Brodheads regulars shook their heads in despair.

Some still had hope for their river. The several pools held for guests at Henryville House were restored by the present Henry family, the sixth generation to shelter anglers. Three momentous decisions were then made for the management of their historic water: Henryville House would post its holdings and manage them like a British trout-fishing inn, stocking would be limited to mature brown trout, and the pools would be restricted to fly-fishing. Henryville regulars followed these rules and paid a daily rod-fee, like fly-fishermen have on European rivers for centuries, for the privilege of fishing—in addition to room-and-board costs at the inn.

The restoration under these rules proved remarkable, and although fly-hatches were meagre the following year, the fishing was surprisingly good. The aquatic hatches have slowly come back in recent years until the sport equals those halcyon days of the brown-trout Renaissance on the Brodheads, when a really accomplished fly-fisherman could average twenty good fish in a leisurely day astream. Each new season has brought better fishing than the last, and with the demise of a four-pound trout in 1961, there was real optimism again on the Brodheads.

Henryville House still drowses in the trees, but the freight wagons and canalboats and steam-driven railroad trains are gone. Modern anglers drive into the Poconos from Philadelphia and New York, and there is an occasional Porsche or Bentley or Mercedes-Benz parked beside the unpretentious buildings and above the best pools. During lunch and dinner, these cars are draped with tackle vests and waders and split-cane rods and drying socks.

The modern Henryville fishermen have included men like

George Kattermann, Stinson Scott, Arnold Gingrich, Richard Wolters, John Randolph, Charles Fox, Samuel Slaymaker, Ted Rogowski, Art Smith, Steve Mills, Ray Ovington, and the late Ken Lockwood.

Kattermann was the acknowledged Dean Emeritus of the Henryville water, having fished it with his father more than fifty years ago, and is a fly-fisherman of the La Branche School. His fly-boxes were limited to two patterns—the delicate Henryville Special first dressed by Hiram Brobst, an old-time Pocono fly-maker from Lehighton, and his own high-floating Kattermann. Both are bivisible-like flies that work well during the several *Trichoptera* hatches that emerge on the Brodheads, especially on pocket-water stretches. When the selective browns refuse these flies, this master angler in the fast-water tradition was content to wait until they cooperated again on his terms.

Stinson Scott is another regular whose devotion to Henryville covers many years, having learned his fly-fishing from Chancellor Levison in 1928. Scott can easily be recognized astream in the distance, because he still goes hatless and regularly requires some fierce sunburns through his thinning silver hackles.

Arnold Gringrich is an accomplished angler who doubles as the peripatetic publisher of *Esquire* magazine. His dedicated angling had its beginnings under the enthusiastic tutelage of the late Ernest Hemingway in the early thirties, and Gringrich has become a Henryville regular since 1961. He likes the skater fished on ultra-light tackle, and can be found with his Young Midge—the Guarneri of split-cane fly rods—plying that refined art on difficult flats like the tail shallows of the Ledge Pool and the Pine Tree.

Richard Wolters is perhaps better known for books like *Gun Dog* and his prowess on the skeet field, but his trout-fishing hours are sometimes spent at Henryville. Perhaps the best-known of the regulars in the years since the flood was the late John Randolph, the familiar outdoor columnist for *The*

New York Times. His columns were an admixture of humor working on two levels—the surface that produced chuckles and wry smiles from his newspaper readers, and the undercurrent of inside jokes that produced belly laughs among the *cognoscenti* and cronies he wrote about. One such column filed from Henryville was included in *The World of Wood, Field and Stream*, the posthumous anthology of Randolph work selected by his friend Richard Wolters. Randolph will be missed at the frenetic midweek lunches of the Midtown Turf, Yachting and Polo Association, an intentionally purposeless gathering of New York friends and disciples who write about shooting and fishing, and he will be missed on the Upper Twin beat at Henryville, the beautiful, rock-filled run that was the last trout pool of his life.

Charles Fox is better known as the leader of a circle of light-tackle experts who frequent the famous Letort Spring Run—and for his recent *This Wonderful World of Trout*—but he has often matched wits with the Henryville browns as well. Fox has continued the tradition of John Taintor Foote, since the final draft of his book was written and polished at Henryville House. Art Smith was outdoor writer for *The New York Herald-Tribune*, and joined the regulars several times in recent years. Steve Mills is a relative newcomer on the Henryville water, but as the youngest member of William Mills & Son—the oldest tackle shop in America—his heritage on American trout water is impeccable and dates back to 1822 with the beginnings of his family as Yankee merchants in Manhattan. His grandfather accompanied Edward Ringwood Hewitt to the International Casting Tournament in London, representing America in the competitions of 1904.

Ken Lockwood was another famous trout-fishing writer who often fished the Brodheads both from Henryville and Analomink. His memorial is the Lockwood Gorge fly-fishing water on the Raritan, where a monument is inscribed with the following lines:

When mists and shadows rob pool and run of shape
and substance
When the voice of the wood thrush stills and the
Dog trout shakes his lethargy
We will remember a stalwart, gentle master of the
Angler's art,
Half submerged in the smother,
Unerringly shooting that long line, watchfully
Mending the drift.
Never more will your skilled hand tempt the
Patriarchs of the flood.
Farewell, old timer.

There are still elegiac moods on the Brodheads too. Death has ended the six generations of Henry family tenure, and its famous mileage of water has passed to a private fishing club. The rambling clapboard inn has changed hands for the first time since 1845, although it has been lovingly restored and is still called Henryville House.

The river remains in good hands. The present Henryville flyfishers are a skilled circle of anglers from all walks of life. Its roster includes board chairmen, publishers, manufacturers, surgeons, psychiatrists, lawyers, toolmakers, computer programmers, architects, police officers, building contractors, professors, poets, and the dean of a major university. Their tastes vary widely from Ramblers to a regal Bentley, and from beer to a fine Pouilly-Fuissé chilled in the river.

Its current is the single theme that unifies their diversity, and the members are a skilled group of light-tackle fishermen. Henryville fish are particularly choosy, because their water is managed on a no-kill basis through the first month of the season. Their diet ranges from the typical eastern mayfly hatches to a marked taste for minutae—the tiny little ants and beetles and jassids usually associated with the limestone streams of Pennsylvania.

The fishing mileage assembled by the Henryville flyfishers has been carefully increased and restored. All of the famous fly-hatches have come back fifteen years after the flood. Fast-water mayflies like the March Browns, Gray Foxes and pale Cahills suffered badly when their clinging nymphs were annihilated in the grinding flood. The bigger drakes were eliminated when high water scoured their burrowing nymphs from the silt beds and flushed them downriver, but the flies have slowly restored themselves. The club has added picturesque little Cranberry Run, which still has wild brook trout, and the Paretta water above Henryville to its holdings. Their pools were once part of the mileage fished from Henryville House in the classic years of the nineteenth century. This past season I fished the deep ledge pool above the Paretta meadows and stopped to daydream in the spring sunlight that warmed the ledges above the pool. Its heat felt good, and I was idly sorting flies when I dropped a Wheatley fly-box that rattled and clattered along the ledge. It stopped just above the pool and when I scrambled down to retrieve it, I found the names of Charles Bryan and Lodie Smith carved into the rock. The date carved beside their names was 1896, the last summer those founders of the Brooklyn Flyfishers came to Henryville.

The fly-fishing pageant at Henryville continues with its passing years and changing cast. New pilgrims come to sample the Brodheads shrine, and some of the old faces are missing. New tales and traditions are evolving into new legends, and the old history is retold in the firelight. Evenings find the regulars tired after pleasant hours astream, and no one fishes seriously at night. The practical observer will tell you they are simply tired, and have settled into the pleasant lassitude of *après*-fishing, but practical minds are seldom right.

There are nights in the Poconos when the wind is high and strange, and on such nights—and others when storms moan in the hemlock ridges and rain cries on the windows— the river belongs to those shadow-anglers who have fished and loved it since aboriginal times. The trout-fisherman with a strain of fantasy in his character can imagine them—Thaddeus Norris delivering his Waltonian dialogues to the worshipful

Luther Henry, Theodore Roosevelt exclaiming to the solemn Pinchot that the Brodheads is a bully river, Hewitt and La Branche continuing their rivalry of cantankerous camaraderie, and puckish Henryville Charlie Ross following patiently behind the political entourage, shaking his head in despair as Coolidge makes another clumsy cast.

More than a century after Joseph Jefferson and Thaddeus Norris and Chancellor Levison, the new regulars still gather to fish the Brodheads. The biggest of little rivers remains as powerful as any trout-fishing Mecca, and Richard Hunt was right when he wrote that it has excellent dry-fly hatches much earlier than its better-known Catskill neighbors. Opening weekends might prove almost subarctic and foul, but bitter or balmy, the regulars will make the pilgrimage and offer their homage to Henryville.

Fishing in
the Land of Fire

THE bad weather sometimes arrived suddenly
on the cool *pampero* winds of February. Its cold interrupted
midsummer life in Buenos Aires, emptying the sidewalk cafes
in the fashionable Avenida Corrientes. The weather is a brief
prelude to the storms of April, and there is always more hot
weather in March while the summer dies.

The late summer storms would build each evening.
Thunderheads tower high in the purple twilight and break
over the city long after midnight. It was necessary to close my
hotel windows against the rain. The wind stripped the green
leaves from the giant gum-trees in the Plaza San Martin, scattering them over the wet streets in front of the Crillon, and
below my balcony, sheets of rain moved down the narrow
Avenida Esmeralda and its shuttered *confiterias* and shops.

Buenos Aires is known for its purple twilight. Evening

crowds walked the cool streets, and the wind stirred in the boulevards of jacaranda trees. Traffic swarmed and circled the giant obelisk in the sprawling Plaza Nueve de Julio. The restaurants were crowded, and it was beautiful in the Avenida Santa Fe when I walked to the Quixote.

Laddie Buchanan was waiting. *¡Hola fisherman!* he shook hands vigorously. *Ready for Tierra del Fuego?*

Buchanan is a well-known sportsman in the Argentine. His wing-shooting exploits on the marshes of his family holdings below Buenos Aires are legendary. His knowledge of the rivers of Patagonia is unequalled, and his horsemanship is known on the polo fields of three continents. Laddie has a boundless enthusiasm for shooting and fishing that spills out in stacatto Cagney-like dialogue and gestures.

It was warm and smoky inside the Quixote. The restaurant was crowded because the unseasonable cold had emptied its sidewalk tables. The smells of good cooking filled the room, and we talked about the salmon fishing in the rivers above Bariloche. Our dinner began with *puchero de gallina* and hot sweetbreads, and we finished with rare *bifes*. The wine began with a delicate Santa Silvia and ended with a rich *tinto* from the foothills above Mendoza.

Laddie explained that Colonel William Lanford, an Air Force officer attached to the United States Air Mission in Buenos Aires, was coming with us to Tierra del Fuego. Dinner ended with *flan con crema* and cognac, and we agreed to meet at the airport just after daybreak.

Hasta pronto! we shook hands.

It was difficult to sleep, thinking about the rivers below the Straits of Magellan. Fishing their runs of legendary sea-trout had long been a dream of mine, and thoughts of Tierra del Fuego were in my head when thunder and driving rain awakened me two hours before daylight.

Tierra del Fuego has some of the worst weather and the best trout-fishing in the world. Its barren islands and skerries and fjords lie barely five hundred miles above Antarctica, between the Straits of Magellan and Cape Horn, in a region that has been called the uttermost part of the earth. Colonies of seals and penguins and sea lions thrive on its remote beaches. Dark mists shroud its mountains and rain forests and glaciers, and its treeless plateaus are bleak with incessant winds.

Magellan sailed his fragile *Vittoria* into its waters in 1520, and his log is filled with observations about its barren landscapes and primitive tribes. The coastal Yahgans used fireboxes in their fishing canoes and built bonfires to mark their villages. Magellan and his crew watched their aboriginal fires in the windy darkness, and they named the place Tierra del Fuego—and it must have seemed to them a bleak and forbidding land of fire.

Tierra del Fuego was settled after 1900. Its pioneer sheepmen established vast grassland *estancias* from its wilderness. Some of these settlers were from England and Scotland, and although their new home was not unlike the moors and highlights of their youth, there were no fish in the rivers. They were homesick for the sport of Devonshire and Scotland, and they brought sea-run browns to Tierra del Fuego in 1934. Since those first stockings, its lakes and rivers have evolved some of the best trout-fishing in the world. The spawning runs begin in late February, the wintry month of midsummer in those latitudes, and the fish average six to twelve pounds.

Buenos Aires seemed to anticipate our trip to Tierra del Fuego. Its storms passed just before daylight, leaving the streets cloaked in mist. Traffic moved slowly through the empty streets. Vehicles passed with their parking lights moving in the darkness, flicking their headlights anxiously at the intersections.

The driver arrived and we loaded my gear. We pulled out into the mist, barely missing a truck that loomed suddenly in the darkness. Our taxi careened wildly through the city, plunging through the intersections with bravado, flushing pedestrians with a rapier flick-flick of headlights. When we finally reached the airport safely, I sighed and relaxed, and we wound out through the grounded aircraft until the car circled under the wing of an ancient DC-3.

Buenos dias! yelled Laddie.

We loaded my equipment while the pilot made his ground inspection. There are no weather reports from the coasts of Patagonia, but operations assured us that the weather was usually good below Bahia Blanca. Colonel Lanford arrived and we were ready.

It was getting light. Sunrise transformed the mist into a flamingo-colored fog, and we taxied out through the silent airfield, with parked aircraft looming in the gathering light. Their tails rose like tombstones. The pilot ran the engines when we reached the runway, and we listened to their deep roar after the first shrill starter-whine and the rough coughing when they caught. Everyone aboard knew that once airborne we were committed to the remote airfields farther south, since returning was impossible in the fog.

Engines sound good, yelled Colonel Lanford.

The plane was rolling now. It shuddered and its tail came up and we could see nothing beyond the wings. Wet concrete and spray blurred past, and we climbed slowly through the mist, turning south in a lazy circle.

The weather report was right, and the cloud cover went thin and patchy below Azul. There were ranches and roads below, and the escarpment of the Sierra de la Ventana was visible in the distance. Tidal flats glittered in the sun below Carmen de Patagones, where Darwin began his overland exploration of the Rio Negro country.

Our flight led south across the Golfo San Matias, and we stared at the penguins and sea lions far below on its barren coasts. The high plateau country of the Somuncura rose toward the mountains, and ahead were the oil-camps and derricks of the Pampa del Castillo.

Commodoro Rivadavia is a new town built on the petroleum from those fields, and we let down into its gravel airstrip to refuel. The downwind approach crossed the rocky beaches, and our shadow hopscotched across the high bluffs when the wheels shuddered down and locked. Outside the brown face of the mountain blurred under our starboard engine. The plane trembled and slipped in its thermals, circling back around the pylon-like outcroppings, and the pilot increased power until the mountain dropped behind and the runway was ahead in the gusting crosswinds.

Dust plumed high behind the rolling plane. The tail dropped and we taxied in slowly toward the fuel trucks in front of operations. The pilot wheeled the plane in a tight circle, scattering gravel with his propellor wash. Colonel Lanford was met by the local Air Force commander, and the fuel truck was already in position. We had a quick lunch of wine and *empanadas* and continued south.

Ten thousand feet above the high altiplano the cabin temperature dropped sharply. We broke into our duffel for parkas and coats. Thousands of sheep were grazing on the pale *barrancas* above Bahia San Julian, where the expeditions of Magellan and Vespucci and Drake once wintered a thousand miles south of Buenos Aires.

The barren coastline was notched with the silt-stained mouths of rivers, and we watched the Rio Santa Cruz where Darwin journeyed inland with whaleboats from the *Beagle* in 1834. Silhouetted in the distance were the Andes, which Darwin sighted but never reached. The afternoon sun was bright on Lago Argentino and its sprawling glaciers—Darwin would have discovered them had his boat-crew not seen an Araucan war-party and turned back.

Rio Gallegos was ahead now. The tide was out and fishing vessels leaned in a jackstraw tangle on its rocky beaches. The pilot circled and studied the airfield, and he settled the plane in a low pass fifty feet above the runway. Hundreds of geese rose clumsily into the wind and the pilot pulled up into a tight climbing turn, coming around fast before the geese could settle back on the gravel strip.

The pilots came back grinning and cursing. *Caucenes!* the

copilot shook his head. *There were caucenes all over the runway out there!*

There were no field lights.

What happens when you run out of daylight? somebody asked absently.

You make your Act of Contrition, said the pilot.

The copilot grinned and watched the geese wheel and settle back on the runway. *Make your Act of Contrition,* he laughed. *Then make your landing!*

The apron crew topped off the tanks. Gravel rattled back over the tail surfaces when the pilot revived the engines and taxied out on the runway. Wind gusted across the field and we climbed toward the south again. Our altitude was low and we crossed a series of somber buttes and saline water holes. There were hundreds of sheep, and ahead were vast gravelly shallows and a glittering reach of water. The pilot came back and pointed west.

Estrechos de Magellanes! he shouted.

The seas were a strange glacier-color in the late afternoon light, and we stared like schoolboys at the Straits of Magellan. Chalky currents patterned against the darker seas, and in the distance we could see the narrows, bright and shining in the sun. Beyond the narrows, the treeless Chilean coasts were lost in line squalls.

Tierra del Fuego reached out barren and forbidding under the starboard wing. There were hundreds of sea lions on the beaches, sheltered under the chalky cliffs, and we started our approach into Rio Grande.

Sleet obscured the grasslands that rose westward from the beaches toward the Darwin Range. The airfield was covered with a passing squall and we circled until it moved across the town toward the sea. The pilot made another low pass to clear the geese and went around again, fighting through the crosswind into his landing roll. We stopped and the flight engineer opened the hatch, and we clambered out into a raw fifty-knot

wind. The plane shuddered and groaned. The engineer struggled to chock the wheels, secure the tail-wheel and fussed
with the tie-down equipment. We walked across the gravel
apron toward the headquarters building.

The windsock was sausage-tight in the gale. *They use
rigid windsocks down here,* somebody laughed.

Frozen? Laddie yelled back.

We shivered in the wind. *Welcome to the Land of Fire,*
said the airport duty officer.

Gracias! we shivered and shook hands.

There was a jeep from the oil-company camp waiting. We
had supper in its commissary and went to bed in the company
barracks. Sleep came soon after fifteen hundred miles in the
DC–3 and the wind scattered gravel against the buildings and
equipment in the compound.

The wind rose all through the night, until it howled across
the kelp-stained beaches to the sea, and our heavy military
blankets were welcomed before morning.

The wind was still fierce at breakfast, and we leaned into
its gusts along the boardwalk to the company mess. We finished breakfast and drove into Rio Grande. It looked like
subarctic towns in other countries. The buildings were
wooden and had corrugated roofs, painted bright colors that
seemed strangely out of place in the barren landscape. The
rigid street patterns were unfinished, and their geometry
looked foolish in the utter emptiness of the land.

We completed our purchases at the Almacen trading-post,
and drove out past the *carneceria* huts where thousands of
fresh sheepskins hung drying in the wind. The river bottoms
were filled with geese, and the deeply rutted road climbed
into the low hills toward the Estancia Maria Behety.

The ranch and its outbuildings are a town in themselves.
It has houses and barracks for its gauchos and shearing men
and their families, as well as a general store and infirmary and
cinema. There are also a constabulary and jail, and the entire

complex is grouped near a vast sheep-barn, with pens and shearing floors for eight thousand Corriedales. The only trees were a line of wind-seared poplars that stood along the lane to the main house.

The door opened and a young man in British riding breeches came outside. *Pafoy Menendez-Behety!* he introduced himself. *Come meet Marucha!*

Lunch was a pleasant two hours over *quiche lorraine* and broiled lamb and Chilean riesling. Pafoy talked about Tierra del Fuego and its discovery by Magellan and the small Spanish harbor in the sherry country where that voyage had started. Magellan started with more than three hundred men and only eighteen reached home. We talked about Darwin and his exploration of Patagonia and Tierra del Fuego on the *Beagle,* and the bloody pioneer skirmishes with the Yahgan and Onca tribes.

Pafoy does not fish his rivers, but he told us about the homesick British ranchers who imported sea-trout eggs, and how the fertile ova had arrived in Rio Grande cradled in moss and packed with ice. These original fish have multiplied until they have distributed themselves throughout the skerries and fjord-like channels and estuaries of a thousand miles of coastline, from Puerto Montt on the Pacific to the Rio Santa Cruz on the Atlantic, including all the rivers of Tierra del Fuego.

The ranchers who control these estancias and their vast watersheds are heirs to the British fly-fishing tradition, and a visiting angler should leave his other equipment at home. These *estancieros* permit hardware in the hands of local fishermen, but consider anything but fly-tackle in the hands of a visitor as poor sportsmanship.

The ranch constable fished the river often and arrived after lunch to serve as our guide. The constable was a happy little man with bad teeth, dressed in a rough wool uniform with red shoulder boards and jack-boots. His information about the fishing was mixed, since the river was slightly high and discolored from two weeks of rain, but the spate would also bring a fresh run of sea-trout across the sand and shallows of the estuary.

Half-wild sheep grazed on the olive-colored hills above the river. There were still traces of high water in the bottoms, and the potholes and sloughs were filled with thousands of ducks and geese. Our jeep caravan followed the bluffs until we dropped down into the coarse grass basin along the river. It looped across the bottoms in the weak sunlight, and we stopped above a series of smooth-flowing pools and rigged our tackle. The wind whistled around the jeeps, and when we stepped out and rigged our tackle, the wind whistled around us. Casting in winds that varied between twenty and sixty knots proved a typical problem, and we learned to pick our positions along the high, looping banks and use the wind to shoot our casts.

The fishing was disappointing that day. The constable fished a five-inch copper spoon that rifled out into the gusts, shuddered and stopped in mid-air, and fluttered awkwardly back into the river on the wind. Several trout were taken, but none were better than four pounds. Laddie Buchanan fished traditional salmon patterns in big sizes, and Colonel Lanford tried trolling-size streamers. Backcasts were almost impossible in the wind, but Laddie showed us how to throw a roll-cast high enough that the gusts caught and lifted it out across the current.

We caught a number of river browns and rainbows, but except for a huge silver-flashing swirl behind my bucktail we saw nothing of the sea-trout, and we left when wind and rain forced us shivering from the river.

Pafoy and Marucha were disappointed. *This is terrible!* said Pafoy. *Two-kilo sardinas are nothing here!*

Marucha agreed. *We have truchas like this!* she gestured with widespread hands. *Big ones!*

It was getting dark when we reached the main house, and we stood outside watching flocks of waterfowl move down-river against the evening sky. The cooks carried our fish into the kitchens. The best was a deep-bellied brown that went twenty-four inches. There was a roaring fire in the sitting room. Marucha served us a fine *manzanillo* that cut the chill of the river, and we sat sipping the sherry until dinner was called.

It comes from the place where Magellan started in Spain, said Pafoy as he poured more sherry. *Sanlucar de Barrameda.* We were cold and tired, and the wind whistled along the roof as we warmed ourselves around the fire.

Our last morning the wind seemed less fierce. The weak sunlight that filtered down into the river bottoms seemed almost warm. There were thousands of sheep, and flocks of waterfowl rose and settled ahead of our jeeps. The trail dropped down past a series of saltpeter marshes, and improbable flocks of flamingos rose into the wind.

Good omen! grinned Laddie.

We left our jeeps in the meadow above the Dos Palos water and the wind diminished slightly. We walked down to the series of channels and pools. There was a yellow tarpon-sized bucktail in my fly-book and I tied it on my tippet. The huge bucktail looped out into the wind, accelerated with a strong double-haul, and dropped across the current tongue. It settled into a deep current-swing before I began a stripping retrieve. When each cast was finished, I moved a half-pace downstream and cast again, covering the pool with a series of concentric retrieves along its bottom gravel. Thirty casts worked out into the wind. Doubt was growing in my mind when there were two gigantic silver swirls that boiled up behind the fly.

Sea-trout! I thought wildly. *Missed him!*

The cast was repeated. The big bucktail worked back deep along the bottom until a heavy strike doubled the rod into a tight circle. The reel rasped and growled, and protested like a siren on the first long run. Twice the fish took me deep into the backing, and on its third run the trout cartwheeled into the air. It was bright silver and fell heavily into the river.

Sea-trout! I shouted into the wind.

The fish fought hard and it was some time before it could be forced into the shallows. The landing net seemed pathetically small. The fish sensed its peril and showered me with water and silt, boring back into the heavy current. Finally it tired and I closed my fingers over its gill covers and wrestled it ashore. It weighed eight pounds.

Our luck had changed. Sea-trout migrate in schools, and a shoal of fresh-run fish are often found together. There were several in the pool. Two casts later I was into a strong twelve-pounder that took line off the reel in huge shrieking jerks. It rolled and wallowed across the surface. Colonel Lanford arrived in time for the *coup de grâce*, and we admired the heavy brace of trout like a pair of schoolboys. Lanford quickly compared notes and hurried back upstream with a selection of big flies from his sheepskin flybook.

Laddie and the constable were both into fish several hundred yards upstream, and scraps of shouted Spanish carried on the wind. Laddie was running and the weak sunlight flashed on his straining rod.

It looked like a heavy fish, and I hurried upstream to watch the excitement. My brace of fish was getting heavy and hard to carry when I reached Laddie. He was into a huge trout and oblivious to the bitter wind. His shoulders were hunched and he looked tired. His goggles were pushed high on his woolen cap, and his salmon rod seemed frozen in a straining circle. It was a stalemate.

Bottom? somebody wisecracked.

Laddie grinned and shook his head. *Make those fish of yours look like bait!* he laughed.

His rod was throbbing wildly again. We stopped wisecracking and got a boat net from the jeeps. The fish made a short run and porpoised in the shallows across the river. It looked large. The floodbanks were steep and crumbling from the high water, and we needed the long-handled net to land the trout safely.

Too bloody small! Laddie laughed at the net.

Big enough! I answered. *You bring that sardine around headfirst and we'll prove it!*

Laddie fought the fish with skill and respect, working it carefully into the quiet bank-currents where I waited with the net, holding it motionless in the water. Twice it came in crosswise and I waited, afraid the net-frame would panic the big fish into wrenching free. Colonel Lanford yelled encouragement. Laddie forced the trout back slowly. When its head crossed the net-frame, I scooped it deep into the meshes and heaved its threshing bulk ashore. Laddie whooped wildly in triumph.

Sixteen pounds! scaled Colonel Lanford.

The entire morning was like that. Sea-trout slashed at our flies until they were stripped of hair and feathers. Lines were lost and reels jammed as big trout ran them bare-spooled into the backing. Flies were torn from heavy nylon on the strike. Pafoy and Marucha never fished themselves, and they had asked us to take anything over four kilos for the smokehouse. We lost count of the eight-pound fish that were loaded into the jeeps like cordwood. Hailstones rattled on the windshields when we left for lunch at the ranch, and there were children playing soccer in the rain.

When lunch was over we gathered in the sitting room to warm ourselves around the fire. Marucha filled our glasses with *manzanillo* and the rich sherry warmed us too. The rain and sleet squalls were ended. The wind was still high, but it was almost sunny outside and we walked down into the gardens to see the pet *guanacos*. Both animals came trotting across the lawn and watched us with their huge liquid eyes and half-comic expressions.

They look like Disney drawings, somebody laughed. *Look at those faces!*

Laddie looked out toward the river. *Shall we try it again?* he grinned. *Quiero mas truchas?*

Siempre, I laughed, *but they've already chewed up all my big bucktails!*

Momentito! smiled Marucha.

We walked back into the house and she disappeared into the library. Marucha returned with a half-dozen tarpon bucktails left by another angler.

Perfecto! I laughed. *Gracias!*

Por nada, she said. *Perhaps my flies will continue your luck with the truchas.*

Marucha was right.

We drove downriver toward Rio Grande, following the high chalk-colored bluffs above the town until we walked to the first pools above tidewater. Gulls wheeled against the dark snow-looking clouds. Steamer ducks were nesting along the river with several black-necked swans, and high on the bluffs we heard the shrill cries of the *tero-tero* birds. The first pool was a vast reach of water that sprawled a thousand yards down a long serpentine curve. Holding currents boiled dark and tea-colored below the floodbanks along the pool.

Colonel Lanford shook his head. *Where do we look for fish in all that water?* he said.

We cast until we get lucky, I answered.

Fishing a big unfamiliar river is half geometry and half prospecting, with a little roulette in the recipe. The pattern of casting must never be random, and it must cover the suspected holding-water with a precise series of current-swings, experimenting with the depth of the fly in the deeper places.

It was difficult to read the river with its high, slightly discolored water, and I walked above its current looking for likely sea-trout places. Several heavy current tongues gathered below some grassy islands and smoothed into quieter shallows near the bank. Our casts reached out and dropped the big bucktails into those likely looking currents. The flies swung deep and worked back erratically over the bottom. We fished each cast through carefully and tried again. Thirty minutes passed without sign of a fish, and then a giant swirl rose behind my retrieve.

They're here! I yelled downriver.

The cast was repeated perfectly, double-hauling the bucktail and dropping it eighty feet out. The current took the line and the swing had just started its deep twitching retrieve when it stopped with a vicious strike. The rod was bucking wildly, and thirteen pounds of sea-trout showered us with dirty water. The reel shrieked and rattled angrily. Finally we beached the fish in the shallows. It measured thirty inches, and we laid its great sea-armored length in the grass.

Beautiful! whispered the Colonel.

Yes! I agreed happily.

The big tarpon-sized bucktail was deep in its throat, and we worked it free and went back to the fishing. Five casts later, there was a marlin-sized strike that showered water downstream on the wind and the reel screamed. This fish was uncontrollable. Sometimes it sounded deep along the bottom, shaking its head angrily like a salmon, and sometimes it threshed wildly just under the surface currents, throwing spray like a whale.

It's huge! I thought wildly. *It's huge!*

Finally it hung stubbornly across the river, resting from its violent acrobatics, and I glanced nervously at the backing. The line had been deep in the river for the entire fight and the white dacron backing disappeared into the dark tea-colored water. The stalemate lasted fifteen minutes. Then the trout moved slowly upstream, telegraphing its mood with an occasional head-twisting wrench that ached back through the rod into my tired muscles. Finally the fish stopped and sulked high up the pool, holding deep in the churning currents.

It rested again and I was unable to force it into fresh action that could erode its strength. I walked slowly along the floodbanks, recovering line until all the backing was on the reel and the fish was directly opposite, lying deep only ninety feet away. The fish was fighting both me and the river now, and when I finally forced it off balance and turned it into quieter water, I began looking for a shallow place to finish the contest.

Maybe! I hoped. *Maybe!*

It was premature, and the fish turned downstream with ponderous dignity and contempt for my straining tackle. The fish had remained hidden in the dark currents throughout the fight. It gathered momentum slowly now, forcing me to surrender the hard-won backing with growing panic, and it started toward the sea.

We were running finally, and twice I stumbled on the soft floodbanks and lost more precious backing. Twice more the fish threshed heavily on the surface. The line dwindled dangerously until I could see the aluminum reel-spool under its remaining turns.

The big trout bulled its way into the gathering tailshallows of the vast pool and I stumbled again, and the rest of the backing evaporated. Unhappily we tried to follow, but the rod was gyrating wildly and it was hopeless. Finally I wrapped my forearm in the backing and pointed the rod at the plunging fish, hoping to save the line.

The huge fish churned and bulldogged angrily into the swift current two hundred yards downstream, biting the white dacron deep into my parka until the heavy nylon leader shuddered sickeningly and separated. Laddie Buchanan arrived too late to help.

What was that? he asked breathlessly.

God knows! I answered unhappily. *I'm not really sure it was a fish!* I selected another bucktail.

Sea lion maybe? Laddie grinned.

Sea tiger! I answered.

My fingers were still shaking, half from the struggle and half from the bitter wind that had been forgotten during the fight. Sea tigers seemed possible, and we walked back toward the jeeps an hour later, struggling to carry six fish better than our eight-pound limit. When we finally reached the road it was raining.

Our last night we gathered in the sitting room to warm ourselves at the fire. Pafoy returned from the library and we registered our trout in his fishing log. Few fishermen have visited the ranch, and the book is limited to trout better than eight pounds, but its list of trophy-sized fish is eloquent testimony to incredible sport. Laddie registered his high-rod trout of sixteen pounds and passed the fishing log to me.

Your flies brought good luck! Colonel Lanford raised his glass and saluted our hostess.

Marucha! we chorused and drank.

Marucha laughed and filled our glasses. *Mil gracias!* she said gaily. *Mil gracias!*

Pafoy raised his glass. *These gentlemen have provided many fish for the smokehouses!* he said ceremonially. *They must come back to Tierra del Fuego!*

There are other rivers, said Laddie.

Tell them about the Rio Serrano! said Pafoy.

Serrano! sighed Laddie happily. *Its fishing is even better than the Rio Grande!*

Better than this? it seemed impossible.

Pafoy nodded emphatically. *There are many more fish,* he smiled, *and they average five kilos!*

Twelve pounds! somebody whispered.

Marucha raised her glass and proposed a toast to the future, and another summer of sport. February was finished and the autumn wind was rising in the darkness. The welcome fire roared and flickered on the hearth, and we stared into the flames. Our trip was finished, and I sat swirling the cognac absently in my glass, inhaling its rich bouquet and dreaming of another summer in the Land of Fire.

Laerdal Memories

For the sake of those anglers who have not had the good fortune to visit the Laerdal in Norway, perhaps some description is necessary to explain the charm which induced us to return season after season, and to leave it with such regret.

—T. T. Phelps[1]

ATLANTIC salmon have been considered the royalty of fishes since Walton enshrined them in his *Compleat Angler* three centuries ago. Fishing them has since evolved overtones of ritual and tradition, until the storied salmon rivers of the world like the Alta and Ballynahinch and Restigouche have a pilgrimage-like fascination for anglers.

The rivers of Norway have surrendered all of the salmon records and are unequalled for trophy fish, and their fishing rights have passed from generation to generation like priceless heirlooms. The past on such Olympian rivers is filled with a long parade of salmon-fishing kings and dukes and princes, and in terms of such tradition, there is no salmon river in the world to equal the pastoral Laerdal for its long history of royalty and riches.

[1] T. T. Phelps, *Fishing Dreams*, Batchworth Press, London, 1949.

Its source lies in the reindeer barrens and snow-melt of the high Fillefjell country, in a region of mountains and glaciers two hundred miles above Oslo. The river drops fifty miles through a spectacular valley of forests and sod-roofed farmsteads and waterfalls, punctuated with the brooding twelfth-century stave church at Borgund. There are salmon in the sixteen miles of river between Ulvisfossen waterfall and the village at its mouth.

Laerdalsøyri is the name of the village. Its charming clapboard houses are clustered along a winding street that ends in the Sognefjord ferry-slips. The pitch-stained church slumbers inside its walled churchyard, almost hidden in a dense cloak of pines. The valley floor is a patchwork of small irregular hay meadows and potato fields. Mountains rise steeply above the valley and the cattle grazing in the sea-grass meadows where the river meets the fjord. There is a waterfall above the center of the village, making its Yosemite-like plunge down the escarpment behind the Lindström Hotel. Its slate roofs and scrollwork Victorian balconies have sheltered salmon-fishing pilgrims since 1845, and the river is the life-blood of Laerdalsøyri.

There are better salmon rivers in Norway. The wild steeple-chase water on the Årøy, which the celebrated Charles Ritz made famous in his book *Fly Fisher's Life*, holds fish of immense size below its Platforms of Despair. Målangsfossen is the best single pool in the world, where the spawning run of a vast watershed is delayed for six weeks below the maelstrom of waterfalls and rapids. The unique Alta lies deep in arctic Lapland, where the fishing is done with graceful Karasjok longboats in the lingering twilight of the Midnight Sun, and is certainly the best salmon river in the world.

Salmon fishermen do not measure their sport in terms of catch alone, and such brawling rivers as the Alta and Målangsfossen and Årøy lack the memorabilia of the past. The history of the Laerdal is richer in both literature and legend.

Its plank-and-timber casting platforms have carried most of the crowned heads of Europe and captains of industry and fishing statesmen from Gladstone to Churchill.

Its character is intimate and less forbidding than its sister Norwegian rivers, with a wading-size friendliness to its silken currents and incredibly clear pools. Such clarity makes each fish visible in the deepest pools, and hooked fish can seem suspended in air rather than in the river. The pools are perfect in size: wide enough to challenge accomplished casters and small enough for the less-skilled, with good wading or bank casting in many places. Picturesque casting platforms are found on some of the famous beats. The current is deceptively swift, swimming flies perfectly in low water and challenging for anglers into heavy salmon. There are few of the problems found on some Norwegian watersheds, like floating timber and excessive poaching or fjord-nets and uncertain fly-fishing, and the Laerdal typically offers good salmon fishing after Midsummer Eve.

Laerdal fishing is usually consistent in a sport known for its fickle moods. The salmon arrive punctually with the first flood-tide in June and migrate slowly upstream until they reach the Ulvisfossen waterfall sometime in August. Sea-run trout enter the river about six weeks after the salmon, but seldom arrive in large numbers until August. The challenge of the river after midsummer is unique, since the flyfisher has good odds for killing a fifty-pound salmon or twenty-pound sea trout in a relatively small river.

Fishing rights on most European rivers like the Laerdal, unlike the relatively open sport familiar to Americans, are privately owned and must be leased through salmon-fishing brokers as much as a year in advance. Such leased sections of river are called beats, and are often named after nearby villages and farmsteads and families.

The fishing at Laerdal is divided into twenty-three beats of varying quality and length, depending upon their location and character. These twenty-three beats total sixteen miles of water. The lower mileage is wide and smooth-flowing, with excellent holding places for both sea-trout and salmon. The upper reach of river between Rikheim and the Ulvisfossen waterfall varies widely in character, from legendary pools like Bjorküm to the moss-covered boulders and wild rapids at Honjüm and the Husum Gorge.

The river has a pastoral charm in the midday hours. Brown cattle are browsing in the water meadows and the farmers are busy with hay-fences and mowing in the fields. The evening comes early in the mountain-walled valley, veiling its pools with a melancholy sense of history.

Midsummer darkness never really becomes night, and the twelve-hour twilight is strange for an angler only hours off the sleek SAS airliner in Oslo. Its light lingers and dwindles imperceptibly until long after midnight, when darkness almost obscures the river, and then suddenly it begins getting light again—living without night is unsettling at times.

Fishing the smooth sea-pools in the tidal meadows has considerable charm in those twilight hours. The waterfall seems louder then, and the music of the river is audible from the hotel when it is swollen with the snow-melt of good weather. Gulls wheel over the quickening current, filling the darkness with their cries.

Down the dark mountain-walled fjord, the sea lies quiet and silvery purple. The night ferry-steamer to Kaupanger sounds its departure, and the deep-throated horn echoes along the mountains. Fishermen row their skiffs patiently in the mingling currents below the river, trolling for mackerel and hoping for a salmon. The tiny freight packet comes down the fjord, carrying its cargo of lumber and machine-parts and cabbages into the Laerdalsøyri landing. The rhythmic *chunk-a-chunk* of its engine is a soft counterpoint above the river sounds. Salmon roll and pirouette restlessly in the sea-pools, the half-remembered intoxication of fresh water in their gill structures, and fall back heavily into the darkening current.

Laerdal has a special place in my remembrances of rivers

past. Its memories include such peripheral pleasures as the flower gardens and print collection of the Lindström Hotel, and the sleep-bringing sounds of its waterfall. There was the calm of village life, with marvelous breakfasts of rolls and sweet butter, brislings and dark goat-cheese, strong English tea and fresh milk from the cows in the water meadows. Breakfasts were sometimes taken on a sun-filled balcony above the street, where I often dressed extra Orange Charms and Black Fitchtails and Hairwing Ackroyds while waiting patiently for an evening beat.

There are also memories of fish and fishing. The swift pools of the Stonjüm reach lie between the fjord and Hunderi, looping across the valley in a long sickle-shaped curve. The river course is lined in places with massive walls of moss-covered granite. Fishing houses and farmsteads with barn-red outbuildings lie along the water. Those pools were filled with fresh-run salmon when I first visited Laerdal years ago.

The fishing rights were held by a young textile engineer from Belfast, who had taken a sentimental fishing leave from his spinning mill in East Pakistan. That first Laerdal fishing was unplanned, since I was travelling north from Oslo to meet Charles Ritz on the Årøy Steeplechase; but when I stopped in Laerdalsøyri for dinner before crossing the Sognefjord on the evening ferry to Kaupanger, the unpredictable Ritz was in the dining room of the Lindström.

But you're fishing the Årøy! I gasped.

His eyebrows arched above his expressive shrug. *The hotel becomes impossible,* he sighed unhappily, *when it interferes with fishing!*

Pierre Creusevaut arrived for breakfast the next morning. Ritz is a fishermen of legendary skills, and Creusevaut is a former world casting champion. Sunlight filled the street as farmers and shopgirls rode their bicycles to work, and the fishing talk at our table was superb. Breakfast was finished, and we shook hands while their driver loaded a mountain of rod cases and fishing duffel and luggage. Their sleek Mercedes purred south toward Oslo and the evening flight to Paris, leaving me without fishing companions.

Hello! it was the young engineer from Belfast. *Understand your fishing arrangements went a bit sour.*

Yes, I nodded gloomily. *Ritz had to leave early.*

Colin Metcalfe! his hand was offered with a grin as warm as two-fingers of Irish whisky after fishing. *You're welcome to have a bash at my water!*

Metcalfe waved aside my polite decline of his offer, and we returned to the breakfast balcony to explore the matter over fresh strawberries and coffee. The young engineer talked about boyhood on the salmon rivers of Ireland, explained that he had missed the sport in Pakistan, and countered my weakening arguments with an old truth: angling is a solitary pursuit, but no angler likes to fish alone.

His fishing rights began at midnight, and we worked his water hard with a mixture of squandered energy and foolishness that spells youth. We killed only two salmon and three grilse, but cemented a friendship possible only among strangers met while fishing. Our sleepless assault on the river came full circle when we overslept the last morning, scrambling to get him aboard the Gudvangen ferry with his huge ferrule-jammed Hardy salmon rod protruding comically from the window of his Mini-Cooper.

There were other memories, like the evening at the Berge farm, where we hiked through steep meadows filled with serpentine hay-fences. Johann Berge expertly fished the eddies of the Honjüm rapids, where the Laerdal narrows and tumbles wildly through silver birches and boulders. We were both fishless that evening.

The salmon cooperated on other days. Memory returns to the bright henfish my first morning on the storied Tonjüm Pool. My host was Thomas Falck of Bergen, an expert salmon-fisherman who holds several of the best pools on the Laerdal. Our riverkeeper was Andreas Olsen, whose sixty-eight summers on the river make him the patriarch of its gillies and keepers. The salmon jumped several times. Both men watched nervously, puffing their pipes and frowning while the fish struggled against my slender fly-rod. Olsen was skeptical about the strange American fly-pattern in its jaw. The salmon had engulfed it surprisingly, after refusing a half-dozen traditional flies like the Durham Ranger and Jock Scott.

The myths and shibboleths of earlier centuries wither stubbornly in men, but the salmon of the Laerdal refused the bright-feathered flies of the past and took drab hairwings like the Silver Monkey and Black Fitchtail.

Have you seen a salmon hand-tailed? I asked.

Both men shook their heads. *You mean you'll just pick the fish up by the tail?*

Yes, I answered happily.

The salmon cooperated well, although Olsen was convinced the fragile six-pound leader would break, and prolonged the fight by following the tired fish through the shallows with his net to salvage it in case of failure. His concern proved unnecessary, and finally the salmon rolled weakly at my feet. There is always a last jump or leader-shearing bolt left in such a fish, and it is best to force that expiring gasp on your own terms. The salmon rested in the quiet currents until I reached down and deliberately stroked its bulk without closing my fingers on its tail. The shallows exploded in a shower of water, but the salmon was finished. It came back stubbornly, and I seated my fingers tightly around the wrist of its tail-structure. Both men applauded happily as we waded ashore with the spent six-kilo henfish, and such memories remain sea-bright in the mind.

There are also memories like the leisurely afternoon at the Rikheim farmstead with Thomas Falck and Sir Thomas Sopwith, whose fame on salmon rivers and grouse moors is less well known than his yachting and legendary pioneering in aviation. Sopwith twice challenged with his *Endeavours* for the America's Cup, and his Sopwith Camel and Hawker Hurricane fighters carried pilots of the Royal Air Force to victories in both World Wars. Fishing that morning had been slow, but the stories of fishing and yacht-racing and flying on the Rikheim terrace were never better.

Laerdal tradition began in 1854, when the British painter James Randell divided a pastoral summer between its salmon and his paint-boxes. Randell lived at Bjorküm in his first Laerdal summers, until he finally settled on a log farmhouse high above the river at Ljøsne. Its walls are still decorated with a thirty-four-pounder he killed in 1863.

Randell fished the river thirty years, paying no fishing rent other than fresh salmon, and published several portfolios of Norwegian landscapes in London. His scenes of Laerdal attracted other fishermen to the region. The principal leaseholder who followed Randell was John Chaworth Musters, who served as Master of the Quorn foxhounds during the reign of Queen Victoria. Musters died in 1891, and his fishing rights at Ljøsne passed into the control of Edward Portman and his brother Lord Henry Portman.

Their tenure on the Laerdal really began three years earlier when they leased the Bjorküm beat from Musters. Edward Portman kept detailed records of his sport, and his diaries tell us that he killed eleven salmon on his first day of fishing. Nine of those fish were taken from the storied Bjorküm Pool. Their party caught 659 salmon weighing over five thousand pounds in 1888. That summer began their twenty-six years of fishing the Laerdal, which ended with the outbreak of war in 1914.

Those years are still remembered in the valley because the Portman family bought out the netting-rights in the fjord, trained riverkeepers and built a hatchery, and began a tradition of fly-fishing that still survives in our generation of anglers and gillies.

Portman wrote in his diary that the best pool on the river in his time was at Bjorküm, which lies between the Honjüm and Seltun rapids. Hundreds of migrating fish stopped there to rest after negotiating the currents below, and before attempting the rapids above. Its holding water measured over two hundred yards until a rock slide spoiled its upper reaches in 1927. Time has improved the pool over the past forty years, until the gillies from Ljøsne counted a hundred fish in its currents one past season.

Bjorküm was the scene of a legendary triumph that occurred eighty years ago. Its sense of chivalry is typical of the sport on great European rivers like the Laerdal. Lord Henry Portman was the lucky fisherman, although his triumph was an accident. His fishing holiday was over, and he travelled downriver to Laerdalsøyri at daybreak to catch the weekly packet-boat to Bergen. Villagers informed Portman that his fjord steamer was delayed at Balestrand, and he hurried back upriver toward his date with fishing history.

Portman arrived on the Bjorküm Pool at noon, and picnicked with his gillies in its boulder-strewn meadows. The gillies loaded an incredible twenty-two salmon into their wagon when he finally stopped fishing. Before leaving for a late supper at Ljøsne, Portman and his riverkeeper ceremonially walked the casting platform, raised their fishing hats, and paid homage to Bjorküm.

Ljøsne farmstead still figures in Laerdal tradition. Its modern owners are the celebrated Astrup family of Oslo, whose business interests are found throughout Scandinavia. Their summer camaraderie is focused upon Nils Astrup and his wife Heddy, both salmon anglers of formidable reputation. The long roster of fishing guests at Ljøsne is a changing cast of family and relatives and friends, including anglers like young Crown Prince Harald of Norway.

The farmstead has changed little. Its site is high on a glacial morraine that commands a panorama of the mountains and the valley floor. Porches were added to the log farmhouse that James Randell bought in 1857. Heddy Astrup has collected goatherd houses from the outlying valleys, restored them carefully and added plumbing, and placed them inside the wall of uncoursed granite that surrounds the farmhouse and its outbuildings. Fishing tackle is kept in the simple keeper's hut, where the gillies sit each evening when they return from the river, drinking *akevit* and telling stories. The mood of life at Ljøsne is almost bucolic, but its true character is found in the clay tennis courts and swimming pool and the costly automobiles parked in its meadow.

Its fishing is an unhurried regimen of early-morning swims and late breakfasts and leisurely meals concluded with Armagnac and vintage cigars on the sitting porch. Salmon are almost a footnote to family activities, although their seemingly off-hand manner conceals a passion for fishing that grips the entire Astrup clan. Their evenings close with midnight suppers of salmon and smoked reindeer and beef tartar after fishing, and the Laerdal tradition continues in their mixture of Olympian sport and elegant leisure.

Invitations to fish the Astrup water are priceless, and my first came unexpectedly in 1963, when I was staying at the Lindström and fishing with Thomas Falck at Tonjüm. Falck called the hotel one morning just as I was loading my tackle in the car to meet him at the Bridge Pool.

Nils Astrup will call at ten o'clock, he said.

The telephone message was on time. *Nils Astrup,* his voice was cultured and faintly Oxonian. *We would like to have you join us for lunch—is it possible?*

Perfect! I answered weakly.

We'll expect you, Astrup continued. *We want you to meet the Crown Prince and see our water and have a look at the American methods we've been hearing about.*

Twelve o'clock, I agreed.

Ljøsne farm lies ten miles above Laerdalsøyri, hidden on its high morraine except for its flag staff. Both the Norwegian flag and the pennant of the Royal Family were flying. The narrow road wound up through the silver birches, and I drove through the gate without meeting the Royal security I had expected on the grounds. Gillies were rigging tackle, and a silver-haired man stopped practicing his switch-cast on the lawn to greet me warmly.

Nils Astrup, he said. *Welcome to Ljøsne!*

Crown Prince Harald was talking with the gillies. Harald is handsome and thirty years old and unmarried. The serious public face, which masks a shyness often mistaken for solemnity, was missing that morning. The young prince was wearing plus-fours and a baggy sweater, laughing infectiously with Olav Klingenberg, his favorite Laerdal gillie.

Prince Harald is a famous sportsman, best known for his many victories in international sailing competition, but he is equally skilled in salmon-fishing. His skills were acquired under the tutelage of his uncle, the late Prince Axel of Denmark, and we were discussing low-water tactics when a great explosion of laughter spilled out from the house. Several young men wrestled and carried a struggling comrade across the yard and dumped him into the pool.

That's my son Halvor, Astrup grinned.

Halvor killed two salmon this morning, Harald explained. *Swimming is the traditional award.*

That includes everybody? I asked warily.

Everybody! laughed the Prince.

That prelude to the fishing at Ljøsne was typical. Life with the Astrups was richly varied, although my experience did not include the two-salmon baptism. Family galleries to watch the fishing at Bjorküm were common in good weather, and we watched Heddy Astrup kill a fine ten-kilo salmon one warm evening to a chorus of family applause. There were several pleasant sessions on the river with Crown Prince Harald and Olav Klingenberg, whose family has gillied for generations, and later I received a note that Prince Harald had taken three salmon his last morning—in bright weather at Bjorküm with one of my low-water Orange Charms.

Crown Prince Harald continues the history of royalty that has fished the Laerdal since the British began its rich tradition over a century ago. Its other royal acolytes have included King Haakon VII and King Olav V of Norway, Kaiser Wilhelm II of Germany, King Edward VII and the Duke of Windsor and King George V of England, King Michael of Rumania, Prince Wilhelm of Sweden, and the late Prince Axel of Denmark.

Fishing members of the British peerage include expert salmon anglers like Lord Portman, Lord Nuffield, Sir Thomas Dunhill, Sir Harold Gillies, Sir Michael Wright, and the legendary Sir Thomas Sopwith.

The list of expert fishermen who have made regular pilgrimages to the Laerdal reads like an Almanac de Gotha of angling, and includes men like the late Per Kampmann and Bruno Jensen of Copenhagen, Roger Gailliard and Charles Ritz of Paris, Odd Jensen and Kristen Mustad and Ragnar Platou of Oslo, Jacques and Albert Bousson and Pierre Creusevaut of Brussels, Thomas and Hans Falck of Bergen, T. T. Phelps and J. C. Mottram of London, as well as celebrities like explorer Fritjof Nansen and fly-fishing statesmen like Gladstone and Churchill.

Laerdal riverkeepers and gillies are human records of the river and its history, and their families have a tradition as rich as the river itself. They have served as fishing equerries to men of royalty and riches for generations, and their profession is passed from father to son with all the mystique of a Medieval guild.

Olav Olsen is typical of such living tradition. Olsen learned his gillying and fly-making from his father Andreas, who has sixty-eight years on the Laerdal and tied flies for Prince Axel of Denmark. His grandfather Ole was riverkeeper and fly-maker for Lord Henry Portman. Olav Olsen is perhaps the best fly-dresser of traditional salmon patterns in the world. His versions of such flies as the Jock Scott and Dusty Miller, which are constructed from hundreds of exotic feathers, are intricate works of art. Crown Prince Harald is a regular customer, and Olsen salmon-patterns are prized in salmon fishing circles on both sides of the Atlantic.

Olsen looks out from his bright-feathered workbench toward the river meadows. *I love the Laerdal,* he smiles. *It has been my whole life for forty years.*

Prince Axel of Denmark had not returned to fish at Laerdal for several years before his death in 1964. Time had sapped his ability to wade strong currents and endure its glacier-cold temperatures, but memories of his fishing years are very much alive in Laerdalsøyri.

The townspeople remember his elegant Rolls-Royce with the royal Danish heraldry discreetly gilded on its door panels. Prince Axel was often seen driving the unpaved roads along the river, with his gillies sitting in the open trunk, holding his salmon rods and dangling their boots in the dust. The front seat was occupied by a great German shepherd that liked salmon-fishing and always came to Laerdal. The shepherd watched each cast attentively and came running when a fish was hooked, barking and running along the water until it was gaffed and given the coup-de-grâce.

Prince Axel and his cronies were also fond of fishing wagers during their Laerdal holidays. One week their pot for total weight caught had accumulated a considerable sum, and Axel accidentally hooked a passing milkmaid with his backcast. The party rushed her to the infirmary in Laerdalsøyri, where the hook was removed and Prince Axel had the farmgirl weighed, easily winning the contest.

Tradition is important on the river. There is a shaped-log fishing house on the grounds of the Lindström Hotel that belonged to Prince Axel and his fishing friends. Most of that circle of famous rods are dead now, and no fishermen return to the charming cottage with wild flowers on its roof. The villagers maintain this simple shrine as it was the last time Prince Axel fished the Laerdal. Its interior remains an intriguing clutter of memorabilia from those years, and each evening the hotelkeeper lights the lamps inside the little fishing house and leaves them burning.